Mrs. Peterson

AMERICAN HISTORY FOR PENNSYLVANIA
BOOK ONE

Drawing by Earl Horter. © *Courtesy The Beck Engraving Co.*
Spanish and Italian galleons were the commerce carriers of the fifteenth century and later.

AMERICAN HISTORY FOR PENNSYLVANIA

BOOK ONE

CHARLES A. COULOMB

ASSISTANT SUPERINTENDENT OF SCHOOLS
PHILADELPHIA

NEW YORK
THE MACMILLAN COMPANY
1933

COPYRIGHT, 1933,
BY THE MACMILLAN COMPANY.

All rights reserved — no part of this book may be reproduced in any form without permission in writing from the publisher, except by a reviewer who wishes to quote brief passages in connection with a review written for inclusion in magazine or newspaper.

Set up and electrotyped. Published August, 1933.

· PRINTED IN THE UNITED STATES OF AMERICA ·

PREFACE

This book presents the history of the United States from the discovery of America by Columbus to the inauguration of George Washington as our first President. The text follows closely the Pennsylvania State Course of Study in Social Studies for grade five as issued by the State Department of Public Instruction.

Through the six units of work the book aims to give to the pupils: a knowledge of the early explorations and discoveries in the New World; an appreciation of the courage and sacrifices of the early settlers; an understanding of the rivalries of the nations of Europe for the control of North America; a knowledge of the causes that led to the separation of the colonies from Great Britain and an appreciation of the sacrifices that the colonists made for what they believed to to be their rights; an understanding of the circumstances that led to the adoption of the Constitution in order to form a more perfect Union; and an appreciation of the need for laws and of the importance of their enforcement as a part of the duties of citizenship.

The vocabulary of the book is within the reading abilities of fifth-grade pupils.

The pictures have been carefully selected, with the objects of giving visual aid in the understanding of the story and of arousing emotional interest in the events portrayed.

The study helps that have been provided are intended, first, to show the need for relating the lessons in the social studies to their geographic situations; second, to indicate ways in which the lessons may be motivated; third, to suggest special topics for independent study by the more advanced pupils; fourth, to indicate a few of the many books which are especially useful in giving pictures of the times or which may be used as storehouses of additional material.

The appendix gives a list by counties of some of the interesting historical places in Pennsylvania. Its study will result in an increased appreciation of the great part the state has played in the history of the nation. Grateful acknowledgment is hereby made for the helpful suggestions of those who aided the author in the compilation of the list.

The author also wishes to acknowledge the courtesy of the many who have contributed to the illustrative equipment of this book. As the list would be too long to give here, individual credit has been given under each picture.

CHARLES A. COULOMB

PHILADELPHIA,
July 4, 1933

TABLE OF CONTENTS

	PAGE
INTRODUCTION	1

UNIT I. PERIOD OF DISCOVERY AND EXPLORATION   9
1. Spanish Discoveries   12
2. Spanish Conquerors and Explorers; The Portuguese in Brazil   30
3. France Seeks Lands in the New World . .   46
4. The Dutch Plan Colonies in America . . .   60
5. England Becomes Interested in America . .   64

UNIT II. PART 1. PERIOD OF COLONIZATION . .   77
1. The Settlement of Virginia   80
2. The Settlement of the Other Southern Colonies .   94
3. The Founding of the New England Colonies .   106
4. The Settlement of New York and New Jersey   128
5. The Settlement of Pennsylvania . . .   138

UNIT II. PART 2. PERIOD OF COLONIZATION . .   177
6. Life and Customs in the Colonies . . .   179

UNIT III. THE STRUGGLE FOR THE CONTROL OF NORTH AMERICA   227
1. The Intercolonial Wars   230
2. The French and Indian War   240

UNIT IV. THE AMERICAN REVOLUTION . . .   261
1. Events Leading to the American Revolution .   264
2. The Colonies at War   283
3. Pennsylvania's Part in the Revolution . .   337

TABLE OF CONTENTS

	PAGE
UNIT V. THE DEVELOPMENT OF THE CONSTITUTION	355
Steps Leading to a New Government	358
UNIT VI. LAWS AND LAW ENFORCEMENT	383
The Good of All Is the Goal of Wise Lawmakers	386
PLACES OF HISTORIC INTEREST IN PENNSYLVANIA	i
INDEX	xiii

INTRODUCTION

A caravan with a load of spices from the Far East
(From De Bry's *India*, published in 1599)

"Ancient Commerce"

European merchants bargaining for the jewels and silken rugs of the Orient (From a mural by A. J. Bogdanove in the Alexander Hamilton High School, Brooklyn)

INTRODUCTION

Learned men of the Middle Ages *From an old print*

Europe before Columbus. For many hundred years before the discovery of America most of the different nations of Europe were governed by kings or emperors who did not have very much real power. In each country there were a great many nobles who lived in strong castles. Many of these nobles were almost as powerful as the king himself. Much of the time they and their men were fighting with one another or with their king, trying to increase their own power.

How the nobles lost their power. As time went on, it happened that the kings finally succeeded in becoming the strongest people in their countries. They forced the great nobles to give up their strong fortresses and to come and live near the palace of the king. The nobles no longer spent most of their time in fighting. Many of them as well as other rich citizens became interested in other things. Some of them traveled through the rest of Europe to learn more about other countries. Others studied some of the books that had been written by the wise men of old Greece and Rome. Still others furnished money to men who were interested in finding out new ways of doing things or who wished to travel to distant places that were then almost unknown. A great many used their wealth to buy beautiful things for their homes and rich clothing and jewels for themselves.

The rich trade of Italy. The chief ruler of Italy, who was called the emperor, lived in Germany, on the other side of the high Alps. The emperor very seldom visited Italy, and so the Italian nobles and the people of the Italian cities found it easy to break away from his control. After this happened, the cities of Italy commenced to govern themselves. Their merchants soon were able to build up a fine trade in the Mediterranean Sea between the people of Europe and the inhabitants of the East.

From the East these merchants brought back the silks, spices, jewels, rare perfumes, and many other articles that the people of Europe so very much desired. Since people were willing to pay high prices for these

INTRODUCTION

goods, the merchants and places taking part in this trade became very wealthy.

Photo by De Cou from Ewing Galloway

A nobleman's castle in southern France built during the Middle Ages

Marco Polo. Two of the rich merchants of Venice decided to travel to the East to see the place where all these wonderful goods came from. Their name was

Polo, and they took their nephew, Marco, with them. They traveled all the way to China. Here the ruler,

A group by Dwight Franklin

Marco Polo telling his adventures to the Great Khan

called the *Great Khan*, thought so much of the ability of young Marco that he persuaded the Polos to stay with him for a while, and he made Marco his chief adviser. After staying at the Khan's court for almost twenty years, the Polos traveled back to their home in Venice, bringing with them such great riches in gold and jewels that all the people of Venice were amazed.

From Sir Henry Yule's "Book of Ser Marco Polo"

Marco Polo's galley going into action in a war between Venice and Genoa

Many years later Marco was captured by a ship from Genoa, which city was at war with Venice. He told his story to a fellow prisoner, who later wrote a book about Marco's travels. For the first time the people of Europe learned about the wonders and riches of the East from some one who had actually seen them. A copy of the book about Marco Polo's travels may still be seen with the margins of its pages filled with notes on the countries of the East in the handwriting of Christopher Columbus, the discoverer of America.

The Turks interfere with the trade to the East. Not long after the book about Marco Polo had been written, the people known as the Turks conquered, one after the other, the countries at the eastern end of the Mediterranean Sea. The Turks did not like the European nations and interfered very much with their trade, especially with that of Genoa. Its trade was almost ruined. Instead of the harbor's and wharves' being busy with shipping and its warehouses' being loaded with rich goods from the East, the wharves were deserted and the warehouses empty.

The caravan routes were constantly beset by robbers, and the pirates made the sea voyages unsafe. Finally came the discovery of the all-water route around the Cape of Good Hope. This route made the bringing of the valuable products of the Far East both easier and cheaper. However, it greatly affected the commerce of the cities that had grown rich by virtue of the Mediterranean trade.

UNIT I. PERIOD OF DISCOVERY AND EXPLORATION

The departure of Columbus from Palos
(From a painting by Ricardo Balaca in the Provincial Museum, Cadiz, Spain)

Columbus sights land.
His captains beg forgiveness for their lack of confidence in him.

FORECAST OF UNIT I

In the study of the early history of our country we first take up the voyages of the bold explorers and adventurers. These men set out in little sailing ships to cross unknown seas and oceans, hoping to bring back the riches of the Far East to their countries and their kings. They were not seeking to discover new lands at first but were trying to find better and shorter routes to the spices and gold and precious stones of China and India.

The ships of Spain took the lead in these adventures. Columbus discovered America. The vessel of Magellan sailed completely around the earth and proved that it was round and that Columbus had discovered not Asia, but a new continent. Mexico and Peru were conquered and brought under the rule of Spain. Lands that now make up the southwestern part of the United States were explored, and Florida and the Mississippi River were discovered.

While the Spanish were accomplishing these conquests, other European nations were not idle. French, Dutch, and English sailors were setting out on expeditions of discovery and exploration. Each of these nations established claims to certain parts of the New World. They planted trading posts and colonies along the Atlantic coast from Virginia in the south to Canada in the north and as far west as the Mississippi River.

As you study this unit, you will learn of the sacrifices the early settlers made in leaving their old homes in Europe to make new homes in America. The slowness and difficulties of travel — it took months to cross the Atlantic Ocean — will impress you. You will also learn about the rival claims of the European nations for lands in the New World.

UNIT I. PERIOD OF DISCOVERY AND EXPLORATION

Photo from Ewing Galloway

The *Santa Maria*, the flagship of Columbus

1. SPANISH DISCOVERIES

Christopher Columbus. We can think of Christopher Columbus as a small boy playing about the wharves of his native city Genoa and being much interested in the wonderful traffic that he saw going on between the people of the East and those of his own city. As he grew up, he saw this trade gradually diminishing until there was almost nothing left of it. In the meantime he had become a sailor and had made various voyages

SPANISH DISCOVERIES

to the west coast of Africa and the western part of Europe, and he may even have traveled as far as Iceland. He read a great many of the famous books, both old and new, that told about other parts of the world. He made notes wherever he noticed anything that told about islands or land to the west of the Azores

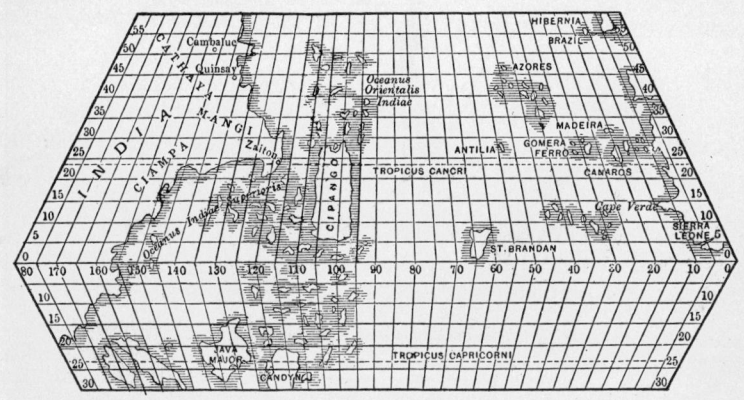

Toscanelli's map — drawn from his own description

and the Canary Islands in the Atlantic. Most of this work was done in Portugal, where he had married a daughter of one of that country's famous ship captains, who gave Columbus the opportunity of studying the maps which he had made on his voyages.

Columbus finally got the idea from his studies and conversations with sea captains and map makers that there was some way of reaching the rich Eastern countries by sailing to the west. The earth, he was sure, was not flat but round.

Columbus appeals to the king of Portugal. Columbus hoped King John of Portugal would present him with some ships and men, so that he could try to reach *Cipango*, or Japan, in the Western Ocean. The king thought that the ideas of Columbus were like fairy tales, but he referred the matter to some expert geographers. These reported against the ideas of Columbus since they found no satisfactory proof that such a place as Cipango existed.

Columbus goes to Spain. Having been refused aid by King John, Columbus decided to try his fortune with the king and queen of Spain. After seven years of urging his claims before friends of the rulers, he finally was permitted to talk with the king. The king referred the plan of Columbus to a group of wise men, who decided, as King John's advisers had done, that there was nothing to his ideas. In desperation he made up his mind to turn to England for aid. In the meantime he sent his brother Bartholomew to the English king to try to enlist his help. Shortly after this, as Columbus was on his way out of Spain, he was called back by a messenger from Queen Isabella, who had been persuaded to help Columbus by two men of her court.

Columbus enlists the help of Queen Isabella. One reason why the king and queen of Spain were slow in coming to the aid of Columbus was that for many years they had been fighting the Moors, a Mohammedan people, who held may rich cities in the south of Spain.

SPANISH DISCOVERIES

In January, 1492, the last Moorish city, Granada, surrendered. Ferdinand, the king, was not so ready to help Columbus as his queen, but, on her threat to pledge her jewels, money and ships were granted for the voyage.

Ferdinand and Isabella sign the commission authorizing Columbus to make his voyage of discovery.
(From a painting by Vacslav von Brozik in the Metropolitan Museum of Art, New York)

The fleet of Columbus. Orders were immediately given to provide three small ships with provisions for twelve months. Joined with Columbus were three brothers of the Pinzon family of Palos. Through their influence crews were obtained to aid in the daring adventure. The total number of men on the three ships was not over one hundred and twenty. The *Santa Maria*, which led the fleet, was the only one of the ships that was fully decked. It was only about ninety feet long. The two smaller vessels, the *Pinta* and the *Niña*, were each about half the size of the *Santa Maria*.

The voyage of Columbus. When all was ready, the three ships left Palos August 3, 1492. Columbus first went to the Canary Islands, where he stayed for a month to make repairs to the *Pinta*. Fortunately no storms were encountered. The length of the voyage, however, soon told on the loyalty of the crew. They were more and more disturbed when they found that the compass no longer pointed to the true north. When Columbus, urged by the sailors to return at once to Spain, persisted in continuing his voyage, plots were laid to kill him or to push him overboard. There was even open mutiny. Columbus was able to persuade the sailors to continue a little longer. Floating logs, flights of land birds, and other evidences of nearness to a coast had been seen during the few days just preceding. At last one night a flickering light was seen, and the morning after that, Friday, October 12, 1492, the voyagers saw before them a small coral island which Columbus named *San Salvador*.

The landing of Columbus. The little company landed, and Columbus, dressed in his uniform of an admiral of Spain and surrounded by his men, took possession of the island in the names of the Spanish king and queen.

SPANISH DISCOVERIES

To the natives Columbus gave the name *Indians* since he believed that he had reached the East Indies. Shortly afterward he learned about the island of Cuba, lying to the west. Columbus did not doubt that it was

The landing of Columbus
(From a painting by John Vanderlyn in the dome of the national capitol)

Cipango. He decided to sail to it and thence to the mainland in order to present to the Great Khan the letters given him by the king. After sailing for some distance along the northern shore of Cuba, Columbus went to Haiti, where the *Santa Maria* ran ashore and became a total wreck.

The return to Spain. On account of the loss of this ship he decided to leave some of his men as a colony while he returned to Spain with the remaining vessels. After a stormy trip Columbus arrived at Lisbon, Portugal, in March, 1493. From here he was invited to visit the king of Portugal, who received him with great honors. From Lisbon Columbus went to Palos, where the whole population turned out in a procession to receive him. He then made his way to Barcelona, where King Ferdinand and Queen Isabella were holding their court. All along the road the people gathered from far and near to see the great discoverer and the Indians and curiosities he had brought with him.

When he arrived in the royal presence, the king and queen rose to meet him and then made him sit beside them to tell his story as though he were the greatest lord in Spain.

Second voyage of Columbus. During the following summer, Columbus was busy making preparations for another trip to the Indies. The king and queen made a grant of five times as much money as they gave for the first expedition. This second voyage was intended to be a colonizing voyage. All sorts of goods were taken, including horses, sheep, seeds, and everything that would be needed for the establishing of a new settlement. Columbus landed on the island of Haiti and began to build the town of Isabella. Only a few months passed before trouble arose. The discontented colonists refused to submit to the authority of the admiral.

Columbus received by Ferdinand and Isabella. Note the Indians and the chest of treasures from the New World.
(From a painting by Ricardo Balaca in La Biblioteca de Sevilla, Seville)

Later on Columbus undertook further explorations of the islands and coasts of the Caribbean Sea. In 1496 the difficulties with the natives as well as with the colonists had become so great that he decided to return to Spain. His story caused the king and queen to decide in his favor and against those who were opposed to him.

Other voyages of Columbus. In 1498 Columbus undertook a third voyage, not only to look after his colony in Haiti but also to make a further attempt to find the riches of Asia. He first sighted the island of Trinidad, off the coast of South America. The next day he discovered the mainland, which he soon decided was not a small island, but was another part of Asia. This belief was held by him throughout the rest of his life.

Meanwhile, affairs had been going badly in the colony. Complaints and rumors of various disorders had reached Spain, and a new governor was appointed in place of Columbus. The new governor on his arrival put Columbus and his brother in irons and deprived them of their property and lands. Columbus was sent to Spain, where he was released by the order of the monarchs, who also ordered his property restored to him.

In 1502 Columbus made a fourth voyage, with the intention of finding a passage from the Atlantic to what he believed to be the Indian Ocean. He sailed along the coast of Honduras as far as the Isthmus of

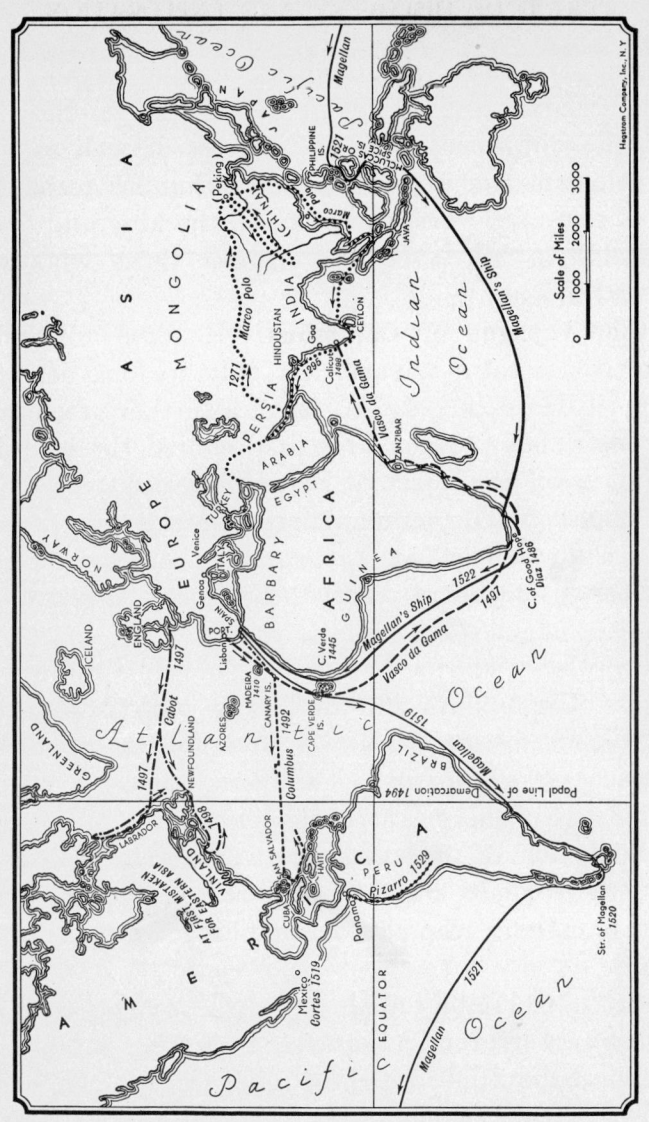

Voyages of discovery

Panama, but no strait was to be found. When he was about to return, his ship had to be run ashore on the island of Jamaica to keep it from sinking. After a year on the island he was rescued and taken to Spain. His health soon failed, and after a lingering illness he died at Valladolid on May 20, 1506.

The claims of Spain. As the result of the discoveries of Columbus and his successors the Spanish monarchs claimed the right to have exclusive power to explore, trade with, and colonize all lands that should be discovered that were not occupied by any Christian prince and that were west of a north-and-south imaginary line drawn one hundred leagues west of the Azores and Cape Verde Islands.

Amerigo Vespucci. Amerigo Vespucci (also called *Americus Vespucius*) was a Florentine who was living in Spain and who was employed in helping to fit out ships to the Indies. Having an opportunity to travel on one of the voyages to what is now South America, he kept complete notes of the voyage, of the new country, and of the things he saw there. On his return Vespucci wrote an account of his trip in letters to friends in Florence. These letters had wide circulation in Europe during the early years of the sixteenth century so that outside of Spain Amerigo Vespucci was a much better known name than Columbus.

How America was named. One of the letters of Vespucci was printed in 1507 in a geography published by Martin Waldseemüller in Lorraine. Waldseemüller thought that Vespucci had discovered the mainland. He proposed in his book that the new world be named Amerige or America since Amerigo discovered it. This

Printing Vespucci's book about America

Note the way the press is built. The man on the right is inking the types. (From a drawing by G. G. White in Bryant's *Popular History of the United States*)

idea was soon copied in geographies and maps and, together with the wide circulation of the letters of Vespucci, served to fix the name *America* on the New World. Vespucci does not seem to have helped in doing this injustice to the memory of Columbus. However, in his letters he does not mention anyone but himself in telling of his voyages.

In Spain the name America was not accepted for centuries. The western world continued to be called *the Indies*. Not until 1758 did Spanish maps contain the name America.

Balboa discovers the Pacific Ocean. Not long after the death of Columbus, Balboa, a planter of Haiti, sailed with an expedition to the mainland of South America. He was heavily in debt and in order to avoid imprisonment he had himself placed in a barrel which was supposed to contain provisions for the voyage. In this way he was smuggled on board the ship. At his suggestion the expedition changed its course and went to Darien on the Isthmus of Panama. On its arrival at Darien Balboa assumed command of the party and made an alliance with some of the native tribes. He also obtained from them food and a quantity of gold. When the Spaniards quarreled over the division of the treasure, a chief told them that across the mountains which they could see was another ocean on which sailed big ships from a land where the people had plenty of gold. In 1513 Balboa decided to find out if this story was true. With about two hundred Spaniards and as many Indian helpers, he set out to cross the low mountains of the isthmus. In eighteen days he reached the last summit and looked out on the broad Pacific, or South Sea, as it was called. Four

SPANISH DISCOVERIES

days later he reached the shore and took possession, on behalf of Spain, of all the lands washed by the great ocean.

This was the most important discovery that the Spaniards had made since Columbus had reached the

The discovery of the Pacific Ocean by Balboa

mainland of South America. Balboa was a wise and just governor and was especially successful in his dealing with the natives. Unfortunately for the Indians Balboa was put to death a few years later by a new governor who had become jealous of his ability.

Ferdinand Magellan's ship sails around the world. A young man named Magellan had been connected with the government of Portugal for many years. He had seen ships return from voyages to India with rich cargoes. In 1505 he went to the East himself, where he remained for seven years. During this time he learned of other islands, far to the east of the Spice Islands, which were even richer than the islands found by Vasco da Gama, a Portuguese navigator, who sailed round the Cape of Good Hope and reached India in 1498 (p. 44). Knowledge that these islands were so far to the east of Asia suggested to Magellan that they were probably close to the west coast of America and so could easily be reached if a passage could be found through the new continent. Not having received any encouragement in Portugal, he went to Spain. At a meeting with the king and his advisers Magellan showed his route on a globe and told the king that he could reach the Spice Islands without going on lands or water belonging to Portugal. He felt sure there must be a strait somewhere between the Atlantic and the Pacific Ocean.

In September, 1519, Magellan left Spain with five small ships and a few hundred men. They followed the coast of South America from Pernambuco to the Plata River, and from there on every inlet of the sea was carefully examined. When he had almost reached the passage for which he was looking, he decided to go into winter quarters. Some of the commanders, wishing to return to Spain, organized a mutiny which Magellan promptly quelled. In the spring the search was renewed, and the entrance to the Strait of Magellan was found. Thirty-eight days were spent in passing through the strait.

When Magellan entered the new ocean, he found it so quiet in comparison with the stormy Atlantic which

Magellan passing through the straits

he had so recently left that he named it the Pacific, or peaceful, Ocean.

The voyage across the Pacific. On the long voyage across the Pacific the provisions gave out, and the sailors were forced finally to eat pieces of leather that formed part of the rigging. The water had become so bad that the sailors had to hold their noses while drinking it, and their biscuit had fallen into a wormy powder. Still Magellan sailed on. Finally the ships reached a group of islands which Magellan called *the Ladrones*, or Islands of Robbers, where provisions and water were obtained and where many of their goods were stolen by the natives. A few days later they reached outlying islands of the Philippines. Here a Malay slave who was with the expedition was able to make himself understood by the inhabitants. Magellan was now sure that he had reached his goal. He was not, however, to return in triumph to Spain, for a little later he was killed in a fight with the natives.

The return to Spain. The expedition was now reduced to two ships and a few more than a hundred men. One ship tried to return to Panama but was obliged to give up the attempt. The other, the *Victoria*, about the size of one of the smaller ships of Columbus, headed for the Cape of Good Hope and Spain. When the sailors stopped at the Cape Verde Islands, the Portuguese, finding that they had been to the Spice Islands, seized a boatload of them, and the little ship was barely able to escape.

On reaching Spain the thirty-one survivors, about one tenth of the number who had left three years before, were received at court by the emperor. The expedition brought back twenty-six tons of spices that were sold for enough to pay the entire cost of the expedition.

What Magellan's voyage proved. The voyage of Magellan had proved the earth to be round. It had also proved that, instead of the earth's being three fourths land and one fourth water, as was generally believed, the proportions were almost exactly the opposite. It had proved that America was far separated from Asia. Finally, it was now certain that the path to India and the East around the Cape of Good Hope was a better way than the passage around the southern end of the Western Continent.

STUDY HELPS

Map Work

On a world map draw the voyages of the important Spanish explorers, including the voyage of Magellan.

Activities

Secure pictures associated with the discoverers, such as scenes connected with Columbus or pictures of places with which he was associated. You should start a scrapbook in which you can place from time to time additional pictures connected with other parts of the history of our country.

Make a model of the kind of ship used by Columbus.

Dramatize such scenes as the landing of Columbus or his interview with the king and queen of Spain when he returned.

Special Work

In the story of Marco Polo find his accounts of the wealth of the East that might induce people to want to find an easier route to that region.

What were some of the new aids to the art of sailing that made it possible for captains to be more certain of their position at sea?

Find out what happened that caused the trade of Genoa and other Italian cities to be almost altogether cut off.

What other group of people explored parts of America before the time of Columbus?

Storybooks to Read

Colum, Padraic: *The Voyagers* (Before Columbus)
Johnston, Mary: *Admiral of the Ocean Sea* (Columbus)
Jordan, Charlotte Brewster: *Discovering Christopher Columbus*
Stapley, Mildred: *Christopher Columbus*

2. SPANISH CONQUERORS AND EXPLORERS; THE PORTUGUESE IN BRAZIL

Cortes. Hernando Cortes was a young man who had gone from Spain to Haiti and later had joined an expedition to settle Cuba. From Cuba an exploring party had been sent to the coast of Mexico and had brought back stories of the great wealth and high civilization of the people. It was then determined by the

Cortes visits the Aztec king Montezuma.

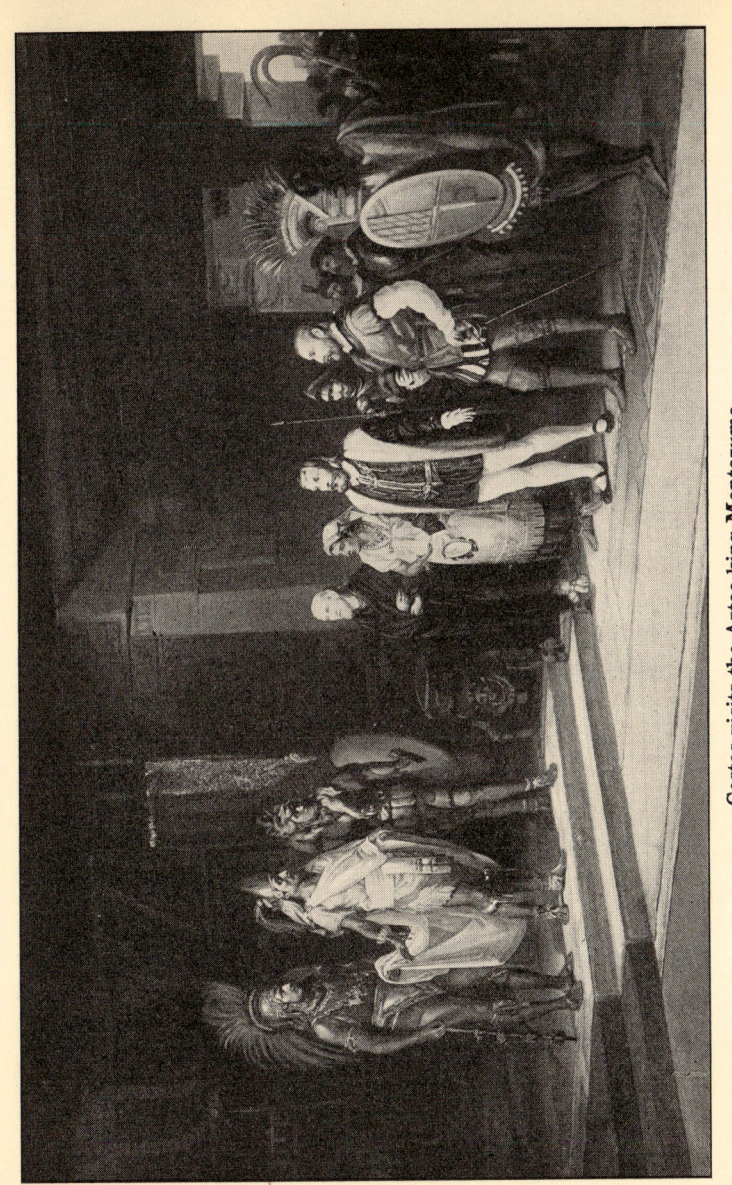

(From a painting by Juan Ortega in San Carlos Academy of Fine Arts in Mexico City)

Spaniards to make a settlement in Mexico, and Cortes was given command of the expedition. When they landed in Mexico, there was a sharp battle with the natives, but Cortes soon established more friendly relations with them.

The Aztecs. *Aztecs* was the name given to a group of three tribes who ruled almost all of Mexico. The most powerful of these tribes held the city of Mexico and the surrounding country. Other tribes of Indians were held in subjection by the Aztecs and were compelled to pay tribute in the form of food and human victims for the religious sacrifices.

Except for this savage kind of religion Mexico was well managed by its Aztec rulers. Much engineering skill was used in digging canals, building roads, and constructing great and wonderfully ornamented buildings. The people knew about the movements of the stars and planets, and had made a calendar by which they could record the dates of events.

The subject tribes were very willing to side with Cortes in the hope that they would be delivered from their Aztec masters. Besides, all these tribes had a tradition that one of their gods, who long before had gone off to the East, was soon to return. Many of the natives believed that Cortes and his white companions were the fair god and his attendants. They thought that the ships of Cortes were great white birds that had brought the god back to Mexico. Thus Fortune set the stage for Cortes!

SPANISH CONQUERORS AND EXPLORERS 33

The capture of Mexico by Cortes. The city of Mexico was situated at nearly the middle of the country on an island in the middle of a lake. It was

The capture of Mexico City by Cortes
The horses of the Spaniards terrified the Aztecs. Note the armor of the Spaniards and the architecture of the house in the background. (From an engraving after a painting by Alonzo Chappel)

connected with the shore by long roads raised above the water level.

Cortes landed at Vera Cruz and then sank his ships so that his men knew that they had no way of retreat. He then advanced to the city and was joined on the way by a large body of warriors from a tribe which just then was at war with the Aztecs. As he approached the city, messengers bearing presents were sent to him by the Aztec king Montezuma, who begged him to stop his advance. Finding that Cortes was determined to proceed to the city, Montezuma sent out an escort which conducted Cortes and his men to his palace.

Cortes fortified the council house in which they had been permitted to live and later seized and held Montezuma and his brother as prisoners. Afterwards, during the absence of Cortes, the Spaniards attacked the Aztecs while the latter were celebrating a festival. The struggle for the city lasted a week, during which Montezuma was killed by his own people for having permitted the Spaniards to enter the city. Cortes and his companions then decided to leave the city of Mexico. After a terrible fight the Spaniards succeeded in cutting their way out. About a year later Cortes returned with reënforcements and more Indian allies and captured the city. The old city was destroyed. Cortes built a new capital and tried in every way to restore order and prosperity to the conquered country.

Mexico under Spanish rule. The chief object of the Spaniards in all their conquests was to obtain gold, silver, and other valuable products to send back to Spain. While actual slavery was forbidden as far as the Indians were concerned, the Spaniards forced them to work in the mines and to till the fields in order that the Spaniards might obtain gold and that the workers might be fed. Many Spaniards came to Mexico to aid in the government and to act as overseers, but their

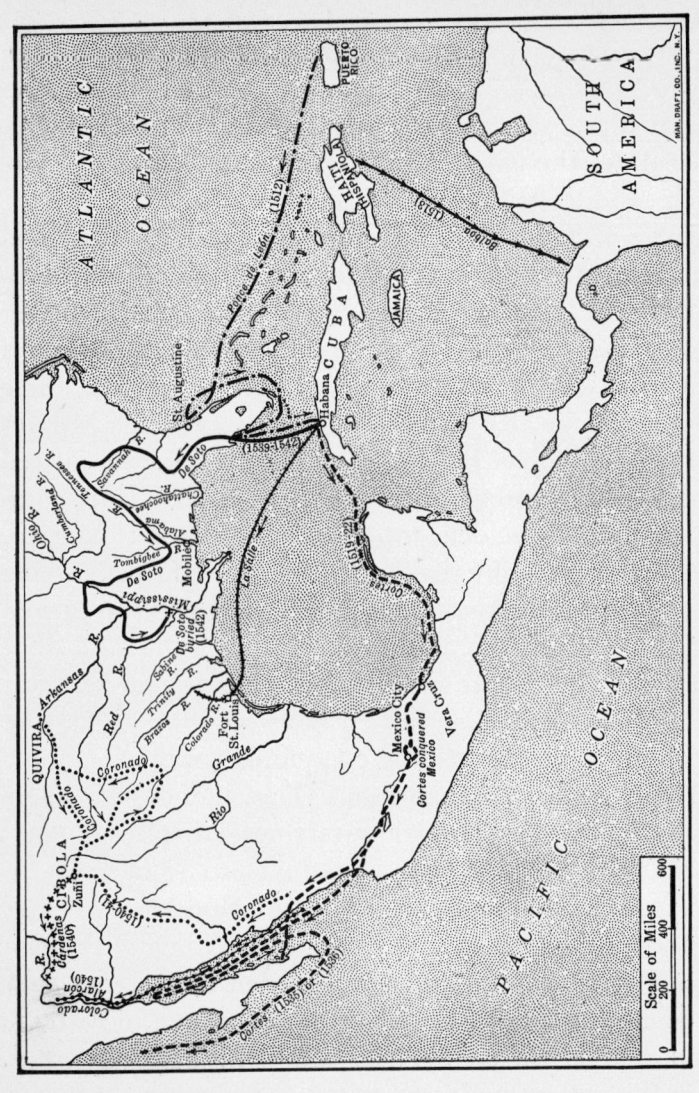

Routes of the early Spanish explorers and of the Frenchman La Salle

chief aims were to get together quantities of gold and silver and to return to Spain with their riches. We must give the Spaniards credit, however, for doing two things: First, they taught the Indians many of the arts of civilization, showing them how best to cultivate their fields and to grow their crops. They taught them also how to use many of the tools and implements that they had known nothing about before the Spaniards came. A second thing that was done by the Spaniards was that they tried to have the Indians give up their old religion and, by means of missions scattered over the country, they taught them Christianity and persuaded them to give up their pagan custom of making human sacrifices.

Pizarro and the conquest of Peru. Francisco Pizarro, after having made several voyages along the northwest coast of South America, led an expedition from Panama to Peru in 1531. His object was to conquer this country and to secure for Spain some of the great wealth of the Peruvian Indians. After many hardships, Pizarro reached Cusco, the capital of Peru. The Inca, or ruler, and his people were at first friendly to the Spaniards. Pizarro determined to seize the Inca and hold him for ransom. A sudden fight was started, and the Inca was seized and imprisoned in his own palace. The Spaniards promised the Inca that he would be released if he would fill a room full of gold. From all over the country his people brought objects of gold from their homes and their temples until the room

SPANISH CONQUERORS AND EXPLORERS 37

was filled to the height of a man. Nearly all the gold and silver in the country had been brought to the capital. Pizarro and his followers seized this immense treasure, but instead of releasing the Inca, they treacherously slew him. Pizarro then seized the government and made Peru a province of Spain. The Peruvians were treated by the Spaniards in much the same fashion as the Mexicans were treated.

Coronado and the exploration of the Southwest. Even before the time of Columbus there were stories told of a mysterious island called *Antilia*, on which were seven cities overflowing with gold. Francisco de Coronado, who was the Spanish governor of northern Mexico, heard a rumor about seven rich cities situated to the northwest of his province. The cities of which Coronado heard were probably the towns of the Pueblo Indians, some of which are still in existence. In some way these two stories got mixed and the cities of the Pueblos were thought to be the same seven rich cities

The last Inca, or king, of Peru, who was treacherously slain by order of Pizarro
(From Herrera's *Historia General de las Indias Occidentales*)

shown on the old maps of Antilia. No time was lost in trying to secure some of this wealth for Spain.

Photo from Ewing Galloway

The pueblo, or town, of Taos, New Mexico

It houses about two hundred families and is one of the towns visited by Coronado. Originally there were no doors, the houses being entered through the roofs which were reached by long ladders. The things that look like large hats are the cooking ovens.

In 1540 Coronado proceeded up the west coast of Mexico, accompanied by two ships in the Gulf of California. When they reached the head of the gulf, the two ships explored the Colorado River as far as the

Grand Canyon. Coronado and the rest of the party turned to the northeast and soon came upon the towns of the Pueblos. The Spaniards captured the town of Cibola, the first of the seven cities, but little or no gold was found. From this point a party was sent to the west, which discovered the Grand Canyon of the Colorado. The expedition then proceeded to the middle of what is now New Mexico, where they stayed all winter. In the spring of 1541 Coronado heard from an Indian of another rich city far to the north called Quivira. He decided to try to find it. After a long journey Coronado with a few followers found Quivira in the present state of Kansas, but there was no gold. Disappointed in his search for gold, Coronado the following spring returned to his province in Mexico.

Spanish remains in the Southwest. The work of Christianizing the natives, as well as that of teaching them the Spanish language and customs, was done chiefly by members of the different religious orders of the Catholic Church. In the Indian villages they built churches, hospitals, and schools in which the children, both boys and girls, were taught Spanish and religion.

Among the wild Indians missionary work was first carried on in the endeavor to convert them to Christianity. The Indians were then gathered in villages, called *missions*, where they were taught not only religion, but various handicrafts. Especial attention was given to agriculture, not only in order to provide food, but also to check the Indian tendency to a wandering life. In time a mission slowly became an Indian village and finally a Spanish town. The natives forgot their Indian language and customs, and the

A Spanish mission — San Xavier del Bol, Tucson, Arizona

village became like the older Spanish towns. Then the line of missions would be pushed still further into the unexplored region beyond.

Many important American cities are located where the Spanish missionaries founded the Indian missions. Among these may be mentioned San Francisco and Santa Barbara in California and Santa Fe and Las Vegas in New Mexico.

Ponce de León and the discovery of Florida. While Juan Ponce de León was governor of Puerto Rico, he heard wonderful tales about an island called *Bimini*. A story of a magical spring on this island that would restore youth to the old was the chief reason that caused Ponce de León to make a voyage to discover it. He secured permission to discover and colonize Bimini and sailed among the islands of the West Indies for several months, trying to find it. Finally, about the time of Easter in the year 1512, he came upon an unknown coast. He named the land Florida, since he had discovered it at Eastertime, the feast of flowers. Ponce de León followed the Florida coast around to the Gulf of Mexico, still looking for Bimini and the Fountain of Youth. Not succeeding, he finally returned to Puerto Rico. Some years later he again went to Florida to plant a colony. In a fight with the Indians he was so badly wounded that he went back to Cuba, where he soon afterward died.

De Soto finds the Mississippi. Hernando de Soto had gone from Spain to the Isthmus of Panama to seek his fortune. While there, he had accompanied Pizarro in the conquest of Peru and had returned to Spain with a fortune of three hundred thousand dollars in gold. At his request the king made him governor of Cuba and Florida and gave him permission to explore and settle in what is now the southeastern part of the United States.

After remaining about a year in Havana to refurnish his ships, he sailed for Florida and landed at Tampa Bay. For three years his expedition wandered slowly

De Soto discovers the Mississippi River.
(From a painting by Stanley M. Arthurs)

through the territory now included in our southern states. He crossed Georgia, followed the Savannah River nearly to Tennessee, and then went southwest to Mobile Bay. Here De Soto again turned to the northwest and traveled until he reached an Indian village in northern Mississippi. A sudden Indian attack almost destroyed the expedition. Undaunted by the disaster, De Soto continued his journey, and at last, in the spring of 1541, discovered the great Mississippi River. After a month spent in building boats, the river was crossed near the present city of Memphis, in Tennessee. West of the river the route of the expedition was mostly within the present state of Arkansas.

The following spring (1542) De Soto died, and his followers, wrapping him in a cloak weighted with sand and stones, buried him at night in the great river which he had discovered. This was done so that the hostile Indians might not know of the death of the commander. The expedition, subjected to constant Indian attacks, slowly made its way back to the Spanish settlements in Mexico.

Historians have pointed out that the year 1542, fifty years after the discovery of America, marks the close of the period of important Spanish discoveries, explorations, and conquests.

The Portuguese and Brazil. Under the famous Prince Henry the Navigator, brother of the king of Portugal, Portuguese sea captains had been accustomed, long before the time of Columbus, to make voyages down the northwest coast of Africa. One of these daring sailors, Bartholomew Dias, had reached the Cape of Good Hope before Columbus discovered

Prince Henry the Navigator discussing plans for exploring the coast of Africa
(From a group by Dwight Franklin in the Brooklyn Children's Museum)

America. A few years after the discovery, Vasco da Gama succeeded in rounding the Cape of Good Hope and making his way to India. Thereafter the Portuguese were as much interested in expeditions to India by way of the Cape of Good Hope as the Spanish were

SPANISH CONQUERORS AND EXPLORERS

in their endeavors to reach India by sailing across the Atlantic. Both Spain and Portugal soon realized that their claims in the East must sooner or later conflict with each other.

The new lands divided between Spain and Portugal; the Line of Demarcation. The king and queen of Spain applied to the Pope to make a division of all the new lands which had been or which might later be discovered. The Pope fixed upon what is known as the *Line of Demarcation.* This line was drawn one hundred leagues west of the Azores and the Cape Verde Islands, which Portugal had occupied about fifty years before. All west of this line was opened to exploration and colonizing by Spain; all east of it was to belong to Portugal. King John of Portugal was not satisfied with this division, and a year later, by the Treaty of Tordesillas, the line of division was fixed at 370 leagues west of Cape Verde Islands. Later, it was found that South America projected so far toward Africa that nearly all of what is now Brazil was east of this line, and so became the property of Portugal. Brazil was held as a province of Portugal until about one hundred years ago, when it gained its independence.

STUDY HELPS

Map Work

On a map of the western continent draw the routes of the principal Spanish explorers. Indicate the regions conquered by the Spanish. Be sure to put the names of the conquerors and explorers where they belong.

ACTIVITIES

Add to your book of pictures some associated with Spanish exploration and conquest, such as pictures of Aztec ruins in Mexico or of old towns of the cliff-dwellers or of old Spanish missions.

Dramatize such scenes as the meeting of Pizarro with the Inca.

If possible, visit a museum that has relics of America before Columbus and tell the class what you have seen.

SPECIAL WORK

Find out what cities the Spanish founded within the present limits of the United States before 1600.

How did the Indians live that Coronado encountered on his expedition?

What names did the Spanish give to the different parts of their claim?

STORYBOOK TO READ

Henty, G. A.: *By Right of Conquest* (Cortes in Mexico)

3. FRANCE SEEKS LANDS IN THE NEW WORLD

France sends Verrazano on a voyage of discovery. Not until 1523 do we learn of any real interest taken by France in the discovery of the new world although

FRANCE SEEKS LANDS IN THE NEW WORLD 47

it is known that fishing vessels from Brittany had gone to the coast of Newfoundland as early as 1504.

Courtesy Chas. Scribner's Sons

The ship of Verrazano exploring a harbor
(From a drawing by A. R. Waud in Bryant's *Popular History of the United States*)

Giovanni da Verrazano was a Florentine who had voyaged much in the eastern Mediterranean region, and while there had learned something of the regions lying farther east. He felt certain that he would be able to reach *Cathay*, or China, by sailing to the north and northwest. Having made preparation, Verrazano set out in January, 1524, going first to the Madeira Islands. Proceeding westward, he reached land in latitude 34° north, on the coast of what is now North Carolina. He then sailed south for about 200 miles, but finding no safe harbor he turned again to the north and explored the coast as far as Labrador.

On the way he appears to have been in New York Bay and Narragansett Bay and to have discovered Block Island. Long Island he thought to be part of the mainland. He described Cape Cod and told of a coast with many islands, which was probably the coast of Maine. After he had sailed along the shores of Newfoundland and Labrador, his provisions gave out and he returned to France.

Results of Verrazano's voyage. In some way Verrazano had become convinced that the New World did not join either Asia or Africa. He thought it possible that it was joined to Europe in the far north by way of Russia or Norway, but he felt sure that it was not and that America was a separate continent inclosed between the Atlantic and Pacific Oceans.

The voyage of Verrazano had two other results: It gave a start to French exploration and settlement of the northern part of this continent, which resulted in the establishment of the French colonial empire in America. In the second place, it became the foundation of all claims which the French later made to any part of North America.

FRANCE SEEKS LANDS IN THE NEW WORLD 49

Jacques Cartier. Ten years passed before the French made another attempt at exploration. In 1534 the French king, Francis I, sent a Breton sailor, Jacques Cartier, to make further explorations and discoveries

A group of Indians at Quebec watching Cartier take possession of the land for France
(From a drawing by George Agnew Reid in the Dominion Archives, Ottawa)

and to find, if possible, a northern passage through to the Pacific Ocean.

Cartier reached the Gulf of St. Lawrence and then went back to France on account of a shortage of supplies. The following year he returned and carefully explored the St. Lawrence River as far as the rapids at Montreal. The explorer named these the La Chine Rapids. *La Chine* is the French name for China, and this name was given them in derision of the idea that people could reach China by following the river.

Because of the severe winter which the explorers had to live through, Cartier took back to France unfavorable reports of the climate. Five years later, however, he established a colony and fort at Quebec. This was soon afterward abandoned on account of disagreement among the settlers and because of shortage of supplies.

Samuel de Champlain founds the first permanent French settlements in America. During the sixteenth century several attempts had been made by French Protestants to settle along the Atlantic coast of what is now the United States, but for one reason or another none was successful. In the year 1600, however, a French company was formed for the purpose of trading in America. On the first voyage a young man named Samuel de Champlain was taken along as pilot. The expedition proceeded as far as Cartier's expedition had gone, nearly seventy years before, and obtained a large cargo of furs. After a second expedition, which settled Port Royal in Acadia in 1605, Champlain was made governor of New France. As a result of his efforts French settlements were established in the St. Lawrence Valley. In 1608 Quebec was permanently founded as capital of the French settlements in America.

FRANCE SEEKS LANDS IN THE NEW WORLD 51

The work of Champlain. Champlain, who was much interested in exploration, traveled about New France, making friends with the Indians and laying the foundations for the rich fur trade which was to become the chief source of revenue from the French possessions.

He explored the Ottawa and Saguenay Rivers in Canada and discovered the beautiful lake that lies

Photo from Ewing Galloway

Champlain's conference with the chiefs of the Algonquins
(From a bronze panel by Mrs. S. J. Farnham in the Pan American Union Building)

between Vermont and New York which now bears his name. Later he got as far west as Lake Huron while searching for a passage to Asia. In 1634 one of his agents reached what is now Wisconsin and made fur-trading agreements with the Indians.

Champlain helps the Algonquin Indians against the Iroquois. In the course of these explorations an event happened which was to have an important result in the struggle between the French and English for control in the New World. Champlain had made friends with the Algonquin Indians of the St. Lawrence Valley. In 1609 he and some of his men accompanied one of their war parties against the powerful Iroquois of central New York. Near Lake Champlain they met a party of hostile Iroquois, who were easily put to rout by the firearms of the Frenchmen. From this time on the Iroquois became bitter enemies of the French as well as of the Algonquins. When the French and English began their struggle for the possession of North America, the Iroquois sided with the English. The Algonquins were driven from their hunting grounds, and the French settlements were repeatedly attacked by their Indian enemies, the Iroquois.

Growth of the French settlements. The French settlements grew very slowly in comparison with those of the English along the Atlantic coast. The French, like the Spanish, were interested chiefly in getting wealth from the New World and very little, if at all, in the founding of new communities that should be self-supporting. The Frenchmen who came over were traders, explorers, soldiers, or officials, whose business it was to take care of the valuable fur trade. Very few of them brought their families with them with the idea of making their homes in New France. They also tried to prevent other nations, particularly the English and Dutch, from interfering with their trade.

As time went on, more settlers and their families arrived who made their homes on tracts of land which had been granted to French noblemen. They had no

La Salle builds the *Griffin* in which he explored the Great Lakes.
(From a painting by Stanley M. Arthurs)

right to participate in the government. They could not hold a meeting to discuss matters which concerned the little settlements alone without the permission of the lord of the land.

Later settlements increased the number of French people in Canada, so that to-day, after almost two hundred years of English government, parts of eastern Canada are very largely French in language and customs. More than half the population of the large cities of Montreal and Quebec speak French and the laws and signs in this part of Canada are printed in both French and English.

The explorations of La Salle. Robert Cavalier, better known as the Sieur de la Salle, arrived in Canada in 1666 and at once began a careful study of Indian languages and customs. He traveled extensively over Canada and through the Middle West, north of the Ohio, founding trading stations, building forts, collecting furs, and exploring unknown regions. Governor Frontenac of New France depended much on La Salle's knowledge of the Indians. La Salle made several trips to France in order to obtain from the king permission to found new settlements and to make further explorations, and especially to get authority to make his way down the Mississippi.

La Salle explored the Great Lakes in a small vessel, the *Griffin*, which was built near Niagara Falls. In this vessel he sailed over the Lakes as far west as the Strait of Mackinac. In the summer of 1681 La Salle

Courtesy Singer Sewing Machine Company

La Salle at the mouth of the Arkansas River taking possession of Louisiana in the name of Louis XIV

began his exploration of the Mississippi Valley. From the Great Lakes he followed the Illinois River to the Mississippi. From this point he sailed down the great river, and near the Arkansas River he took possession of the entire valley and named it *Louisiana* in honor of Louis XIV, king of France. A few years later he endeavored to found a colony in Louisiana. He sailed from France for the Gulf of Mexico but was unable to find the entrance to the Mississippi. La Salle divided his party, leaving half in the new colony and intending with the other half to make his way to Canada for help. On the way La Salle was killed by some of his companions.

The French missionaries. The task of converting the Indians to Christianity was one of the conditions on which the French king permitted companies to trade in the French possessions in America. This labor fell on the shoulders of Catholic missionaries, who were members of religious orders, just as the missionaries in the Spanish colonies were. These faithful and devoted men followed the rivers and lakes far into the interior of the country, converting the Indians and preparing the way for the trade which followed them. The most important of these missionaries were Fathers Hennepin and Marquette. Hennepin explored the region of the Great Lakes and was probably one of the first white men to see Niagara Falls.

Marquette's labors took him farther west. Accompanied by Louis Joliet, a fur trader, he came in **1673**

FRANCE SEEKS LANDS IN THE NEW WORLD 57

upon the northern waters of the same Mississippi River that the Spaniard, De Soto, had first discovered far to the south more than a century and a quarter before. Marquette and Joliet explored the river as far as the mouth of the Arkansas.

Courtesy Chas. Scribner's Sons
The discovery of Niagara
La Salle or Father Hennepin probably was the first white man to see Niagara Falls. (From Hennepin's *A New Discovery of a Vast Country in America*)

French traders. The French, like the Spanish, wished for new territories and new wealth, and they were anxious to convert the heathen Indians. They were very willing to take whatever furs or other valuables the Indians brought them without trying to

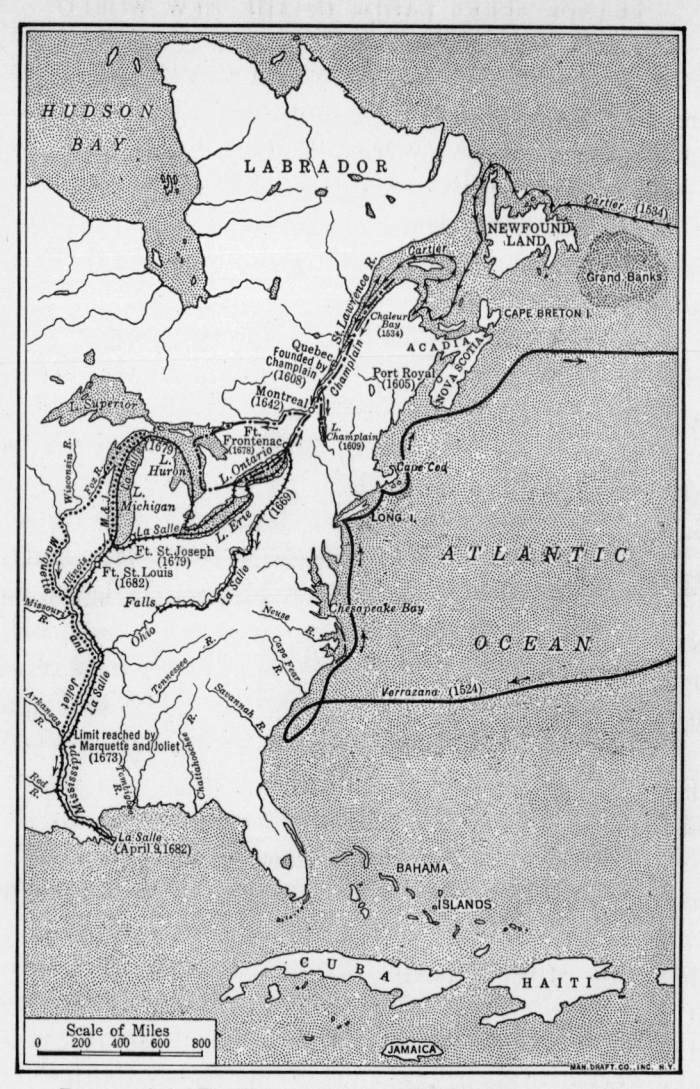

Routes of the French explorers and the French line of forts

force the Indians to adopt French ways. In fact the French traders were much more apt to adopt Indian ways. Often they married Indian wives and were adopted by the natives into their tribes. This method of dealing with the Indians proved very helpful to the French later when the conflict arose between them and the English.

We do not find in New France forced labor, or forced tribute from the natives, as we found in the Spanish possessions. In time the Indians found some of the French ways good and adopted them. But there was no attempt to make the Indians live like Frenchmen. On the other hand, the French did not try to form self-supporting colonies in America such as the English founded. There were no factories and few farms. Nearly all the food and other supplies had to be brought from the homeland. These were paid for with furs and fish, which were almost the only products of New France.

Claims of France in the New World. As a result of the explorations and settlements made by Cartier, Champlain, La Salle, and other French explorers, France laid claim by right of discovery and occupation to all that part of North America belonging to the valleys of the Great Lakes and the St. Lawrence and the valley of the Mississippi, including that of the Ohio. It may help you to remember that these valleys were claimed by France if you note that these rivers and lakes form a large irregular *F* on the map of North America.

4. THE DUTCH PLAN COLONIES IN AMERICA

Spain and Holland. About the time the larger nations of Europe were making discoveries and explorations in the New World, Holland had come under the control of Spain. Later, when religious troubles arose in Europe, Holland became rebellious. A long struggle followed between Spain and the unruly provinces, during which Holland was aided with money and soldiers from England.

By the end of the reign of Queen Elizabeth of England, in 1603, Spain had given up hope of winning back these provinces though she refused to acknowledge their independence until nearly fifty years later.

The discoveries of Henry Hudson. In 1609 the Dutch, as the people of Holland (or the Netherlands) are called, sent out Henry Hudson, an English sea captain, to discover a way to India by going around the north of Europe. He got as far as Novaya Zemlya, an island in the Arctic Ocean north of Russia, but found his way blocked by ice. He then turned and sailed for Newfoundland and traveled as far south along the coast as Chesapeake Bay. On his return he entered the Hudson River. Here he spent a month in exploration and in trading with the Indians. A few years later a fort was built on Manhattan Island, and exploration was continued.

Later the Dutch chartered a company for trading in *New Netherland*, as the country discovered by Hudson was called. It extended between Virginia and New France, from the fortieth to the forty-fifth degree of north latitude. No conflict with the English was intended since the charter was for trading purposes only.

Henry Hudson and the *Half Moon* in the harbor
(From a group by Dwight Franklin in the Museum of the City of New York)

The Dutch settlements in New Netherland. Nevertheless, the Dutch West India Company proceeded to send out a number of parties which were the first attempts of the Dutch to found colonies in America. One party under the command of Captain Cornelius May sailed to the Delaware River, where they erected a fort near the present site of Gloucester, New Jersey, called

Fort Nassau. Another party went up the Hudson River and built Fort Orange, where Albany now is.

Peter Minuit succeeded May as governor of New Netherland in 1626. He bought from the Indians the whole of Manhattan Island for goods and trinkets worth

Courtesy Title Guarantee and Trust Company, New York
Peter Minuit buying Manhattan Island for twenty-four dollars' worth of goods

about twenty-four dollars and established a settlement which was called New Amsterdam.

Other small settlements were made from time to time, and eventually, as we shall see, quarrels with the English and other neighbors broke out.

The Dutch claim in North America. The claim of the Dutch to territory in America was founded on the explorations of Hudson and his successors. During the

THE DUTCH PLAN COLONIES IN AMERICA 63

wars in Europe, which continued through the seventeenth century, Holland got possession of territories and colonies in Africa and the East Indies. Holland later gave up its claims to lands in America in order that it might hold its possessions in Africa and the East, which were thought to be more valuable.

STUDY HELPS

Map Work

On a map of North America draw the routes of the explorations of the French and Dutch. Shade in different colors the claims of France and Holland.

Activities

Add to your book pictures connected with the French and Dutch explorations, such as pictures of St. Malo, in France, the port from which Cartier sailed, or pictures of the St. Lawrence River and Lake Champlain.

Make a model of a Canadian Indian village.

Dramatize a scene in which the French king grants Cartier permission to find new lands in America.

Special Work

What were the names of some of the important forts built by the French in what is now the United States?

What American cities have grown up on the sites of some of these forts?

Do the French now have any possessions in North America? If so, where are they?

What explorations did Henry Hudson make for the English?

Storybooks to Read

Marquis, T. G.: *Marguerite de Roberval*
Munroe, Kirk: *The Flamingo Feather*

5. ENGLAND BECOMES INTERESTED IN AMERICA

John Cabot. You have already learned that Columbus, discouraged by his treatment in Spain, sent his brother to England to try to get the aid of the king of that country for his plans. The king, Henry VII, made some promises, but when the brother reached Spain with the promises, Columbus himself had just returned from the voyage in which America had been discovered.

King Henry resolved to make up what he could of his lost opportunity. He granted a request from an Italian sailor named John Cabot for authority to discover and govern any new land which he might discover in America. Cabot did not receive authority to explore in the southern seas since the king wished to avoid a conflict with either Spain or Portugal.

The voyage of Cabot. Cabot seems to have had the idea of reaching the East by sailing west even before the voyage of Columbus. In May, 1497, Cabot sailed from Bristol in a small ship. He first went to the northwest and then to the west. After sailing four hundred leagues, he reached the mainland, probably near Labrador, which he thought to be the lands of the Great Khan. Cabot then followed the coast to the southwest for nearly a thousand miles as far as South Carolina and then returned to Bristol.

Cabot's voyage, giving, as it did, promise of England's sharing in the supposed wealth of the New World, aroused great excitement in England. The king gave Cabot only a small sum of money, but later

From an old print
Cabot leaving Labrador to return to England

he awarded him a pension of twenty pounds a year which would be worth to-day about twenty-five times as much.

Another voyage possibly was made by Cabot in 1498, but very little is known of it. The story of the second voyage was told by John Cabot's son Sebastian. In his story he claims most of the credit for John Cabot's discoveries. There is no real proof that a second voyage ever was made.

England's claim based on the discoveries of John Cabot. The importance of the discoveries of Cabot lies in the fact that they laid the foundation for English claims to part of North America. These claims resulted in the settlement of the thirteen continental colonies as well as of numerous others in the islands of the West Indies. The French and Indian War, which was the result of conflict between these claims and the claims of France, gave England the control also of the great Dominion of Canada.

The struggle between England and Spain. During the later years of the sixteenth century Spain and England were really in a state of war with each other, though war had not actually been declared. Holland had rebelled against the control of Spain, and England aided Holland in the fight. Another reason for England's attitude toward Spain was that English commerce had been rapidly growing. This growing trade interfered very much with the established trade of other nations of Europe, particularly with that of Spain and Portugal.

Ever since the time of Cabot English sailors had become more and more adventurous in their voyages. This brought them and their government into constant disputes with Spain, since the hardy English sailors frequently made their way south of the Strait of Gibraltar into waters that Spain claimed as its own. The Spaniards also treated English sailors very badly when they reached Spanish ports. It was natural, therefore, that the English captains should take revenge as best they could even though England and Spain were supposed to be at peace.

Sir Francis Drake. The most daring of these English sea captains was Sir Francis Drake. Drake had been a pilot on some English ships that had taken slaves from Africa to the West Indies, which was against the laws of Spain. Driven by storms, he took refuge at Vera Cruz in Mexico. Although the Spanish authorities at first agreed not to harm the English, their treasure was seized and their ships were destroyed. The Englishmen were just able to escape with their lives. Drake then and there resolved some day to punish the Spaniards for their treachery.

Drake attacks the Spanish West Indies. A few years later, Drake gathered together a little squadron and sailed for Spanish America. At the Isthmus of Panama he attacked the Spanish settlements and gained considerable booty. He marched across the Isthmus, saw the Pacific, and resolved to make further exploration in that ocean. He then returned across the Isthmus and went back to England. When Drake reached England and told the results of his expedition, there was much excitement. Spain protested, but Queen Elizabeth did not punish him although according to law he was a pirate because he had gone on a sea-roving expedition without any authority from the queen. Besides, England was not at war with Spain.

The *Golden Hind*
The ship of Sir Francis Drake in which he raided the Spanish towns of South America
(From a book published in Leyden in 1588)

Drake's voyage around the world. The relations between England and Spain were rapidly approaching a state of war, and Drake was soon able to organize another expedition against the Spaniards. With five well-equipped vessels he sailed again for the Spanish settlements. This time he resolved to do his work in the Pacific. By the time he had passed through the

ENGLAND BECOMES INTERESTED IN AMERICA   69

Strait of Magellan, he had but one ship. The others were lost or had returned home.

Sailing up the Pacific coast, he stopped at many of the Spanish ports, took them by surprise, and loaded

Queen Elizabeth knighting Francis Drake

his vessels with the gold, silver, and jewelry, worth millions of dollars, that he captured from them.

Drake returns to England by way of the Pacific Ocean. Drake sailed north as far as the present state of Oregon, looking for a northern passage back to England. On the way, he landed near where San Francisco is now and took possession of the country in the name of Queen Elizabeth. Not finding the passage that he looked for and not daring to return home through the seas where the Spaniards would be on the watch for him, he boldly sailed across the Pacific and Indian Oceans and finally reached England. The Spanish ambassador to England made many and violent protests to Queen Elizabeth concerning Drake's exploits. He called Drake a pirate and threatened open war. The queen answered the protests of the ambassador by making Drake a knight.

The voyages of Sir Humphrey Gilbert. A man who was firmly convinced that a northwest passage to the Pacific existed was Sir Humphrey Gilbert. He also had the idea of founding a colony of Englishmen in America. The charter granted him by the queen provided that the colonists were, among other rights, " to enjoy all the privileges of free persons native of England." This right, in one form or another, was put into all the charters which later were granted for the colonization of America.

Gilbert was accompanied on his first expedition by Sir Walter Raleigh, his half-brother, who had become interested in the plan of founding a colony. After having passed through several heavy storms and having had a fight with some Spanish ships, the expedition returned to Ireland without accomplishing anything.

A second expedition reached Newfoundland, but the climate was so unfavorable that Gilbert concluded to try farther south. However, he became discouraged by the discontent and desertion of the crew; so he resolved to return to England. On the way back, during a storm, the lights on Gilbert's own small vessel suddenly disappeared, and neither the ship nor any of its passengers were ever seen again.

Sir Walter Raleigh attempts to plant an English colony in America. Sir Walter Raleigh, who had accompanied Gilbert on his first voyage, now undertook to carry on the work of colonization. Raleigh was at this time a great favorite with Queen Elizabeth, whose gifts and honors had made him a very rich man.

In preparation for his adventure he caused a pamphlet to be written telling of the advantages to England of colonizing America. He succeeded in obtaining the authorization of the queen to make the attempt and in having the authorization confirmed by Parliament.

A settlement is made on Roanoke Island. Raleigh first sent out an exploring expedition which he directed southward in order to avoid the cold weather that had interfered with Gilbert's attempt to found a colony. This expedition selected Roanoke Island, south of Albemarle Sound, as a suitable place for a colony. The queen suggested, when they had returned, that the new country should be called Virginia.

The next year (1585) a fleet of seven vessels was fitted out which took about two hundred settlers to Roanoke Island. The commander of this fleet was Sir Richard Grenville, afterward commander of the

Raleigh's expedition sails for America in 1584 to find a site for a colony. (From a mural painting by C. Y. Turner in the Hotel Raleigh, Washington, D. C.)

ENGLAND BECOMES INTERESTED IN AMERICA

Revenge during the great fight the English made against the Invincible Armada of Spain.

Troubles of the first Roanoke colony. During the winter and spring after the arrival of the settlers food became scarce and there was much trouble with the Indians. Not long afterward Drake, on his return from one of his expeditions, appeared with a number of ships and offered to take the colonists back to England. The settlers accepted Drake's offer and abandoned the island. They brought back with them to England two new products that were destined to become very important. One of these was the white potato and the other was tobacco.

A few days after Drake had sailed away, ships that had been sent out from England by Raleigh with colonists and supplies arrived at the island.

Some time was spent in a search for the colonists who had been taken away. Raleigh's ships then returned, leaving fifteen people to retain possession of the colony.

Raleigh again attempts to found a colony. Raleigh was disappointed at the results of his attempts to plant a colony in the New World, but the good reports of the country made by members of the expedition led him to make a third attempt. So in 1587, about one hundred and fifty settlers sailed for Chesapeake Bay. On the way they were to stop at Roanoke to take off the fifteen men who had been left there. When they arrived at Roanoke, the pilot refused to go farther; so the colony was established at the old site.

Grenville's men could not be found. It seemed that they had been attacked and driven off by the Indians. Governor White tried to make friends with the Indians, but he had no success except with the tribe of Croatoan, a near-by Indian village.

The lost colony on Roanoke Island
(Drawn by W. L. Sheppard for Bryant's *Popular History of the United States*)

When White returned to England for more supplies, he found England threatened with the attack of the Spanish Armada. Every ship was needed for the defense of the home country.

The settlers abandon the Roanoke colony. It was four years before help could be sent to the little colony at Roanoke. Raleigh had spent much of his fortune, but with the help of others he raised money to send

Governor White back to Virginia. When he reached Roanoke, he found the word "Croatoan" cut into a tree. It had been agreed that, if the colonists abandoned the colony, they were to leave some sign telling where they had gone. If they left on account of danger or distress, they were to add a cross to the sign. No cross had been added to the word, so it was supposed that the settlers had gone to Croatoan of their own free will.

On account of a storm it was not possible to visit Croatoan. Later there was a legend that most of the settlers were killed after living at Croatoan a few years and that others were carried off and adopted by the Indians.

Later life of Sir Walter Raleigh. Until his death Raleigh held to his faith in the future of English colonies in America. Because of Raleigh's hostility to Spain and the desire of King James of England to please that country, a charge of treason was brought against him, and he was imprisoned. In 1616 he was released by the king in order that he might attempt to find a gold mine in Guiana in South America, which he claimed to have heard about on one of his earlier voyages. He was not, however, to interfere with Spanish settlements. Unluckily Raleigh got into a fight with the Spaniards near the Orinoco River. On his return the Spanish ambassador complained, and, in order to satisfy Spain, the king caused Raleigh to be executed on the old charge of treason.

STUDY HELPS
Map Work
On a map of the Western Continent indicate the regions explored by the English, including those connected with Sir Francis Drake. Shade the claims of the Spanish, French, Dutch, and English and note where they overlap.

Activities
Put into your book pictures connected with the English explorations and discoveries, such as Spanish places attacked by Drake, or of English ships of the time.

Dramatize the scene in which Drake returns and meets Queen Elizabeth after his raids on the Spanish settlements.

Special Work
What other famous sea captains made voyages to the New World?

Why did Queen Elizabeth refuse to punish Drake for his acts against Spain?

What is the story of the Spanish Armada? Of Sir Richard Grenville in the *Revenge?*

Storybooks to Read
Johnston, Mary: *Croatan*
Kingsley, Charles: *Westward, Ho!*
Limpus, Aitken: *The Sea Lord* (Francis Drake)
Westerman, Percy F.: *'Gainst the Might of Spain*

UNIT II. PART 1. PERIOD OF COLONIZATION

From Cook Studios

Captain John Smith
He is dressed in the uniform worn by soldiers at that time.

Photo from Ewing Galloway

Monument erected at Jamestown, Virginia, in **1907** to commemorate the first permanent English settlement in America

FORECAST OF UNIT II

In Unit II you will learn some of the reasons that led courageous and self-sacrificing men and women to leave their old homes in Europe in order to build up new homes in America.

From time to time, beginning with the settlement of Jamestown, groups of people or companies settled and traded in the English land along the Atlantic Ocean. You will learn that these little settlements later grew into thirteen colonies, spread along the coast. Although they adjoined one another, they looked to England rather than to one another for help.

Most of the colonizers had come from England, but many groups of brave men and women came from other countries of Europe. All sought freedom from oppression and better living conditions in America.

There were differences in soil and climate and varying opportunities for making a living to be found in the different colonies. Besides, the settlers brought with them from their homes in the Old World different manners and customs. You will find that the result was that industries and ways of living were not the same in all the colonies.

Pennsylvania with a favorable climate and soil, together with the wise provisions for its government that had been made by William Penn, its founder, attracted settlers from all the countries of western Europe and soon became one of the most prosperous of the colonies.

You will find that there is a great contrast between the life of the early days with the difficulties of transportation, the struggle for a living in a wilderness inhabited by Indians, and with few comforts and conveniences and the life of to-day with easy transportation, quick means of communication, and comforts and luxuries such as have never been known before in the history of the world.

UNIT II. PART 1. PERIOD OF COLONIZATION

Welcoming an English ship at Jamestown — *From an old print*

1. THE SETTLEMENT OF VIRGINIA

Why Englishmen wished to settle in America. The attempts of Raleigh to found colonies, though not successful, served to keep up among Englishmen an interest in the New World. There were, besides, other reasons for founding English colonies along the Atlantic coast of North America.

Scarcity of land in England. In the first place, much of the land in England had been taken away from the farmers and had been made into great sheep pastures. The landlords thought that they could make more money by selling the wool from the sheep than they could by renting the land to farmers.

Besides, many people who had been employed on the farms became idle and had a very hard time to make a living. Some of these idle people wandered about the country in groups, committing crimes and causing disorder and giving the government much trouble.

Many persons also thought that there were too many people in England, and efforts were made to remove some of them from the overcrowded parts of the country.

Religious troubles. About this time, also, many people had come to believe in new forms of religion. These differences in religious beliefs brought on quarrels which often became very bitter, and sometimes even led to war. In England the people who did not agree with the state religion were frequently prosecuted under the severe laws and were punished for their beliefs. Their only escape was to move to some country, like Holland, where people were permitted to worship as they pleased.

Growth of English trade and commerce. Still another reason for founding colonies was the great development of English trade and commerce during the reign of Queen Elizabeth. About 1550 a company was founded for trading with Russia. Later, other trading companies were organized to trade with other parts of the world. In the year 1600 the great East India Company was founded for trade with India and the East.

We can see that it was very natural for men to want to form other companies to trade with the new lands in America. In 1606 a charter was obtained from King James, who had followed Queen Elizabeth as the ruler of England, for two trading companies. One of these was called the London Company; the other was called the Plymouth Company.

The charter claimed for England all the land in America between what is now South Carolina and Maine. The London Company was granted the right to make a settlement in the southern part of this territory.

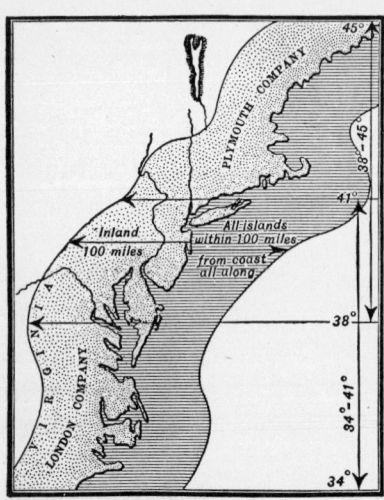

The Charter of 1606 provided for two colonies.
The first might be made anywhere on the coast between 34° and 41°; the second anywhere between 38° and 45°. The two colonies must not, however, be within 100 miles of each other.

The English settle at Jamestown. In a few months the London Company had prepared an expedition. It sailed for Chesapeake Bay, which was reached in April, 1607. For two weeks the colonists searched for a good site for their colony. Finally they decided on an island about thirty miles up a river that flowed into the bay. The river they named the James, and the settlement they called Jamestown, both in honor of the king.

Troubles of the colonists. Trouble with the Indians began almost at once. Besides, the long voyage had cut down the food supply of the colonists. After some quarrels among the leaders Captain John Smith was put in charge of the food supply and was successful in getting corn from the Indians.

The owners of the company who had been left in London wanted to get immediate cargoes of valuable goods from the colony. This caused the leaders to have the colonists work cutting down cedar wood to send to England and to search for gold, instead of planting corn. The climate, too, was hard on the settlers and many died.

Smith soon proved himself the most energetic of the leaders and finally was made the president of the colony.

Captain John Smith. Captain John Smith was born in England in 1579. He spent many years in fighting the Turks and had many hairbreadth escapes. One time he was captured and sold as a slave to a rich Turkish woman, who put him in charge of her business affairs. Finding a good opportunity one day, Smith killed three of his Turkish guards and made his escape.

Many stories are told of Smith as leader of the colony. One of his rules was that, if a man was found swearing, he was to be punished by having his arm held up and cold water poured down his sleeve. If a man refused to do his share of the work, Smith refused to permit him to have any food.

Pocahontas saves Captain John Smith.

Some think that this incident never happened, but Captain Smith, who tells the story himself, has been generally found to be truthful. (From *General History* by Captain John Smith)

THE SETTLEMENT OF VIRGINIA

The story is also told that, on one of Smith's visits to the Indians, he was seized and condemned to be killed. As a warrior was about to strike him with a club, Pocahontas, the chief's daughter, ran forward and asked that Smith's life be spared, a request that her father granted.

The Starving Time. For several years the colony barely managed to exist. Once the supply of food was so nearly gone that Smith separated the colonists into three groups and sent them to different places at some distance from the colony so that they could live off the fish and shellfish that they could get from the waters of the rivers and bays.

In 1609 Smith went back to England, having been injured by an explosion of gunpowder. For a time things went from bad to worse. The Indians refused to furnish supplies to the settlers. Instead, they killed the settlers, stole the hogs, and drove away the deer. This resulted in what is known as the "Starving Time." It occurred during the winter of 1609-10. Out of more than five hundred colonists in Virginia in the summer of 1609 only sixty were left in the spring of 1610. These were saved only by the timely arrival of a ship with supplies.

Planting tobacco saves the colony. The beginning of prosperity in the colony dates from 1612. In that year the colonists began to plant tobacco. It brought a high price in England and in other countries where its use became very popular. It soon became the most important product of the colony. Taxes were paid in tobacco. The salaries of governors, judges, other officials, and even of clergymen were paid in pounds of tobacco.

About this time, also, the colonists were each given a few acres of land, which they were allowed to cultivate for their own benefit instead of doing all their work for the settlement in general. This made the colonists more interested, especially those who were energetic and anxious to make homes for themselves in the new country.

Slavery is introduced into the colony. As the planting of tobacco increased, it was soon found that a great deal of labor was required in order to take care of the tobacco plants. Besides, it was much more profitable to grow this product on large farms, or plantations. These required many farm laborers. Efforts were made to get colonists from England who could be hired to work on the plantations, but enough of these could not be had.

In 1619, a Dutch sea captain arrived in the James River with a cargo of negro slaves that he had obtained in Africa. By this time tobacco was worth about one dollar a pound, and the more a planter could raise the richer he would become. The demand for this new kind of labor was so great that the Dutch captain had no trouble in selling his human cargo at good prices. In this way slavery was introduced into the English settlements.

It was soon found that the negroes were more able to work in the hot climate of the lowlands, that they could be trained in agriculture, and that the work they did was worth much more than it cost to keep them. As a result negro slavery extended in time through all the settlements in the southern part of the country.

Kinds of settlers in Jamestown. The people that came to Jamestown in the different supply ships were from all classes of the population in England. Some of them were wealthy people who preferred the freedom of the new country. Others were poor folk who had their passage money advanced to them by the company. This money was to be repaid by requiring the colonists to work for the company in Virginia for a term of years. These people were called *redemptioners* because they could, in the course of a few years, redeem themselves.

Later on women were brought to the colony in order that homes and families might be established in the new settlement. In this case the husband paid for the passage of his wife. The first shipload of women came to Virginia in 1619.

The Virginia colonists get the right to govern themselves. The charter of the London Company allowed the owners in England to appoint the governor and other officials of the colony in Virginia. The governor ruled like an absolute monarch. The colonists had nothing whatever to say about their government or about the laws under which they lived.

Finally the stockholders in England became divided into two groups. One group wanted to continue the arbitrary rule of the colony. The other group was more liberal and thought that the prosperity of the colony would increase if the settlers were allowed to own their lands and to have a share in the government.

The first women to arrive at Jamestown to become wives of the settlers

The first law-making assembly in America. In the end the liberal party won, and Governor Yardley was sent out with instructions to put the new plan into operation. Settlers were granted lands by the hundreds of acres in proportion to the amount of money they had expended.

On July 30, 1619, the first law-making assembly in America met in the old church in Jamestown. Besides the governor and council there were two representatives from each of the ten little settlements in the colony.

Virginia becomes a royal province. A few years after this a sudden Indian uprising resulted in one fifth of all the inhabitants of the colony being killed. It was claimed that this was caused by the neglect of the company to contribute to the protection of the settlers, and a complaint was made to the king. The king took away the company's charter. Virginia was made a royal province and was governed in such a way as the king and his council might decide. The king now appointed the governor, but the assembly of citizens elected by the settlements continued to share in the making of the laws.

Virginia becomes a prosperous colony. Virginia became increasingly prosperous as time went on. When the war between Parliament and the king broke out in England, Virginia remained loyal to the king. When Parliament gained the upper hand, many of the merchants and nobility of the king's party came to Virginia, adding to the numbers of the better class of the population.

Meanwhile Parliament had passed the first of the Navigation Acts, which prohibited all commerce except with England and with English vessels. Later, other acts interfering with trade and commerce were passed. Although the colonists persistently disobeyed these laws, they caused much loss to Virginia.

The Virginians object to the tobacco tax. As soon as Virginia raised tobacco in large quantities, the government decided to impose a tax of one shilling a pound on all the tobacco raised in the colonies. It also required that all tobacco be sent to England. In time the colonists produced so much tobacco that the price

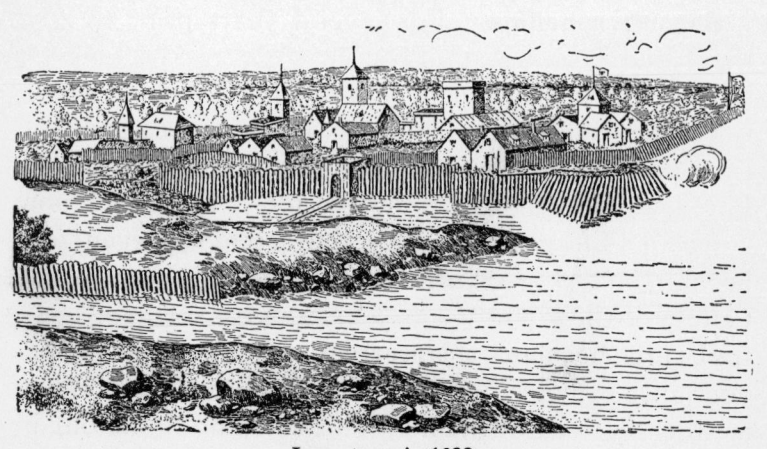

Jamestown in 1622
Note the palisade around the town and the ditch to protect it from sudden attack by the Indians. (From a Dutch print of that time)

in England was lowered. This gave rise to much distress in the colony and to constant quarrels between the government and the colonies. When the value of tobacco went down, the price of everything else went up since prices were all measured in pounds of tobacco.

The colonists firmly believed that this trouble was due to the Navigation Laws, which forced them to sell

THE SETTLEMENT OF VIRGINIA

their tobacco for a lower price in England than they could get elsewhere. The Virginians, therefore, got into the habit of evading the laws whenever they could. They sent their tobacco to New Amsterdam and to other foreign ports on this side of the Atlantic and even to Europe.

Bacon's rebellion. For several years prior to 1676 there had been great unrest in some of the outlying settlements of Virginia. This was caused by a continuation of the quarrel between those who had favored the king and those who had been on the side of Parliament.

About the same time the Indians became hostile and began to attack the settlements. Appeals were made to Governor Berkeley, but neither he nor the council took proper steps to protect the people. Finally a young man named Nathaniel Bacon raised a force of three hundred men and marched against the Indians. Berkeley proclaimed him a rebel and marched after him.

While Bacon was destroying Indian villages, and Berkeley was trying to capture him as a rebel, the people at Jamestown, who sided with Bacon, upset Berkeley's government. A civil war between the two parties in the colony followed. Many colonists were killed and Jamestown was burned. Bacon died of a fever, and in a few months the rebellion broke down. Berkeley caused thirteen of the rebels to be put to death but was soon afterward recalled from the governorship.

Governor Berkeley threatening Nathaniel Bacon
(Drawn by J. E. Kelly for Bryant's *Popular History of the United States*)

THE SETTLEMENT OF VIRGINIA 93

From this time on the part of the story of Virginia that is interesting to us becomes a part of the story of all the colonies and will appear from time to time in later sections.

STUDY HELPS

Map Work

On a map of the eastern United States, show the grant of land to the London Company and the location of Jamestown.

Activities

Put into your book pictures which have relation to the settlement of Jamestown, such as the old church, the present appearance of the site, and pictures of tobacco growing.

Dramatize the scene in which Nathaniel Bacon and his friends demand that Governor Berkeley take steps to protect them from the Indians.

Make a model of the old Jamestown church or of an Indian village of this part of the country.

Special Work

What is the story of the early life of Captain John Smith?

What is the story of the later life of Pocahontas?

Make a list of the food plants that were cultivated by the Indians.

Storybooks to Read

Chatterton, Edward Keble: *Captain John Smith*
Cooke, John Esten: *Stories of the Old Dominion*
Cooke, John Esten: *My Lady Pokahontas*
Johnson, Rossiter: *Captain John Smith*
Knipe, E. B. and A. A.: *Cavalier Maid*
Seaman, A. H.: *Little Ma'mselle of the Wilderness*

2. THE SETTLEMENT OF THE OTHER SOUTHERN COLONIES

The Settlement of Maryland

Lord Baltimore obtains a grant of land in America. At the time of the struggle between the king and Parliament, Catholics were persecuted just as others were who differed from the Established Church. Desiring to provide a place where Catholics would not be subject to the oppressive English laws, George Calvert, the first Lord Baltimore, obtained (1632) a grant of part of the territory of Virginia. He was given the land that fronted on the ocean and on Chesapeake Bay north to the fortieth parallel and west to the headwaters of the Potomac River. George Calvert died before the paper describing the grant was made out; so it was issued in the name of his son Cecil Calvert.

Cecil Calvert founds Maryland. An expedition was soon made ready. It sailed for Chesapeake Bay under Leonard Calvert, the governor, who was Cecil Calvert's younger brother. The news of the coming of this group of settlers reached Virginia long before they arrived. Both the Virginia settlers and the Indians were much disturbed because they were afraid that the new colonists would interfere with their lands. On his arrival Leonard Calvert reassured both the Indians and the Virginians, telling them that whatever settlement he would make would not interfere with any of the Virginia settlements and that he would buy the land that he needed from the Indians.

After a search for a suitable site, Calvert finally decided on a place on the St. George River. Here he laid out the town of St. Marys as the capital of his new colony.

Cecil Calvert, Lord Baltimore
(From an engraving after a portrait attributed to Sir Peter Lely)

Success of the new colony. From the first the colony was fortunate. The colonies in Virginia and New England had become so firmly established that they could be drawn on for food supplies. It also happened that the Indians in that neighborhood had decided to remove to Virginia, leaving the cleared and tilled fields to the newcomers. The Maryland colonists immediately planted tobacco and corn. They had a shipload of surplus corn the very first year.

Tobacco in Maryland. Calvert was anxious to establish cities and towns in his colony. The people, however, found so much profit in raising tobacco that they almost all engaged in agriculture for a living, rather than in trade or manufacturing. In this way Maryland came to resemble Virginia in its manners and customs rather than the colonies of New England.

The Maryland colonists obtain self-government. The grant to Lord Baltimore gave him almost as much power in Maryland as the king had in England. For a time he tried to enforce these rights in his colony, but the people of Maryland had no intention of being governed in this way. After a few years of struggle with the representatives whom he had selected from the various towns, he agreed to permit the colonists to elect their own representatives and to join in making the laws.

This assembly adopted a plan of government very much like that of Virginia with a lower house elected by the people.

Maryland is made a royal province. For some years Maryland remained a Catholic colony. When the struggle between the king and Parliament came on,

Protestant settlers seized the governor and imprisoned many of Lord Baltimore's officials and friends. A civil war ended with the adoption of a provision that none should be molested on account of his religious beliefs. This did not satisfy some of the people, and for some years Lord Baltimore's authority was taken away and Maryland became a royal province. Not long afterward, however, it was restored to the heirs of Lord Baltimore.

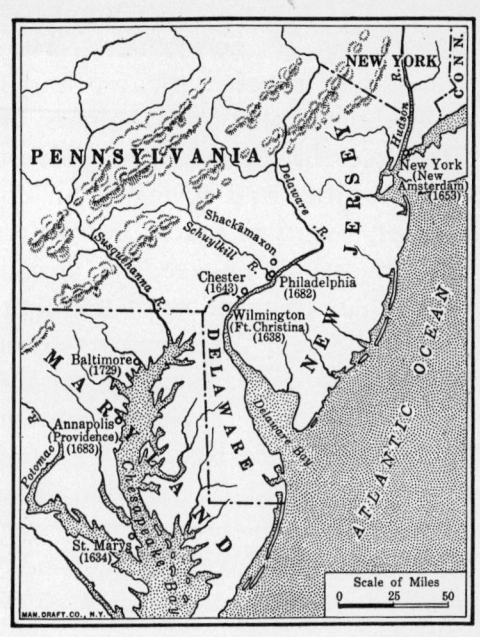

Early settlements in Pennsylvania, Maryland, and Delaware

The Settlement of the Carolinas

Charles the Second grants a charter for settling the Carolinas. In 1663 Charles II granted to a group of English noblemen the lands which are now North and South Carolina. Sir Ashley Cooper was the chief one named in the grant. Among those joined with him were Berkeley and Carteret, who were also the pro-

The first settlers arriving in Maryland
(From a painting by F. B. Mayer in the State House, Annapolis)

Photo from Ewing Galloway

SETTLEMENT OF OTHER SOUTHERN COLONIES

prietors of New Jersey. The charter was very liberal and the proprietors, like Lord Baltimore, had as much power within their grant as a king would have. They had to have, however, the consent of the colonists in making laws and were subject to the Navigation Laws of England.

A settlement is established at Charleston. After several attempts at settlement a colony was finally sent out which, after some trouble, succeeded in reaching the mouth of the Ashley River. Here Charleston was founded in 1669.

The harbor of Charleston, South Carolina, in 1739
(After a drawing by B. Roberts)

The usual story of scarcity of provisions is part of the history of the first years of the colony. Help was obtained from Virginia, New England, and the Barbados; so the settlement did not have to be abandoned.

Charleston becomes an important city. The site chosen for Charleston proved healthful and soon the colony was on its way to success. Settlers were induced to come from the Barbados. Later on French Protestants, or Huguenots, arrived. Swiss immigrants founded New Bern, and a large number of Scots went to Port Royal, South Carolina, instead of settling in New York as they had first intended. The settlement at Charleston was moved across the river to a more

From an old print
The governor's palace at New Bern, North Carolina

favorable location, and in a few years it became the most important city in the colonies south of Philadelphia.

South Carolina becomes a royal province. In the Carolinas the usual quarrels occurred between the people and the proprietors in regard to the share the colonists were to have in making the laws. These disputes continued for many years. At last in 1719 the colonists rebelled and a royal governor was appointed.

Ten years later the charter was canceled. Both North and South Carolina became royal provinces. The governor and the council were named by the king, and the people of the colony elected the lower house of the legislature.

Rice and indigo in the Carolinas. In South Carolina there were many rich planters who had obtained from the proprietors large tracts of land. These were usually lowlands along the rivers and were very favorable for the growing of rice and indigo. Rice soon became one of the great staple products of South Carolina and brought great wealth to the colony. About the time of the war between the North and the South in 1861, the farmers of Louisiana and Texas found out how to grow rice on higher land. Until then the Carolinas remained the chief rice-producing states. The cultivation of the indigo plant later became another important industry and brought much wealth to the planters.

The Settlement of Georgia

General Oglethorpe decides to help poor English debtors. For many years England saw the need for the establishment of a colony between the older colonies and the Spanish and Indian lands to the south and west. While plans for such a colony were being considered, General Oglethorpe, a charitable Englishman, became interested in poor debtors.

At this time it was the custom to put people in prison if they did not pay their debts. These poor people had to stay in jail under the most horrible conditions, although the longer they stayed in jail the less likely it was that they would be able to pay their debts.

Oglethorpe had the idea that if these people were given a little start they might succeed in a new country.

Oglethorpe founds Georgia. Many wealthy people subscribed to a fund to start a new colony in America which was to be called Georgia in honor of George II, who was at that time king of England. The grant of land included very nearly all that is now included in the state of Georgia. The objects of the settlement were, first, the relief of the poor debtors and, second, the protection of the frontier lands of the Carolinas against attacks by the Spanish and Indians.

General James Oglethorpe, founder of Georgia

The provisions of the Georgia charter. Since the government was to be largely a military one, no provision was made for a representative assembly. No profits were expected to be made from the colony, and full reports were to be made to the king. Religious liberty was granted to all, and slavery was prohibited so as to discourage the forming of large plantations. No rum was to be imported into the colony, and a license was required to trade with the Indians.

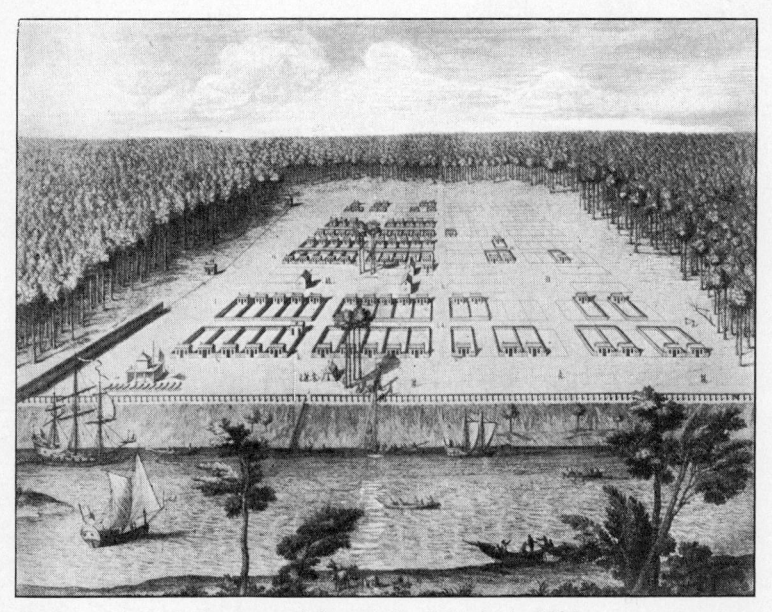

The town of Savannah, Georgia, in 1734
(From a contemporary copy in the possession of the Historical Society of Pennsylvania)

Progress of the colony. Oglethorpe sailed with about one hundred settlers in 1703. He went first to South Carolina, so that he might have time to purchase from the Indians a site for his colony. A tract was secured near the mouth of the Savannah River, and a treaty of friendship was made with the Creek Indians. Oglethorpe gave each settler fifty acres of land, including a town lot and a garden.

The people of South Carolina gave much help to the new Georgia settlers. A quantity of food was given to Oglethorpe's party, and a troop of soldiers and an armed vessel were lent to the colonists to protect them from attack until they were able to defend themselves.

In 1734 some Germans came from Salzburg and settled not far from Savannah. These were followed by other Germans whose settlements extended along the river.

Later on several hundred people from Scotland settled on the Altamaha River on the southern boundary, where a frontier fort was erected for defense.

The settlers join in the government. Georgia repeats the story of disputes between the governors and the settlers that is found in the history of almost every colony.

It was not long before the colonists complained that the growth of the colony was interfered with by the prohibition of slavery. It was found hard to get enough white labor, and the introduction of slaves was urged. Finally, in 1754, the charter was surrendered to the king and Georgia became a royal province, in which the people elected the assembly and so joined in making the laws of the colony.

STUDY HELPS

Map Work

On a map of the eastern United States show the location of Maryland, the Carolinas, and Georgia, with the places of first settlement.

Activities

Add to your book pictures relating to the Southern colonies.

Get specimens, if possible, of the rice and indigo plants.

Dramatize the welcoming of General Oglethorpe and his settlers when they stopped at Charleston on their way to Georgia.

Make a plan of the city of Charleston or of Savannah.

Special Work

Find out how Leonard Calvert treated the Indians.

Find some reasons why Charleston became the largest city in the colonies south of Philadelphia.

What troubles did Georgia have with the Spaniards?

Where had these Spaniards come from?

The Georgia colonists were forced to plant mulberry trees and grow silkworms. What was the result of this plan?

What were the disadvantages of using so much land for growing tobacco?

Storybooks to Read

Bennett, John: *Barnaby Lee* (Maryland)
Oertel, Theodore Eugene: *Jack Sutherland* (Georgia)
Simms, William Gilmore: *The Yemassee* (Carolinas)

3. THE FOUNDING OF THE NEW ENGLAND COLONIES

The Settlement of Massachusetts

The Puritans. You have already learned about the religious disputes that took place in England and continental Europe about the time of Queen Elizabeth. By the time the English were making settlements in America, most of the English people had accepted the beliefs of the Church of England. As time went on, many of these came to believe that the Church of England was still too much like the older church. They wished, as they said, to purify it. These people were, therefore, called *Puritans*.

Another group wished to leave the Church of England altogether, permitting each congregation to make its own rules. These were called *Separatists*. In time most of the people who called themselves Puritans actually became Separatists.

The Pilgrims. A small congregation of Separatists that belonged to Scrooby, in the north of England, decided to avoid trouble by moving to Leyden, in Holland, where they could worship as they pleased.

The Pilgrims leaving Holland to make their homes in America
(From a painting by Robert W. Weir in the National Capitol)

They took the name of *Pilgrims* because they traveled about on account of religion like the Pilgrims of the Middle Ages. They remained in Holland for about twenty years.

The Pilgrims leave Holland. Having lived so long in Holland, the Pilgrims felt that their children were growing up to be Hollanders instead of English men and women. They did not like the ways of the Dutch people, many of whom did not live the way the Pilgrims believed they should.

After much thought, the Pilgrims decided to move elsewhere and determined to come to America. They believed that they could live better in America. They also had in mind that they would be able to convert the Indians to Christianity.

The Pilgrims come to America. Accordingly a grant was obtained from the London Company permitting them to settle within its territory in America.

In July, 1620, they set out from Holland for England. At Southampton they were to be joined by others from London in the *Mayflower*. They had sailed about 300 miles from Southampton when they found the *Speedwell*, in which they had come from Holland, was in danger of sinking. They then returned to Plymouth. From there about 100 people sailed in the *Mayflower* on September 6, for America.

The Pilgrims had intended to land at some point south of the Hudson, but, when they reached America, they found themselves near Cape Cod. They decided

FOUNDING OF NEW ENGLAND COLONIES

to settle somewhere near the place at which they had reached land.

The Mayflower Compact. Before landing, the Pilgrims drew up an agreement called the *Mayflower Compact*. They made themselves into a government and

The Mayflower in Plymouth harbor
(From a painting by William F. Halsall in Plymouth Hall, Plymouth)

agreed to submit to all laws that might be made by themselves for the general good of the colony. John Carver was chosen governor, and Myles Standish was elected captain.

The Pilgrims found Plymouth. The Pilgrims stayed on the ship for over a month, while Captain Standish and others explored the country. The exploring party finally found a good harbor where there was a good stream of water and plenty of Indian corn-

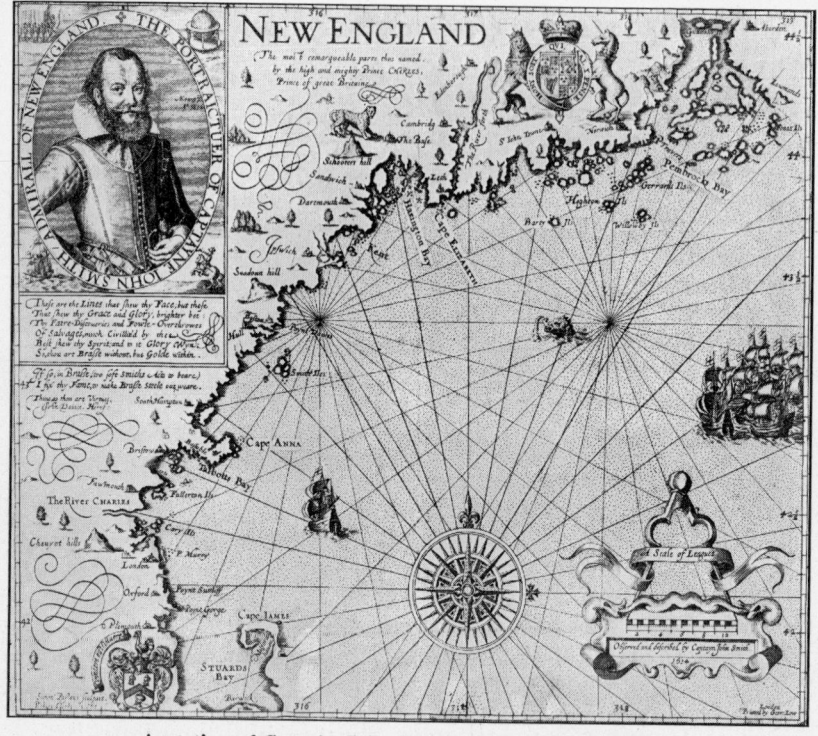

A section of Captain John Smith's map of New England
Cape Cod is named Cape James on the map, and the word " Plimouth " is just above the coat of arms in the lower left-hand corner.

fields. The rest of the company crossed the bay in the *Mayflower* and landed at Plymouth on December 21, 1620.

The place had been called Plymouth on Captain John Smith's map of New England. The Pilgrims adopted this name for their settlement, as it was the name of the town in England from which they had sailed.

The first year at Plymouth. A few days later the men of the colony began to build cabins, the women, the children, and the sick living on the ship.

The cold and exposure and bad food gave rise to much sickness. During the winter more than half of the little company died. Fortunately there was not much trouble with the Indians. A pestilence of some sort had much reduced their numbers and had caused them to abandon many of their cleared fields. The colonists, therefore, used these fields to grow corn.

Relations with the Indians. For a time the Indians avoided the whites, but the next spring an Indian, Samoset, who had picked up a few words of English from fishermen, came into the settlement and welcomed the English. Not long after he returned bringing with him Squanto, an Indian who had been taken to England a few years before and later had been brought back to his tribe. Through these two a treaty of peace and friendship was concluded with the chief, Massasoit. Squanto remained with the settlers and helped them very much in putting the colony on a successful basis.

Squanto shows the settlers how to plant corn. Squanto obtained corn from the Indians for the settlers and showed them how the Indians planted it in hills and rows. This method of planting had not been known to Europeans before this time. He also showed the colonists how to fertilize their crop by putting a small fish in each hill with the seed corn. Both of these methods of planting corn were adopted by the colonists. During the following summer the settlers harvested a good crop of corn, finished their cabins, and collected many beaver skins.

Photo from Ewing Galloway
Myles Standish and his company exploring the country under the guidance of Samoset

When the winter's supply of wood and food had been stored away, Governor Bradford appointed a day for Thanksgiving. All their Indian friends were invited to the feast. Everyone contributed and had a share in the good time. This was the first Thanksgiving Day ever celebrated in America.

FOUNDING OF NEW ENGLAND COLONIES 113

Indian troubles. A new danger soon arose from the Indians. Canonicus, the chief of the Narragansett Indians, sent a challenge in the form of a bunch of arrows tied with snake skin. Acting on the advice of Myles Standish, Bradford promptly stuffed the skin

The first Thanksgiving
What kinds of food do you see in the picture?

with bullets and sent it back to Chief Canonicus. This fearless reply kept the Indians from carrying out their plan of attack, but from that time on the settlement was fortified, and a strict watch was kept up.

More settlers reach Plymouth. In the spring a new shipload of settlers arrived but no supplies. Only the

Plymouth in 1622

Note Governor Bradford's house with the fence around it.

From an old print

arrival of a ship from Jamestown, Virginia, whose captain shared his supplies with them, prevented another period of famine.

For several years the success of the colony was threatened from time to time by the arrival of new groups of settlers poorly supplied with food. These had to be given the food that the settlers so badly needed for themselves.

Finally Governor Bradford decided to assign a tract of land to every family instead of having the lands shared in common. The result was as satisfactory as it had proved to be in Virginia. At harvest time there was plenty of corn, and thereafter there was no want or famine during the history of the colony.

The Massachusetts Bay colony. Not long after the founding of Plymouth, some merchants of Dorchester, in England, established a fishing station at Cape Ann. This was soon abandoned and the settlers removed to what is now Salem. John White of Dorchester promised these people that he would get them a grant of land and money and supplies for trade.

In accordance with White's promise a patent was obtained, in 1628, from the Council for New England, for the land from three miles north of the Merrimack River to three miles south of the Charles. It happened that other grants had been made which included this land; so the Massachusetts Bay Company in England tried to get a royal charter to protect their rights.

The charter of Massachusetts. Through the help of friends at court the king was induced to grant the request for a charter. According to this charter the governor and council were to meet once a month.

Early New England settlements

FOUNDING OF NEW ENGLAND COLONIES

Four times each year the whole membership was to assemble to elect new officers and to make new laws for the company. The charter did not provide that the company should meet in England; so the following year, at a meeting of the leaders, it was agreed to transfer the headquarters of the company to America. Those officers who did not wish to leave England resigned, and others who were willing to come to the new country were chosen in their place, John Winthrop being made governor.

John Winthrop
The first governor of Massachusetts Bay colony in America

Growth of the colony. About this time King Charles I decided to rule without Parliament. He put into prison many eminent men who were not in agreement with him. In a few months thousands of wealthy and influential persons decided to emigrate to America. Since most of those who differed with the king were either Puritans or Separatists, they came chiefly to the New England settlements. In the twelve years from 1628 to 1640, more than 20,000 people left old England for New England.

The settlement of Boston. When Winthrop arrived at Massachusetts Bay, he found the Salem colony in much distress. His own party was not much better off, for they had accidentally left behind in London a quantity of supplies. The two colonies were merged and after a short time the settlers moved across the Charles River to the present site of Boston, where there was plenty of good water.

During the winter the suffering was great and the colonists lived chiefly on the fish and clams from the bay. Winthrop appointed a day of fasting to be kept, but, before that day came, a vessel arrived with supplies, and a day of thanksgiving was substituted for the day of fasting. From that time on the colony prospered.

No religious freedom in Massachusetts. We have learned that the people of Plymouth and the people of Massachusetts came to America to get freedom of worship. But they did not wish to grant the same freedom of worship to others. It was not long before the Puritans became Separatists and joined with Plymouth in keeping away from the neighborhood all those whose religious opinions were different from their own.

King Philip's War. From time to time troubles arose with the Indians. The Connecticut settlers had a war with the Pequot Indians in 1636, in which that tribe was almost wiped out. About forty years later King Philip, chief of the Narragansett Indians, incited his people to war against the settlers. In a speech he said that the whites would cut down the forests, spoil their hunting and planting grounds, and would at last drive the Indians from the lands and council fires of their fathers.

The war lasted three years, with many raids by the Indians on the outlying settlements. Finally the fort of the Narragansetts was surrounded, captured, and burned, and a thousand members of the tribe were killed. King Philip escaped, but he was hunted from place to place by the colonial soldiers. He was finally shot by one of his own people. This war was the last of Indian troubles for many years.

The Quakers in New England. When the society of Quakers, or Friends, arose in England, many of them came to New England to live. Most of them settled in Rhode Island, where for a time they controlled the government.

The first Quakers that reached Massachusetts were sent back to the place from which they had come, and a law was passed forbidding Quakers to live in the colony. Many Quakers were imprisoned and banished under this law. Still others that returned to the colony after banishment were put to death.

Witchcraft. For centuries many ignorant people had believed in witches. Witches were supposed to be in league with Satan, who had given them power to bring misfortune, sickness, or even death to their neighbors.

In England laws had been passed making witchcraft a crime to be punished by death. These laws were copied by Massachusetts. Some young women of Salem began to act strangely, and people said that they were bewitched. When asked about it, the girls agreed that they had been. At first they named three persons and, later, still others whom they accused of bewitching them. Soon a number of the men and women of Salem and its neighborhood were imprisoned. A special court was called to try the cases, and some people were put to death.

This wicked belief spread. Many of the leading people of the colony, including the wife of the governor, were accused of being witches.

Suddenly a change of feeling came about and the persecution stopped. The people of Massachusetts decided that a great wrong had been done and that many innocent people had been put to death. A day of fasting and prayer was set to atone for the mistake. But this did not bring back to life those who had been put to death as the result of this strange and wicked notion.

The Founding of Rhode Island

Roger Williams. Roger Williams was a young minister who differed from the Puritans in respect to their beliefs. He denied that civil magistrates had the right to punish for Sabbath breaking and similar offenses.

He was first prevented from preaching at Salem and soon afterward was banished from the colony. He

FOUNDING OF NEW ENGLAND COLONIES 121

then settled near Plymouth with the Indians, among whom he had made many friends. At the request of Massachusetts the authorities at Plymouth told him that he had better move, for they did not wish to displease this colony.

Roger Williams welcomed by the Indians at Rhode Island
(From an engraving after the painting of Alonzo Chappel)

Williams settles at Providence. From Plymouth Williams went to Rhode Island, where, in 1636, he established a settlement called Providence on land which he had purchased from the Indians. Later many people from Salem who agreed with Williams joined him in the new colony.

Anne Hutchinson. Anne Hutchinson was a woman of Boston who had made herself very helpful in that colony. She had become prominent in church affairs and later had taken up the work of nursing sick people in the colony. Since there were few doctors, those people whom she had helped when they were ill were grateful to her and sided with her in her disputes with the officials. Soon she began to hold meetings of the women, in which she urged beliefs that did not please the ministers of the church. She was banished from the colony and followed Roger Williams to Rhode Island. Even here messengers from Boston came to try to have her and her husband punished. To escape them she moved to the Dutch settlements near New Amsterdam, where she was killed in an Indian attack.

Other settlements in Rhode Island. Later some settlers went to the southern part of the island and established the town of Newport. The town of Warwick was settled by some who had been driven from Massachusetts and afterward from Providence, where they had refused to submit to the laws. All these settlements finally came together and organized a government under a charter for Rhode Island and Providence Plantations which Roger Williams had succeeded in obtaining.

Liberal government of Rhode Island. The government adopted under the charter granted freedom of worship and full civil rights to all who believed in God. This toleration brought many to the colony, not only

Courtesy Chas. Scribner's Sons

The trial of Anne Hutchinson for defying the church authorities
(Drawn by Edwin A. Abbey for Bryant's *Popular History of the United States*)

from the neighboring colonies of Massachusetts and Connecticut, but also from England.

Massachusetts was jealous of the success of the Rhode Island colony, and, when the New England Confederation was formed (p. 126) for protection against the Indians and Dutch, Rhode Island was not permitted to join.

The Settlement of Connecticut

The first settlement at Windsor. In 1633 Plymouth sent out a colony which built a fort at Windsor, about ten miles above Hartford. Meanwhile the Dutch from New Amsterdam had already established a settlement where Hartford now stands. When Boston heard of the Dutch and Plymouth settlements, people from the towns near Boston made their way to the Connecticut River and established settlements there.

A large part of the congregation of the Reverend Thomas Hooker at Cambridge sold their lands and emigrated to Hartford, and other settlers from Massachusetts founded other towns in the Connecticut Valley. About the same time Massachusetts built a fort, which was called Saybrook, at the mouth of the Connecticut River.

Connecticut establishes its own government. When Massachusetts permitted its people to settle beyond the bounds of the colony, it provided that the settlements should remain under the control of the home colony. So in the beginning Massachusetts had the right to govern these new settlements.

FOUNDING OF NEW ENGLAND COLONIES

Later the three towns, Hartford, Windsor, and Wethersfield, organized an independent government of their own under the name of Connecticut. The representatives of the three towns drew up a constitution called the *Fundamental Orders*. This did not recognize any authority in England which they were bound to obey.

Courtesy Chas. Scribner's Sons

The first Sunday at New Haven
(From an engraving after a drawing by A. C. Warren in Bryant's *Popular History of the United States*)

In 1662 Connecticut was granted a charter much like the Fundamental Orders, which gave the settlers almost complete independence. It also granted to Connecticut all the land from Long Island Sound to the Massachusetts boundary and from Narragansett

Bay to the South Sea, or Pacific Ocean. This last provision gave rise later to boundary disputes with New York and Pennsylvania.

The settlement at New Haven. New Haven was settled by a group of people who came from England under John Davenport, a clergyman. They did not believe that laws should be written out but that they should be taken directly from the Bible. They first stopped at Boston, but, thinking they could not live as they wished in Massachusetts, they proceeded to the place where New Haven now is. Here they made a settlement. New Haven was united with the other Connecticut settlements under the charter of 1662.

THE UNITED COLONIES OF NEW ENGLAND

The New England colonies unite against the Dutch and Indians. In 1643, after several years of discussion, the colonies of Massachusetts Bay, Plymouth, Connecticut, and New Haven made an agreement to join together under the title of the *United Colonies of New England*. The object was to form a league for offense and defense and for mutual advice and help upon all proper occasions for their common safety and welfare. Among the reasons for this union was fear of the Dutch of New Amsterdam and of attacks of hostile Indians.

Rhode Island and the settlements in New Hampshire were not permitted to join because they differed in religious beliefs from the other colonies.

This union was of great usefulness in settling disputes

and in providing for combined action when it seemed necessary. It worked well for about ten years until Massachusetts refused, on one occasion, to raise troops for an expedition against the Dutch.

This was the first occasion on which the colonies of America joined together of their own free will in order to provide for their common safety.

STUDY HELPS

Map Work

On a map of eastern United States show the New England colonies with the places of early settlement; also show the location of Jamestown.

Activities

Get for your book pictures relating to the New England settlements, such as Plymouth Rock, pictures of Boston in colonial times, the Pilgrims going to church, the first Thanksgiving, etc.

Dramatize the scene when the challenge was received from Canonicus and it was determined, on the suggestion of Captain Standish, to return the snake skin filled with bullets.

Dramatize the first Thanksgiving.

Make a model of the Plymouth settlement.

Special Work

Find out why the Indians near Plymouth had deserted their fields.

What was the Mayflower Compact?

Who were the Indians that were friendly with the whites? Why did the Indians later become hostile?

What were some differences between the people that settled New England and those that settled Jamestown?

Storybooks to Read

Austin, Jane Goodwin: *Standish of Standish*
Barbour, Ralph Henry: *Giles of the Mayflower*
Dix, Beulah Marie: *Soldier Rigdale* (with Myles Standish)
Hall, Ruth: *Boys of Scrooby*
Hawthorne, Nathaniel: *Grandfather's Chair*
Stimson, Frederic Jesup: *Philip of Pokanoket*
Usher, Roland G.: *The Story of the Pilgrims for Children*

4. THE SETTLEMENT OF NEW YORK AND NEW JERSEY

The Dutch Settle New Netherland

The patroon system. You have learned already about the founding of Fort Orange and of Fort Amsterdam (p. 62) as the result of the expeditions of Henry Hudson and the Dutch explorers.

At first there was little agriculture in the Dutch settlements and their populations were very small. The Dutch tried to remedy this condition by giving

SETTLEMENT OF NEW YORK AND NEW JERSEY

great tracts of land to men who would agree to bring over a certain number of settlers and start them on farms. These settlers were to be provided with cattle, tools, and seed and were to be given assistance in constructing their houses and barns. The amount of land granted was in proportion to the number of settlers. These great estates fronted on the Hudson River for miles and extended far back into the country. The owners, called *patroons*, charged rent for the land.

Governor Peter Stuyvesant. The patroons soon interfered with the profits of the companies that had given them their land. Several governors were sent out in order to protect the interests of the company.

In the meantime the Swedes had made settlements within the limits of the Dutch claims along the Delaware River, and the English were making settlements along both shores of Long Island Sound. As a result many disputes arose.

Finally Peter Stuyvesant was made governor. He was very energetic but very quarrelsome. He made the Dutch colonists of New Amsterdam angry by his domineering ways and by his determination to keep them from sharing in the government. He depended on English residents of New Amsterdam for support, but, since these could not hold office, they were not of much help to Stuyvesant.

Meanwhile the fort was falling into decay. Stuyvesant's pleas for better defenses were not heeded,

Governor Stuyvesant berating his council for surrendering New Amsterdam to the English
(From a group by Dwight Franklin)

although the English were gradually settling in the territory claimed by the Dutch.

The English capture New Amsterdam. To the claim of the Dutch that the English were trespassing on their lands, the English replied with a similar charge against the Dutch. Besides, the English fur trade

Photo from Ewing Galloway

Dutch houses in New Amsterdam
Note the odd style of the houses; the City Hall is in the center.

had been much reduced, and there were other disputes with the Dutch over matters of trade in far-off Africa and in the East Indies.

The English finally decided to seize the Dutch settlements in America. In 1664 an expedition was organized, and a governor was appointed for the territory which the English expected to conquer. The English fleet suddenly appeared before New Amsterdam and demanded its surrender. Stuyvesant stormed around the room, swearing he would never yield to the English. His council, however, knowing the weakness of their defenses, did not wish to have the town battered down around them. They sent out a flag of truce to the English commander and surrendered New Amsterdam to the English.

New Amsterdam becomes New York. After the capture of New Amsterdam its name was changed to New York in honor of the Duke of York, brother of the king of England, who had been granted the land which had just been captured from the Dutch.

The English governor made every effort to conciliate the Dutch colonists. Although English names were given to many of the Dutch settlements, the settlers were allowed to retain their language and customs. Trade and settlement were encouraged, the shipping of the colony was increased, and treaties were made with the Indians.

The government of New York. The Duke of York was opposed to self-government, but he especially charged Governor Nicolls to model the government of New York on that of an English city with a mayor, a sheriff, and other officers. No provision was made for an assembly; so Governor Nicolls drew up a code of laws known as the *Duke of York's Laws*. These were based on provisions from the laws of Massachusetts and Connecticut. Full toleration of religion was allowed.

The lack of a representative assembly at once made trouble with the English settlements on Long

Courtesy Title Guarantee and Trust Company, New York
Signing a deed in colonial times
Note the way the men are dressed. An hourglass in front of the magistrate serves to tell the time.

Island, which had been under the rule of New Haven in Connecticut. These people refused to assent to the laws and declined to pay taxes even for defense.

New York becomes a royal province. In 1673 war again broke out between the English and the Dutch, and New York was captured and held for a year by its first owners. At the close of the war it was given to the English by treaty.

The Duke of York again became the proprietor. When he became the king of England in 1685, New York became a royal province.

The Beginnings of New Jersey

The first settlements. Almost as soon as New Netherland had been granted to the Duke of York, he gave that part of it between the Hudson and Delaware Rivers to John Berkeley and George Carteret, who had helped his father, Charles I, during his struggle with Parliament. The land was given the name of New Jersey in honor of Carteret's former office as governor of the island of Jersey in the English Channel.

People from New Amsterdam had already established Dutch settlements in northern New Jersey at Bergen, Weehawken, and other places near New York Bay.

Governor Nicolls of New York, who did not know about the grant to Berkeley and Carteret, made liberal offers to settlers from New England and Long Island. As a result Elizabeth, Shrewsbury, and places in their neighborhood were settled.

The government of the colony. The proprietors issued a form of government known as *The Concession*. The laws provided for liberty of worship, the right to hold property, and permission to elect representatives to aid in making the laws.

The colony is divided into East and West Jersey. Berkeley soon tired of his share in the colony. New

Courtesy Chas. Scribner's Sons
Sir Philip Carteret takes possession of his colony of New Jersey
(Drawn by Edwin A. Abbey for Bryant's *Popular History of the United States*)

Jersey was divided into East and West Jersey by a line which ran from Little Egg Harbor to a point on the Delaware River, a few miles northeast of the Delaware Water Gap.

West Jersey, which was Berkeley's share, was sold to Edward Byllynge, an English Quaker, who had the idea of providing a refuge for some of his persecuted brethren.

Almost immediately Byllynge got into money troubles and had to sell his share in West Jersey to William Penn and some others. After this settlements were made, chiefly by Quakers, at Burlington and other places along the Delaware.

Prosperity of the colony. The colonists who bought land in West Jersey from Penn and his friends had a very liberal charter which was the wisest and best that had been granted up to that time for any colony. It provided for a governor and a freely elected assembly that should have entire control of passing laws which were not against the laws of England. Freedom of worship was established; there was to be no imprisonment for debt; and the people had the right of trial by jury. Under these liberal laws West Jersey prospered and largely increased in population until 1702, when it was united with East Jersey as a royal province.

STUDY HELPS

Map Work

On a map of eastern United States mark the extent of the Dutch claim and the places of early settlement whether in New York or elsewhere. Mark the division

SETTLEMENT OF NEW YORK AND NEW JERSEY

between East and West Jersey; indicate the location of Jamestown and Plymouth.

Activities

Get pictures of events connected with colonial New York and New Jersey.

Dramatize the scene in which the town council surrenders New Amsterdam to the English in spite of the protests of Governor Stuyvesant.

Make a list of places in New York that have names given by the Dutch.

Make a model of the Dutch settlement at New Amsterdam.

Special Work

Why were the English anxious to obtain New Netherland?

How did the Dutch get the right from the Indians to settle on Manhattan Island?

Why was the name "Fort Orange" given to the early settlement at Albany?

Why was Jersey divided into East and West Jersey?

How was Cape May named?

Storybooks to Read

Belden, Jessie V.: *Antonia* (New Amsterdam)
Brooks, Elbridge Streeter: *In Leisler's Times*
Knipe, E. B. and A. A.: *A Maid of Old Manhattan*
Malkus, Alida Sims: *Pirates' Port* (New Amsterdam)

5. THE SETTLEMENT OF PENNSYLVANIA

William Penn and the Quakers. William Penn, whom you have read about in connection with the Jerseys, was the son of Admiral Sir William Penn of the English navy. He had been brought up as a young nobleman and had been educated at Oxford. Here he had become a convert to the new sect of Quakers.

Penn's father, the Admiral, became angry at his son and sent him first to Paris and later to Ireland. In Ireland he was to have charge of his father's extensive estates. One day he met Thomas Loe, an Irish Quaker, and listened to his preaching. Penn turned back to the Quaker beliefs that he had years before embraced at Oxford.

For the remainder of his life his influence and money were used to help the Quakers escape the persecutions to which they were subjected in England. It was for this reason that Penn became interested in the Jerseys, and for the same reason he founded Pennsylvania.

The Holy Experiment. At the death of his father William Penn received much wealth. He discovered, also, that the king owed his father a large sum of money. Then Penn conceived the idea of asking for land in America in payment of the debt. On this land he could establish not only a place where the Quakers would be free from oppression but also a place where everyone of any race or creed could have full religious

Admiral Penn quarrels with his son William.

William Penn sending his son from home because he has joined the Quakers, or Friends. (From a mural painting by Violet Oakley in the Governor's reception room in the capitol at Harrisburg)

© *Curtis & Cameron*

freedom and could live under laws of their own choosing.

This plan of Penn, as he tells about it in his writings, is called "The Holy Experiment."

The king gives William Penn a charter for Pennsylvania. In 1681 the king, in accordance with Penn's wishes, gave him a part of the land which had already been given to the Duke of York but which the Duke was willing to release. By direction of the king the territory was named Pennsylvania.

Penn proposed to call his new land *Sylvania*, to which the king prefixed the name *Penn*. Penn said that this would seem to his friends to indicate pride on his part. The king told him that the name Penn had been added not to honor him but to honor his father.

The land extended from the fortieth to the forty-second degree of north latitude and for five degrees of longitude west from the Delaware River.

Penn sails for Pennsylvania in the *Welcome*. The following year Penn, having organized his company, sailed for his new province in the ship *Welcome*. Sickness broke out on board, and a third of the new settlers died on the voyage. The Delaware River was reached on October 12, 1682.

Penn finds settlers in his province. The Dutch had made a few settlements along the Delaware about 50 years before. They had been followed by companies of Swedes, who had made settlements at what is now Newcastle in Delaware, Chester in Pennsylvania, and

THE SETTLEMENT OF PENNSYLVANIA 141

other places on the west bank of the river. These people had heard of the new proprietor and his liberal

Penn's first view of the shores of Pennsylvania as the *Welcome* ascends the river
(From a mural painting by Violet Oakley in the Governor's reception room in the capitol at Harrisburg)

plan of government through Penn's agents, who had come to pick a site for the new Quaker settlements, and to make other preparations for Penn's arrival.

Peter Minuit and the Swedes establish the first settlement on the Delaware River at Fort Christina
Note the dress of the Indian chief who is bidding them welcome. (From a painting by Stanley M. Arthurs)

THE SETTLEMENT OF PENNSYLVANIA

Penn meets the Dutch and Swedish settlers at Upland. Penn had representatives of the Dutch and Swedish settlers called together at Upland, now Chester. Here he offered to the people his plan of government called the *Great Law*. This resembled very closely the law which Penn's friends had made for West Jersey in its liberality and in the freedom of government and religion which it gave to the people.

Penn proceeds to Philadelphia. From Upland Penn proceeded to the site which had been selected for the new city Philadelphia. Here the Swedes already had some small settlements.

Penn met the Indians under a large elm tree at Shackamaxon, now Kensington, within the present limits of the city. He made a peace treaty with them in which it was agreed that the Quakers and the Indians would remain friends " as long as the sun and moon should shine."

A wise Frenchman, Voltaire, once said that this treaty was the only treaty that had never been sworn to and that was never broken. It was kept for many years and was not violated until the government of the colony had passed from Quaker control.

Indian tribes of Pennsylvania. The Indians of Pennsylvania belonged to two great groups. The Algonquins, of whom there were many separate tribes, or clans, occupied the western and eastern parts of the state. In the central part, however, there was the long peninsula of Iroquois tribes which extended down from

William Penn making a treaty of friendship with the Indians

The houses in the background were built by Swedish settlers. (From an engraving after the painting by Benjamin West)

THE SETTLEMENT OF PENNSYLVANIA 145

New York state, where this group was the most numerous. The chief tribe in the vicinity of Philadelphia was known as the Lenni Lenape, one of the Algonquin tribes. These Indians lived in small villages, usually along the rivers. They lived chiefly on the game and fish that they were able to get from the forests and streams.

In many cases, however, the Indians had cleared small areas of land, on which they cultivated corn, beans, pumpkins, and a few other vegetables.

In times of peace the government of the tribes was in the hands of *sachems*, or wise men, who decided questions of peace or war and other matters that concerned the tribe. If war was decided upon, prominent warriors, who were known as *chiefs*, would gather others about them and go off on an expedition against the settlers or against other tribes.

Relations with the Indians. You have learned already of the treaty of friendship which Penn made under an elm tree at Shackamaxon, near Philadelphia.

From time to time, as he disposed of the lands that had been granted to him, Penn made purchases from the Indian tribes of whatever right they had to the land that he desired. A large number of treaties were made. In some cases it was arranged to buy a certain tract of land which was afterward to be exactly marked out.

The Walking Purchase. Such an early treaty was one that Thomas Holme, Penn's agent, had agreed upon with the Indians for land stretching back from

Wrightstown on the Pennsylvania side of the Delaware near Trenton. The distance was to be as far as a man could walk in a day and a half.

When the time came to carry out the provisions of the treaty, Edward Marshall, a famous walker, was engaged to do the walking on behalf of the proprietor. For some days before the event was to take place, Marshall and his companion trained themselves so that they would be able to walk as fast and as far as possible. When the day of the walk came, the party started out, but to the dismay of the Indians Marshall continued almost without stopping during the whole thirty-six hours and covered a distance of about seventy miles. The Indians had expected the walkers to proceed in a leisurely way, stopping to rest from time to time and camping at night. In this case the walkers would probably have covered a distance of about thirty miles.

The Indians felt that they had been cheated for another reason. It had been agreed that a line should be drawn from where the walk stopped to the Delaware River. When this part of the boundary came to be drawn, instead of extending to the nearest point of the river, it was drawn at right angles with the line of the walk, thus taking in a great many additional square miles of land.

The Indians thought that they had been very badly treated in the carrying out of this treaty. As the frontier settlements encroached more and more on the

Indian land, the natives were less willing to deal with the whites, and the remembrance of the way they had been treated made them more ready to take up arms and organize war parties against the settlers.

Philadelphia. Philadelphia, Penn's capital, was located on the peninsula between the Schuylkill and Delaware Rivers. The site had been selected before Penn's arrival. The streets were made wider than was usual and crossed each other at right angles. Penn urged that they be planted with trees so that his city would be " a green country town, which will never be burned and always be wholesome."

Penn arranged with the Indians and the settlers the title to the site of the town. All colonists purchasing tracts of land from Penn were entitled to a building lot within the city limits.

Penn advertises his colony. Penn widely advertised his colony not only among the Quakers in England but also among the many who lived in Ireland and Wales. The latter were very poor and were glad to come to Pennsylvania where they could get cheap land.

Pamphlets were also printed and sent about among the Germans of the Rhine Valley, many of whom held religious beliefs similar to those of the Quakers.

This advertising, together with Penn's wise and liberal plan of government, soon brought many new settlers to the colony. In a few years it rivaled Virginia and Massachusetts in population and wealth.

Early in the following century a strong tide of immigration from the peasantry of northern Ireland arrived. These people were known as the Scotch-Irish. They belonged to a colony of Scotch who had been induced to migrate to Ireland in the hope of bettering their

Courtesy Philadelphia Commercial Museum
William Penn's house
This house was built for Penn's daughter Letitia. It now stands in Fairmount Park, Philadelphia.

condition. These people felt that they would be still better off in America.

Then followed a second wave of emigrants from the Rhine region which was so great that there was fear that the colony would become German instead of English.

THE SETTLEMENT OF PENNSYLVANIA 149

Where the newcomers settled. It was not long before the fertile valleys of the southeast were taken up and settled for the most part by Germans. The Scotch-Irish pioneers, however, being of a more restless disposition, pushed westward into the mountains and into the Great Valley. Thence they gradually made their way north into southern New York and south as far as the southern border of Virginia.

The growth of Philadelphia. Penn's first step was to lay out his city on the site chosen by his commissioners. The principal streets extending from river to river were named after the trees of the forest. The north and south streets were numbered beginning with each river, until Broad Street was reached.

Where Broad Street and High (Market) Street met, there was a large square where the City Hall now stands. Other squares were located in each quarter of the city.

When Penn first landed, there were few houses for the colonists to live in. So for some years many of the settlers lived in caves dug in the high banks of the river. Penn had arranged that artisans of all kinds should be attracted to his colony; so in the short space of two years six hundred houses were built.

Great increase in immigration. In 1684 it was estimated that the population of Pennsylvania had increased to 4000. Many other thousands were coming yearly from almost every country in Europe. During the first two years more than fifty vessels came to Philadelphia with settlers and their goods.

In the German towns where Penn had advertised his colony, companies were formed under leaders who purchased tracts of land in Pennsylvania and then were brought over in a group to settle. In one year as many as 12,000 Germans arrived in the colony. It is estimated that 16,000 men, women, and children from the

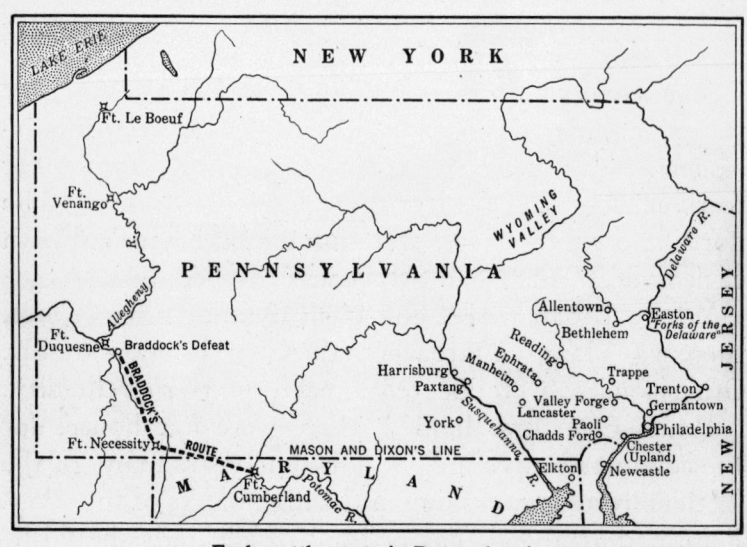

Early settlements in Pennsylvania

Rhine country camped near London, in 1690, many of them waiting for a passage to Pennsylvania.

Industries of Pennsylvania. Most of the settlers of Pennsylvania took at once to agriculture. The rich limestone valleys of the southeast made this an exceedingly profitable occupation. In less than twenty years after Penn's arrival the markets of the West Indies

Old Swedes Church in Philadelphia, built in 1700
Some of the carved ornaments contain Bible verses in Swedish.   It is on the site of a blockhouse church that was built in 1677.   (From a painting by Stanley M. Arthurs)

were glutted with flour, meats, and other provisions from Pennsylvania, according to the statement of a traveler. The principal exports were grain, salt beef, and salt pork. The Indian corn that was grown was used chiefly for feed for cattle.

Manufacturing in Pennsylvania. Spinning and weaving were carried on in the homes of the settlers. Only the coarsest stuff was woven in the colonies. When finer qualities were wanted, they had to be imported from England. Hat making was a common industry in all the colonies because the large number of fur-bearing animals provided the material for the felt of which hats were made. Later this industry became so important that it interfered with the trade of English merchants, and an act was passed forbidding hats to be exported.

Ironworks. The first iron furnace in Pennsylvania was established in Berks County in 1720. Because of the large quantities of iron ore and limestone to be found in the state, many other iron furnaces were established, especially near the ore beds. At first charcoal was used to smelt the iron. Not until much later was it discovered that iron could be smelted with coal. In 1750 nearly 4000 tons of iron were exported to England.

Many other industries were early established. Among the more important products were paper and leather and the products of the flour and lumber mills which were generally run by water power.

THE SETTLEMENT OF PENNSYLVANIA

The commerce of Philadelphia. In the beginning the commerce of Philadelphia consisted of exchanging the products of the new country for such manufactured products as were needed from England. As soon as the colony commenced to manufacture many of the articles needed, it was found more profitable to ship the surplus products to the islands of the West Indies and to bring back such tropical products as sugar and molasses directly to Pennsylvania instead of having them reach the colony by way of England. In 1701 the customs duties amounted to 8000 pounds sterling, a large sum to come from a colony that had been founded only twenty years before.

Later on the English government began to enforce the Navigation Acts, the first of which had been passed in 1651. In spite of these acts, however, Pennsylvania, in common with other colonies, carried on considerable illegal commerce with the French and Spanish colonies in the West Indies.

Pennsylvania a refuge for the oppressed: John Kelpius. You have learned that Penn founded Pennsylvania principally that his fellow Quakers might find a place where they could worship in the manner they thought best. Penn also invited the oppressed of every nation to come to Pennsylvania. John Kelpius was the leader of a group of Germans, called *Pietists*, that arrived in Philadelphia in 1694. They came from Germany to seek toleration of worship. Their belief seems to have been somewhat mystical. The day of

The harbor of Philadelphia in 1702
(From a painting by Stanley M. Arthurs)

THE SETTLEMENT OF PENNSYLVANIA

their arrival they went to Fairmount, just northwest of the city of Philadelphia, and performed some mysterious rites, in which they made a great fire on the hillside and then scattered the burning brands down the slope. Later on they moved up the Wissahickon to what is known as the Hermitage Estate, where they built a monastery. Here Kelpius lived for a time in a cave in the hillside.

The Dunkers founded Ephrata. The Dunkers was the name given to a German religious sect which was much persecuted in the homeland. Gradually a little settlement was formed at Ephrata in Lancaster County. Here they formed a self-sustaining community following such trades and occupations as would enable them to be independent of outsiders. They established a printing press and built a paper mill. They printed many books. One of them, called the *Ephrata Music Book*, was probably the most ornamental piece of printing done in the colonies. Some of the Continental money was printed at Ephrata during the Revolution.

In the beginning they practiced a great deal of self-denial, eating no flesh foods. They used wooden blocks for pillows and thin pieces of boards for plates. They made their drinking vessels and their forks out of wood. Later they built two cloisters, or houses, one for men and one for women, in which each group lived separately.

Baron Stiegel. Henry William Stiegel was a German nobleman of much wealth who came over with a colony of Moravians and founded Manheim, which was located

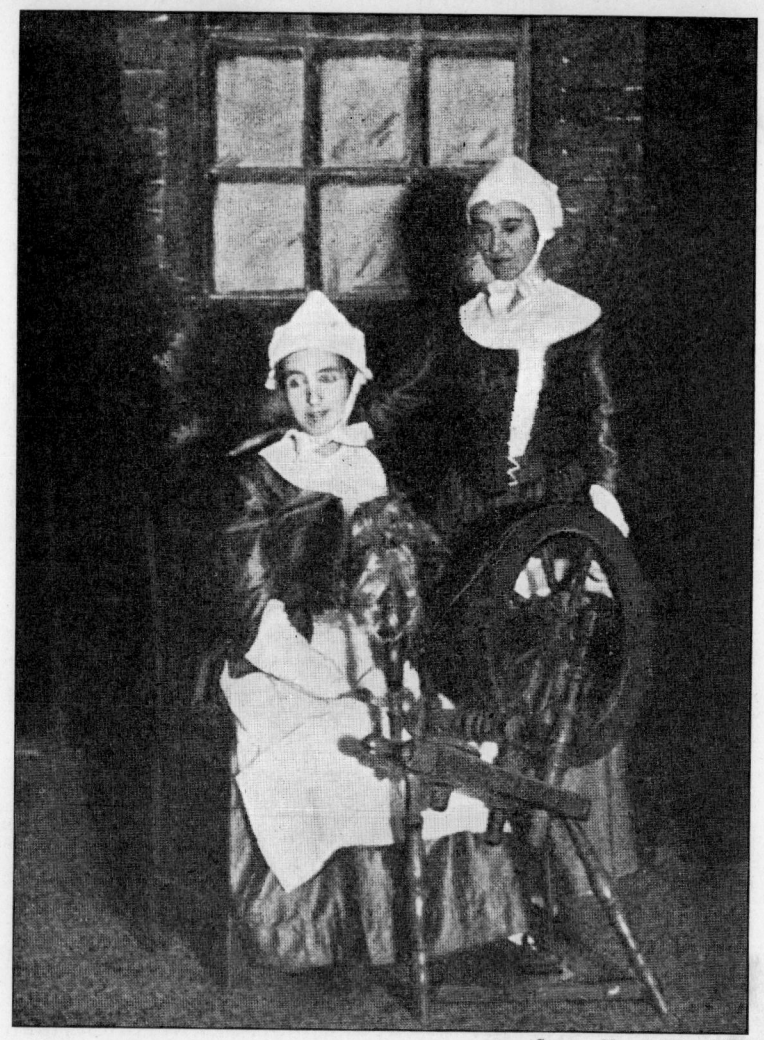

Courtesy Mrs. J. Upton Myers
Moravian women spinning in the Sisters' House, Bethlehem

THE SETTLEMENT OF PENNSYLVANIA 157

not far from Ephrata. Here he established factories for the production of iron and glass. The glass is much sought after to-day by collectors of the interesting manufactures of olden times. Stiegel stoves were famous even in colonial times.

Pastorius settles Germantown. Very soon after Penn founded his colony, Francis Daniel Pastorius, a native of Frankfort, Germany, had, with some others, bought 10,000 acres from William Penn as a site for establishing a settlement.

Courtesy Harrisburg Evening News
The pulpit in the Cloisters at Ephrata

When Pastorius arrived in Philadelphia, in 1683, to select the land, Penn refused to give it to him until he had the settlers to put on it. In the meantime a group of Germans from Krefeld on the Rhine arrived and asked Pastorius to become their leader. Pastorius agreed and succeeded in persuading Penn to give them the land which is now included in Germantown. Here the colonists erected houses and planted vines and flax so that they might carry on the industries that they had carried on in Germany. Finding that these products were not well suited to the climate, they soon turned their attention to the raising and manufacturing of wool, an industry for which Germantown is still noted.

Courtesy The Moravian Book Shop

A reproduction of the first house in Bethlehem, Pennsylvania, on Revolutionary Burial Hill

Count Zinzendorf and the Moravians. Many of the settlers who came to Pennsylvania were men of wealth and position in the old country. Among these was Count Zinzendorf, a leader of the Moravians. He bought 10,000 acres of land near the junction of the Lehigh and Delaware Rivers and founded the town of Bethlehem in 1740. This settlement soon became a

THE SETTLEMENT OF PENNSYLVANIA 159

center from which the Moravians sent out missionaries to the Indians, many of whom became converts. Most of the settlements of Christian Indians were in the southeastern part of the state, though others were to be found far in the west and in the north of Penn's province. Among the most famous of the Indian converts was the great chief Tedyuscung, who unfortunately often forgot the Moravian belief in nonresistance and joined Indian war parties. These Christian Indians many times saved the lives of the settlers by giving warning of hostile raids.

Conrad Weiser a peacemaker with the Indians. For many years Conrad Weiser had lived among the Indians of New York, where he had learned their language. Having come to Philadelphia to act as an interpreter when they made a treaty, he was persuaded to become the agent of the province in its dealings with the Indians. For many years he participated in making almost all the treaties and agreements with the natives. He never tried to cheat them or deceive them in any way; so the Indians had great confidence in him, and whatever advice he gave they were usually ready to accept.

Many times Weiser urged the province to wiser and more honest ways of treating the Indians in order that attacks on the settlers might be avoided. He kept the Indians from being cheated in land purchases and always insisted that their lands should be protected from encroachment by the whites.

The German Lutherans in Pennsylvania. Another group of Germans who had been persecuted in the old country were the Lutherans. Hundreds of these people came to Pennsylvania in 1741. Most of them came from what is known as *The Palatinate*, which was along

Courtesy the Rev. P. C. Croll, D.D.

Conrad Weiser and his wife
Weiser was an important man in the colony, and he dressed suitably to his position

the upper part of the Rhine Valley. Their settlements in Pennsylvania were chiefly along Perkiomen Creek, near what is now Pottstown. They first settled at a place called *the Swamp* under the leadership of Doctor Henry M. Muhlenberg.

THE SETTLEMENT OF PENNSYLVANIA 161

They made many other settlements in this neighborhood. At the village of Trappe there is an old stone church which is one of the first places of worship built by the Lutherans in the United States. Peter Muhlenberg, a son of Doctor Muhlenberg, followed in his

Courtesy the Rev. P. C. Croll, D.D.

A blockhouse church
This is the first church of a group of people from the Palatinate in Germany, who settled at Newburgh, New York.

father's footsteps as a preacher. During the Revolutionary War he preached a sermon urging his congregation to resist oppression and the thwarting of their rights by tyrants. Suddenly he threw aside his clergyman's gown and his congregation beheld him dressed in the uniform of an officer of the Continental army. Almost all the men in his congregation joined him in the fight for independence.

The affair of the Conestoga Indians. You have already learned that Moravian missionaries had succeeded in establishing a number of Christian Indian

The interior of the old church at Trappe
Note the simplicity of the architecture.

villages. One of these villages was at Conestoga in Lancaster County. In 1763 a number of armed men belonging to the frontier rangers of this neighborhood, who lived in a village called Paxton or Paxtang, made an attack on Conestoga. Several families of white settlers had been murdered, and the rangers believed that the murderers were concealed in the Indian village.

"There is a time to pray and a time to fight."

The Reverend Peter Muhlenberg calling on the men of his congregation to join the patriot army. (From a painting by Stanley M. Arthurs in the Lutheran Theological Seminary, Gettysburg, Pennsylvania)

Most of the Indian men were away hunting or at Lancaster trading their furs. The attack was made in the middle of the night. All those in the settlement were killed by the frontiersmen, and their dwellings were burned to the ground.

The authorities at Lancaster gathered together the Indians who had not been present on the night of the attack and confined them in the stone workhouse or jail at Lancaster, where it was supposed they would be safe until they could be moved to Philadelphia. The Paxton men, as the rangers were called, were not satisfied and decided to exterminate the tribe, saying that one or two of the hostile Indians were among those at Lancaster. Suddenly riding into the town, the band overpowered the keeper of the jail. They rushed into the prison and killed all the Indians, about fourteen in number. An alarm was raised, but before the citizens could assemble the murderers had fled.

Moravian Indians from Wyalusing and Nain had already been brought to Philadelphia for protection. The Paxton men decided to march to Philadelphia and destroy these Indians. Meanwhile the Indians had been placed in charge of the garrison of the city. The Paxton men reached the Schuylkill, but, finding several companies ready to repel the expected attack, they returned home.

The Cornplanter Indians. The Cornplanter Indians were named after Cornplanter, a famous chief of the Seneca Indians, who were the most numerous and most

THE SETTLEMENT OF PENNSYLVANIA

warlike of the Six Nations. During many years and through various treaties they were deprived of one piece of their land after another. Cornplanter was allied with the French, during the French and Indian War, and he opposed the Continental troops during the Revolution. After the war he became the fast friend of the United States, for he found that the Indians had not been protected by the British when the treaty of peace was made. Because of this friendship the state of Pennsylvania gave him a fine reservation on the Allegheny River.

His tribe was not satisfied with Cornplanter's attitude toward the new government. Red Jacket, a rival chief, sought to undermine the popularity of Cornplanter and urged his tribe to fight the white settlers. During the Indian wars from 1791 to 1794 Cornplanter pledged himself that the Senecas would remain friendly to the United States. He often gave notice to the garrisons of forts of attacks of hostile Indians, and he often risked his life on missions to other tribes. After peace was finally established between the Indians and the United States, Cornplanter devoted his time to his own people. He always aided the efforts of missionaries among members of his tribe, yet until his death he himself held to many of the peculiar religious ideas of the Indian faith.

The Welsh settlement in Pennsylvania. About twenty years after Penn founded his colony, a group of Welshmen, many of whom were Quakers, purchased a tract of 40,000 acres, extending across the lower end of Montgomery County and into Chester and Delaware Counties. This was known as the Welsh Tract. Many of these Welsh people were of good family and education.

They made many settlements within this tract. The first one they called Gwynedd, or North Wales. A number of townships were established, among them Haverford, Merion, and Bryn Mawr, all of which names were derived from favorite places in Wales.

The Welsh settlers were very industrious. They had very good farms and raised many cattle so that they became as wealthy as any group in the province.

About one hundred years later there was a large emigration of Welsh people to the central part of Pennsylvania for the purpose of working in the mines of that neighborhood. The township in which they settled was called Cambria after the old name of Wales. Afterward the same name was given to the county.

Redemptioners. The slave labor that proved so profitable in the colonies of the South was not used to a like extent in Pennsylvania or the more northerly colonies. There were two reasons for this: first, the climate of the North was not suitable to the growing of the plantation crops that seemed to make slave labor necessary. The second reason was that the long period of forced idleness in wintertime made slave labor very costly.

Courtesy Dauphin County Historical Society

The original log-cabin home of John Harris at Harris's Ferry
The tree on the right is the one to which he was tied by the Indians

The cheap labor used on the farms in Pennsylvania and in many of the other colonies was furnished by men called *redemptioners*. These people came from the very poor classes in England and other countries. They had agreed with the ship captain that he might sell their services for three years to pay him for bringing them to America. Men who were sometimes called *soul-drivers* would bargain with the captains for these people and then take them around the country to the farmers, who would buy the services of the redemptioners.

A story is told about a driver whose group of redemptioners had been reduced to one person. One night they stayed at an inn. The redemptioner got up early the next morning and passed himself off as the driver and sold the driver to the landlord for a good sum of money.

These poor people were treated not much better than slaves during the time for which their services had been sold. After that they became free men, could work for whom they pleased, and in many cases became prominent in the affairs of the colony.

John Harris. The first John Harris came from Yorkshire, England, to America not long after the year 1700. He first settled in Philadelphia and later moved to the present site of Harrisburg. He built his house on the river bank just below where his grave now is. Harris established a ferry at this point in order to help in his trading with the Indians and also to aid people who wished to settle beyond the Susquehanna River.

THE SETTLEMENT OF PENNSYLVANIA 169

He made friends with the Indians of his neighborhood and carried on an extensive trade with them for skins and furs. These he would send to Philadelphia to be sold. The pack horses on their return would bring back provisions and articles for trade.

Courtesy T. B. Keener

The grave of John Harris

John Harris died in 1748, and his grave can still be seen in the park on the banks of the Susquehanna. He owned at his death about 900 acres of land where Harrisburg now is and had considerable other land in the neighborhood.

The founding of Harrisburg. John Harris, his son, inherited and bought a total of about 700 acres. He had an extensive farm and traded with the Indians as his father had done. He would sometimes have ten or twelve wagonloads of furs stored away at a time.

Harris's Ferry, as the settlement was called, soon became a place well known even in Europe. The younger John Harris believed that his farm would eventually become the seat of the state government. He stated this belief to a friend at least twenty years before Harrisburg was founded.

The law creating Dauphin County and making Harris's Ferry the county seat was passed in 1785. Harrisburg was laid out the same year. Harris gave to the commissioners for laying out the city four acres of land on Capitol Hill, east of the present State Capitol, to be used for whatever public purpose the legislature might decide. It seems certain that he had in mind the possibility that the future capitol of the state would be built on this site.

Stories of the Harris family. One day a band of Indians came to the house of the elder John Harris. They asked for some rum. Harris, seeing that they were already drunk, refused to give them any. Very much angered, they seized Harris and tied him to a mulberry tree, intending to burn him. Fortunately some friendly Indians came up and released Harris and drove off his attackers. At his death Harris asked that he be buried at the foot of the tree at which the Indians intended to burn him. This request is said to have been carried out.

Another story is told of his son John. When news of the passing of the Declaration of Independence reached him, he read to his wife the Declaration from a Philadelphia newspaper. He said, "The war in which we are about to engage cannot be carried on without money. We have £3,000 in the house, and, if you are agreed, I will take the money to Philadelphia and put it into the public treasury to carry on the war." She did agree, and he carried the money to Philadelphia and gave it to the treasurer of the Continental Congress.

The boundary dispute between Penn and Lord Baltimore. William Penn's grant of land from the king provided that the southern boundary of his province should start at the Delaware River and then follow along a circle drawn twelve miles from Newcastle until it reached the fortieth parallel of latitude. From this point it was to extend westward along the parallel a distance of five degrees of longitude.

Lord Baltimore, who had received his grant some years before, had been given the land extending to the fortieth parallel if it were not already settled. When Penn came to survey his lands, it was found that the maps had been inaccurate, and that the proposed twelve-mile circle would not touch the fortieth parallel.

A dispute soon arose between Penn and Lord Baltimore. If Penn's claims were allowed, Baltimore felt that he would be deprived of lands rightly his. If Lord Baltimore was allowed the lands up to the fortieth parallel, Penn's new city of Philadelphia would come

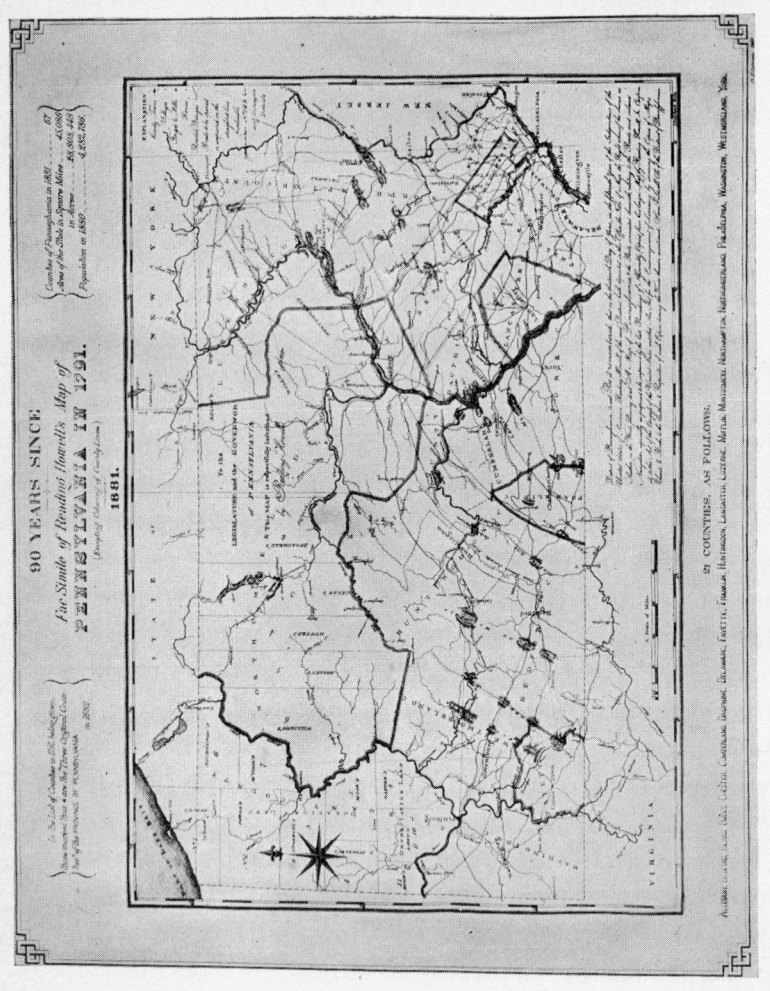

Map of Pennsylvania in 1791

At this time there were but twenty-one counties in the state. The old trail from Shippensburg through Bedford to Pittsburgh shows faintly at the lower left side. (Engraved from a map in the possession of Mr. Norman C. Koontz, Superintendent of Schools, Indiana, Pennsylvania)

THE SETTLEMENT OF PENNSYLVANIA

into the possession of Lord Baltimore. The fortieth parallel passes through the upper part of what is now Germantown, some miles north of Penn's original city.

Mason and Dixon's line. In 1766 two English surveyors, Mason and Dixon, were employed by the two colonies to survey what is now the southern boundary of Pennsylvania. Starting with the Delaware River, they first surveyed the twelve-mile circle. Then they ran a line up the middle of the land between Delaware and Chesapeake Bays to find the boundary between Delaware and Maryland. From a point on this line fourteen miles south of the southern boundary of Philadelphia, they surveyed a line as far west as the Monongahela River, where they were stopped by Indians.

Later on in the history of our country the states lying north of this line abolished slavery and the states south of it retained slavery. The line became famous as Mason and Dixon's line which marked the boundary between the slave and the free states.

Pennsylvania's land dispute with Connecticut. The grant of land made to Connecticut provided that its land should reach to the South Sea. If this boundary had been carried out, it would have given Connecticut almost one half of Pennsylvania.

This quarrel between the two colonies did not become serious until settlers from Connecticut and from Pennsylvania had pushed into this disputed region, especially in the neighborhood of the Wyoming Valley. A war between the two groups of settlers and their Indian allies then broke out, called the Yankee-Pennamite War. During this war much blood was shed and much cruelty was practiced, especially by the Indians.

The dispute was brought to the attention of the Continental Congress after the close of the Revolution. It was finally settled by Congress giving the land to Pennsylvania and repaying the Connecticut settlers the money they had expended.

Courtesy Chas. Scribner's Sons

The landing of Lord de la Warre, for whom the state of Delaware was named

(From a drawing by W. L. Shepard in Bryant's *Popular History of the United States*)

Delaware created out of the three lower counties. In the same year that Penn received his grant from the

THE SETTLEMENT OF PENNSYLVANIA

king, he also obtained the rights of the Duke of York to what is now the state of Delaware. You have already learned that in this territory settlements had been made at Newcastle and other places by the Swedes and the Dutch.

This part of Penn's possessions was generally referred to as the "Three Lower Counties on the Delaware." At first they were annexed to Pennsylvania and delegates from them sat in the Pennsylvania assembly. But soon the people of these counties felt that their interests were being sacrificed for the benefit of Penn's larger colony. In 1704 they were given the name Delaware and were allowed a separate assembly although they had the same proprietor and often the same governor as Pennsylvania.

STUDY HELPS

Map Work

On a map of eastern United States show the extent of the grant to Penn; the location of the other colonies that had been founded up to this time. Indicate on the map Philadelphia, Harrisburg, Fort Duquesne, Chester, Bethlehem, Lancaster.

Activities

Make a model of Penn's town, Philadelphia. Make a model of a fort or a blockhouse (one that was located near where you now live, if possible).

Collect, if you can, relics and articles used in colonial times.

Dramatize the scene in which Charles II granted Pennsylvania to Penn. Dramatize the arrival of Penn in his colony or his treaty with the Indians.

Get for your book pictures connected with the settlement of Pennsylvania.

Visit the most interesting historical site near your home.

Visit a museum and describe to your class some of the interesting colonial furniture.

Special Work

Find out how Penn advertised his colony.

Why did Penn call his colony " a Holy Experiment "?

Find out about the early life of Penn before he became a Quaker.

Storybooks to Read

Butterworth, Hezekiah : *Wampum Belt*
Holland, R. S. : *William Penn*
Kaler, James Otis : *Stephen of Philadelphia*
Walton and Brumbaugh : *Stories of Pennsylvania*

UNIT II. PART 2. PERIOD OF COLONIZATION

A night watchman on his rounds with his lantern and staff
(From a painting by Stanley M. Arthurs in the Wilmington Society of Fine Arts, Wilmington, Delaware)

Courtesy Metropolitan Museum of Art

A lady's costume of colonial times. The chest of drawers is called a high boy. The wall paper shows Chinese scenes.

UNIT II. PART 2. PERIOD OF COLONIZATION

Courtesy Title Guarantee and Trust Company, New York

Winter sports in colonial times
Note how the sleigh is built and the costumes of the people.

6. LIFE AND CUSTOMS IN THE COLONIES

Classes of People

The wealthy and ruling class. In all the English colonies as soon as they became well settled a wealthy and ruling class arose. This group was composed in part of people of high social position from England and other countries who were looked up to by the other settlers. Another group consisted of those colonists who, through fortunate business ventures in commerce or trade, became wealthy. In the South the members of this second group were colonists who had succeeded in obtaining large quantities of land on which they had established plantations for the growing of tobacco.

The free working man. Next below this ruling group was a very great number of small shopkeepers and artisans of every sort, who carried on the industries of the town, and the hunters, trappers, farmers, millers, and tanners, who carried on chiefly the industries of the country districts.

The slaves and redemptioners. As you have learned already, the people of the South carried on their plantations with the aid of negro slaves. The first of these had been brought to Virginia from Africa in 1619, and from that time on large numbers of negro slaves continued to be brought to the Southern colonies. These came not only from Africa but also from the islands of the West Indies.

Many efforts were made by the colonies to stop the slave trade, but without success since high officials in the English government were interested in this traffic.

In the Northern States the work for the most part was done by free people, who for one reason or another had to depend on others for the opportunity to make a living, or by indentured servants or apprentices or by redemptioners. The indentured servants were usually young persons who agreed to work for an employer for a number of years in return for board and clothes and the chance to learn a trade or occupation. The redemptioners, or people who agreed to work for a number of years in order to pay for their passage to America, have already been told about. It must not be understood that negro slavery did not exist in the Northern colonies. It simply was less common.

Courtesy Chas. Scribner's Sons
The way wealthy colonists dressed about 1650

Classes in the colonies of other nations. In both the French and Spanish colonies in America the governing and wealthy class consisted of noblemen and other important people who had come to America in order to acquire additional wealth in the New World.

As to the rest of the population there were important differences. In the first place, neither France nor Spain made any effort to bring settlers to this country in large numbers. They did not intend to build a new nation in America. All they wished to do was to get from America gold, silver, furs, and other important and valuable products. The few people that they brought over with them were their own servants, soldiers, and traders whom they expected to help obtain these valuable products.

In the Spanish colonies slavery was absolutely forbidden. The Spaniards, however, forced the Indians to live in villages near the missions and to labor in the fields and in the mines. It is very likely that the actual condition of these Indians was no better than that of slaves.

In the French settlements the Indians were treated as fellow members of the community, since to treat them badly would have interfered with the plans of the French for a rich traffic in furs.

Homes and Social Life

Types of houses. The cold winter climate of the New England colonies caused the settlers there to build small houses that would not be too hard to heat. They had few windows and doors so that as much as possible of the cold winter winds would be kept out. Huge fireplaces were the means by which the houses were warmed. The barns and other outbuildings generally adjoined the house or were connected with it by means of a covered passageway. In this way, in wintertime, when everything was snowed up, the cattle could be attended to and the supplies of food and fuel in the barn could be reached.

In the Southern States the houses were much larger and were generally more open. Frequently a large hall

An early New England farmhouse
Note how the buildings all adjoin one another.

extended from front to back through the house so cool breezes could blow through. Here, during the hot summer months, was a place where the family could spend their time in comfort while the plantation hands were in the fields cultivating the tobacco crop.

In the South, also, the kitchen was frequently in a separate building so that the house itself would not become heated from the fires used for cooking. The barns, storehouses, and the quarters for the slaves were usually situated at some distance from the house.

From Cook Studio

The hallway of Westover, on the Potomac River
This was the home of Colonel William Byrd, governor of Virginia and a wealthy plantation owner.

In the Middle colonies the houses tended to be somewhat like both of these types. Since the winters were cold, the houses ordinarily had few and small windows and were heated with fireplaces. On the other hand, since the deep snows of New England were not common in the Middle colonies, we find the large barns situated near the house but not attached to it.

Neither in the Middle colonies nor in New England was there any need for providing quarters for the slaves. Where the people of these colonies had slaves, they were

From an old print

A home in New England
Note the simple furniture, the bellows for blowing the fire, the gun over the mantel, and the powder horn.

usually house servants and lived in the homes of their owners.

Colonial homes lacked comforts and conveniences. Colonial homes had few of the comforts and conveniences that we think so necessary to-day. Since the houses were all heated in wintertime with open fireplaces, the rooms were cold and uncomfortable at even a few feet away from the fire. All the cooking and other work requiring the use of heat had to be done at this same open fireplace. Stoves were not used until about the time of the Revolutionary War, and such a thing as heating the whole house from a single central heating plant had not been thought of.

Courtesy Metropolitan Museum of Art
Colonial metal work
A handsome pewter tankard and a pitcher

Furniture of the homes. The log cabin of the pioneers generally contained a table made of a split log, the legs of which consisted of lengths of saplings stuck into holes bored into the underside. The seats or benches were made in similar fashion. The wardrobe consisted of rows of pegs driven in between the logs. The few kitchen utensils were hung on similar pegs. Often the bed was made by rolling a small log three or more feet from the wall and then filling the space with dried branches and leaves which were then covered with a blanket or with furs.

There was always a large pot in which the meals were cooked. Sometimes, however, meat was roasted on iron rods, or spits, hung in front of the fire. Bread was sometimes baked on the hearth in front of the fireplace. Often it, as well as the meats, was cooked in a sort of oven, which was open at one side, the open side facing the fire.

The pioneer family may have been provided with a few pewter plates and spoons. These, with their iron knives and forks, had been brought with them from the older settlements. Bowls and drinking vessels were made out of wood, or perhaps half of a gourd was used.

With increasing prosperity the furniture of the home became better made. Though plain and substantial, it was generally much the same as is found in more modest homes to-day. Tables and chairs, huge four-poster bedsteads, china cupboards, chests of drawers, and long settees could be found in almost every farmer's home as well as in the houses of the workingmen of the town.

When the growth of commerce gave rise to a rich class of merchants, furniture and other household comforts were imported from England. The tables were furnished with china and silverware, and the kitchens with a complete assortment of pots, pans, and other cooking utensils.

Not long before the Revolution carpets began to be

used on the floors of the wealthy, and, it is said, visitors would often walk around the edge of the carpet so as to avoid soiling it by walking on it.

Photo from Ewing Galloway

This colonial kitchen is in the old Wayside Inn.
This is where Longfellow's story of Paul Revere's Ride is supposed to have been told. How many objects can you recognize in the picture?

The water supply usually was got from wells, even in the towns. In a few cases some of the larger towns brought the water to public fountains located every few blocks. Here the people would come with their jars and cans to obtain water for their household needs, just as is done in some of the older towns of Europe to-day.

LIFE AND CUSTOMS IN THE COLONIES

The walls of the room were usually of plain wooden boards, and the floors, if covered at all, may have had a covering of rushes or of fine, clean sand.

The colonial homes had no gas or electric lights. When people read or worked at night, they used the light of candles. These were made by the people themselves out of tallow made from the fat of animals. A few of the wealthier class used lamps in which they burned whale oil. Kerosene was not known at that time.

COLONIAL SPORTS AND PASTIMES

Recreations and amusements. There was very little opportunity for recreation in colonial times. Life in the new country was so hard that the whole family, children included, had to join in making the home. There were no art galleries, museums, libraries, theaters, concerts, or " movies."

One of the recreations of the colonists was the opportunity of making trips to the near-by towns on market days. On these occasions they visited stores to purchase supplies or to sell produce to the merchants. Occasionally they had the opportunity to see traveling showmen and entertainers. Sometimes these shows were of wild animals that had been captured alive and were exhibited in cages for the education of the townspeople. Sometimes there would be a puppet show. Often the entertainment appealed to the more brutal feelings. Bears or other animals were fastened by a strong chain to a heavy stake. Dogs were then set upon them, and a bloody fight followed among the animals. In the country districts contests in shooting at marks and wrestling, jumping, or other athletic competitions were common forms of amusement.

But public entertainment in the form of shows or other exhibitions was rare. The result was that the people took advantage of every possible excuse to get

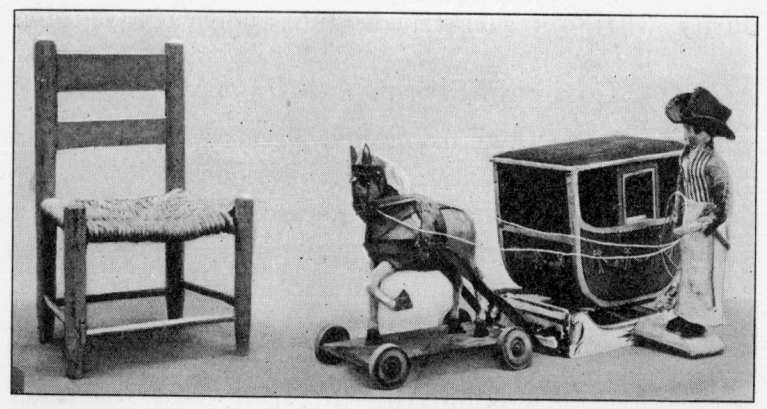

Toys of colonial children

together for a good time. Spelling bees were often held in the schoolhouse. Old and young took part in order to show off their learning, and the schoolmaster acted as judge.

Singing schools would be held, sometimes in the church and sometimes in the schoolhouse. These singing schools were especially needful since the strict Puritan churches were not furnished with organs or other musical instruments to accompany the singing.

LIFE AND CUSTOMS IN THE COLONIES

The need for coöperation in getting certain kinds of work done was also made an excuse for a social time. So we find the womenfolks getting together at each other's houses to make wadded quilts or comfortables on large quilting frames. At harvest time there would

Courtesy Metropolitan Museum of Art

In colonial times girls spent much time in making samplers like the one in the picture to show how well they could use the needle.

be a succession of husking bees. The townspeople, young and old, would go from one homestead to another and husk out the ears of corn. When the task was over, all would join in one of the old-fashioned barn dances. Helping the new neighbor build his home was one of the important occasions for getting together.

If a log cabin was to be built, there would be a log-rolling, in which the newcomer would be helped in putting the logs one on top of another until the cabin was built. Sometimes better houses would be built out of squared timbers or boards. Then the frames for each side would be made on the ground. When all was ready, the neighbors would be invited over. Everybody would help raise the frames up straight and then fasten them with beams and joists so that they would not fall down.

Travel in Colonial Days

Difficulties of transportation. The first settlements in the colonies were located along streams. For many years afterward the almost total absence of roads made water transportation the most convenient, both for people and goods. As the settlements pushed farther and farther into the interior, rapids or falls in the river were reached. Here the goods had to be taken out and carried around the falls or rapids to the smoother waters above. Often these carrying places, or *portages*, became later the sites of important towns.

The first method of transporting goods overland was by means of pack horses, such as John Harris used in taking his furs to Philadelphia and in bringing back the needed supplies (p. 169). Later on, the paths followed by the pack trains, which were usually old Indian trails, were widened into roads. It then became possible to use wagons. Since these roads were merely cleared

LIFE AND CUSTOMS IN THE COLONIES 193

trails through the forest, they often became impassable in wintertime and after heavy rains, and the wagons needed many horses or oxen to pull them through.

Passenger travel in these times was either by horseback or by stagecoach. On account of the bad roads it took several days to make the journey by coach from

A pack train *Photo from Brown Bros.*
Such a train usually consisted of from fifty to one hundred horses, each carrying about two hundred pounds.

New York to Philadelphia and nearly a week to reach Boston.

The inns, or taverns, in which travelers had to stop along the road were just as uncomfortable as the homes of the settlers. Often they had only two sleeping rooms, all the men travelers sleeping in one and the women in the other.

Roads to the West. The first settlers made their homes on the Coastal Plain between the Appalachian Highland and the Atlantic Ocean. When most of the fertile lands east of the mountains had been taken up, newcomers sought to cross these mountains to reach the rich lands in the Mississippi Valley.

Photo from Publishers' Photo Service

The first stagecoach from Baltimore to Washington leaving Waterloo Inn

There are not very many places where the Appalachians can easily be crossed. One of these places is in the state of New York, where the Mohawk River comes from the west and flows into the Hudson near Albany. The people from the Hudson Valley could follow the Mohawk River over a series of low hills and finally reach the Great Lakes.

The next-best place to cross the mountains was

LIFE AND CUSTOMS IN THE COLONIES

reached by going from Philadelphia to Lancaster and the Susquehanna River and then through Carlisle and Chambersburg to Bedford. Another road to the west followed the Potomac River to Cumberland, Maryland. From there an old Indian trail led to Pittsburgh. South of the Potomac there is a passage through the mountains at Cumberland Gap, at the southwest corner of Virginia.

When the settlers in central Pennsylvania found their way to the west blocked by the Appalachians, a few of them pushed to the north into New York. Most of them, however, went to the south through the Great Valley, which lies between the Alleghenies and the Blue Ridge. They finally reached Cumberland Gap and pushed through the gap into Tennessee and Kentucky.

Daniel Boone in hunting dress. Note the fur-trimmed coat, the coonskin cap, and the long rifle.

(From an engraving after a painting by Alonzo Chappel)

Among the families that made this move were those of

Abraham Lincoln and Daniel Boone. Lincoln's family finally reached Illinois. Daniel Boone was born in Berks County, Pennsylvania. When he was sixteen years old, his family moved to Virginia and thence to North Carolina. Later Boone himself went through

Daniel Boone's fort at Boonesborough, Kentucky
Note that the doors all open to the inside of the fort.

Cumberland Gap to Kentucky, where he founded Boonesborough. He finally reached Missouri, where he passed the later years of his life.

How the Colonists Solved Their Food Problem

Food and its preparation. The food of the first colonists consisted of such supplies as they had brought with them, helped out by the game that they could obtain from the forests or could purchase from the Indians.

LIFE AND CUSTOMS IN THE COLONIES

For a few years at least their food continued to be of a very simple sort and was chiefly the grains and vegetables, such as Indian corn, beans, and squash, which the Indians had learned to grow successfully.

Colonists making hominy
The corn is placed in the hollowed-out stump and is broken into hominy by the pounding of the short log attached to a sapling.

As time went on, plants with which the people had been familiar in the old country were grown and domestic animals were imported and raised. The production of grain and of animals for food soon became so successful that the colonists were able to export their surplus to England and to the West Indies.

The farmers, in their anxiety to prosper, generally lived off the less salable grain, such as rye and corn, and sold their wheat. By doing this a farmer soon could save money enough to buy a farm for his son.

Photo from Ewing Galloway
Old grist mill near New London, Connecticut
Built about **1650** by John Winthrop, this mill continues to grind corn and other grain for the farmers of the neighborhood.

On the frontier pork and cracked corn, or hominy, formed the regular dishes for breakfast and dinner. At supper corn-meal mush and milk was the common meal. The mush was often eaten with molasses or gravy from the roasted meat. The molasses was brought from the West Indies. Sometimes the settlers used sugar which they obtained from the sap of the maple trees. At times on their hunting trips the men would find a hollow tree in which wild bees had accumulated a store of honey which the pioneers could use in place of sugar or molasses.

When the settlers went into the interior of the country, they were able to obtain more game, such as deer and wild turkey. The cereals, however, were often difficult to obtain, especially when frost or insects caused a failure of the grain crops. In such a case the housewife had much trouble to disguise the meats so as to make them an acceptable substitute for bread and vegetables. It may seem strange to us that pioneer children would cry for bread, when it was possible for them to have roast turkey every day.

How the Colonists Dressed

Clothing of the working people. The clothing of the early settlers was made to last as long as possible. Usually, if it were made of cloth, it was the result of the work of the women members of the families. Most of their time that was not taken up with the ordinary household duties was spent in spinning yarn, both from wool and from flax. This was afterward woven into coarse kinds of cloth on huge hand looms.

The most common kind of cloth was linsey-woolsey, in which the warp threads were made of flax, and the

From Earle's "Home Life in Colonial Days"

Spinning flax by hand. A reel to hold the yarn is at the left. The spinner is dressed as in colonial days.

cross threads made of wool. Farmers and workmen generally wore breeches and aprons of leather because of its stoutness and its wearing quality.

Little skill in tailoring was displayed in making garments. It is said that the man of the house would lie down on the floor and his wife would draw a chalk mark around his body. From this a pattern would be cut and the clothes would be made. It is not likely that they would look very handsome or that they would fit very well.

In wintertime working people would put on one linsey shirt after another until they had enough on to keep them warm. Then they would top the whole off with a leather jacket.

Because of the large amount of fur to be had, the making of felt hats early became a common industry. The hunters and trappers usually wore hats or caps made of the skins of animals with the fur still on them.

The dress of the women belonging to the households of the traders and farmers was usually just as simple as that of the men. It was generally made from the same kinds of material except that leather was not so often used.

Shoes were heavy and were poorly made. Many people wore what were known as *pacs*, which looked very much like an Indian moccasin. Later on, however, much finer kinds of shoes were made. The story is told of a young lady who bought a pair of fancy satin shoes to wear to a wedding party. When she had put them on, she was unable to walk down the stairs because the heels were so high.

Dress of the rich colonists. The more wealthy people in all the colonies, both north and south, wore clothes as fine as those worn by people of similar social

Courtesy Title Guarantee and Trust Company, New York

The home of a wealthy colonist

A reception given to Governor Franklin of New Jersey at the Jumel Mansion in New York City

position in England. Fine broadcloths, silks, satins, and laces formed part of the wardrobe not only of the women, but also of the men of the wealthy classes. The clothing of the men of the upper class in colonial times had plenty of color and ornament. Rich mer-

A pioneer repairing his shoes

chants and officials would wear suits of red, blue, or yellow velvet, or plush, trimmed with fine lace around the collar and cuffs. With this they would wear a long figured-satin waistcoat, or vest, with gold or jeweled buttons. Silk or satin stockings to match, and shoes with silver or gold buckles completed the costume.

Later, when some of the commoner people became rich, laws were sometimes passed to prevent them from wearing the same kind of garments as the upper classes were permitted to wear.

None of these rich and expensive materials were produced in the colonies. All had to be imported from England at the cost of much money and trouble.

Dress of the children. Boys and girls, as soon as they became old enough to wear clothing other than that of infants, usually were dressed very much like their elders. A little girl twelve years old wrote in her diary that she went to a party dressed in a yellow coat, with black feathers on her head, and wearing an imitation diamond comb and marquisite and jet pins, together with a silver plume, a locket, rings, black mitts, yards of blue ribbon, and silk shoes. This seems to be very different from what a girl of twelve years would wear to-day.

In the same way boys of all classes dressed like their fathers. If they belonged to the working class, they wore leather aprons and breeches and heavy hobnailed shoes. If the boy's father was a rich merchant or official, his clothes would be made out of the same kinds of velvets, satins, and laces as were those of his father.

How the Colonists Made a Living

Occupations in the South. As you have learned, the lands in the Southern colonies were divided up into large plantations for the growing of tobacco and, in the Carolinas, for the production of rice and indigo. The production of other food supplies on these plantations was just enough for the needs of the owners and their slaves.

Each plantation was a self-sustaining community. Many slaves became skilled at carpentry, weaving, and other kinds of work needful on a great plantation. There was little or no other industry in the South.

In the larger cities commerce was carried on, and the few artisans were those engaged in the building trades.

Industries in New England. In New England the cold climate and the rocky soil kept agriculture from becoming an important industry. It was soon found, however, that the shallow waters off the New England coast were teeming with fish, and the numerous bays and inlets formed by the irregular coast line and the islands afforded safe harbor for the fishing fleets that soon were built. The New England forests contained fine ship timber so that shipbuilding became an important industry of the Northern colonies.

In New England the mountain system is not far back from the sea. Most of the rivers and streams have a rapid current and a considerable fall. This made it very easy for the people to obtain water power. They very quickly took advantage of this opportunity to construct mills in which lumber was cut, and a number of other industries requiring the use of water power were carried on.

The New Englanders used the ships that they built to carry their fish and their lumber products to the West Indies and to England. Soon a great commerce was developed which became important enough for

Shipbuilding in colonial days

England to interfere with it by the Navigation Laws and other restrictions.

Occupations in the Middle colonies. As you have already read, there were no large plantations in the Middle colonies on which the labor was performed by slaves. The work on the farms was usually performed by the owner with the aid of redemptioners or other hired servants. The farms, especially of Pennsylvania, were of very rich soil and produced large quantities of agricultural products.

The forests of Pennsylvania were probably as extensive as those of New England. Shipbuilding, therefore, became an important industry in Pennsylvania.

Courtesy The Moravian Book Shop
First water works in America at Bethlehem

The extensive commerce which soon developed through the city of Philadelphia was chiefly in wheat, flour, and salted meats, as well as live cattle and horses. The Middle colonies produced so much grain and flour for export that they were sometimes called " the bread colonies."

With the growth of the colony and the increase of the wealth of the colonists, all kinds of industries were soon established. The building trades were, of course, among the most prominent, since it is reported that within two years after Penn's landing several hundred houses were built in Philadelphia. The Germantown settlers devoted themselves to spinning and weaving. It is said that some of these people were goldsmiths and silversmiths, although it is not likely that this kind of work was much in demand until the number of rich people in the colony had greatly increased. Flour or grist mills were found in almost every settlement. Almost as numerous were paper mills, tanneries, and sawmills.

When the colonists pushed up the rivers to the mountains, beds of iron ore and limestone were found, and charcoal could be obtained from the extensive forests. Soon iron furnaces were established in many parts of Pennsylvania where these three things could easily be obtained.

Religion in the Life of the People

The Puritans in New England. You have learned that the Puritans came to New England for the purpose of securing the privilege of worshiping as they pleased. You also recall that they were not willing to permit other people who differed in religious belief from themselves to stay in their colony. No person who was not a member of the church congregation in any of the

LIFE AND CUSTOMS IN THE COLONIES 209

Massachusetts settlements could either vote or hold office.

Truly religion must have formed a large part of the lives of these people. It almost seems as if their daily tasks became religious duties. Even days that we now

Pilgrims at church. Note that the church is built of roughly hewn planks like the cabins of the settlers.

consider to be especially days of happiness and rejoicing were observed with great solemnity in New England. The town crier would be sent around, ringing his bell and announcing that there would be " no Christmas this year."

Religion in the Southern colonies. All the Southern colonies except Maryland had been settled by people who had belonged for the most part to the Church of England. These people were much more liberal in their religious views. While they were just as sincere as the Puritans, they were much less solemn in the way they observed Sundays and the festivals of their church.

Old Bruton Church, Virginia, in the time of Washington
(From a painting by A. Wordsworth Thompson in the Metropolitan Museum of Art)

In these colonies, also, a person had to be a member of the church to take part in the government. Every landholder had to pay a tax for the support of the church whether or not he was a member of the Church of England.

Religious freedom in other colonies. The colonies of Rhode Island, Maryland, Georgia, and Pennsylvania had all been established as refuges for people who were oppressed and persecuted either for political or religious reasons.

The settlers who came to these colonies were, therefore, of many religious beliefs. In order that these

Old Friends Meeting House in Philadelphia

people with differing religions might get along peaceably together, it was necessary that each should respect the differing beliefs of his neighbors. In these colonies, therefore, we find congregations of many different religious beliefs dwelling alongside of each other in harmony.

How Offenders Were Punished

Curious laws. In colonial times the laws provided very heavy and severe punishments for all serious offenses. In England, at the time Penn founded his colony, more than two hundred crimes were punishable by the death of the offender. In most of the colonies these severe English laws were copied.

One of the important provisions of the Great Law which Penn's plan of government contained was that only two crimes, treason and murder, should be punished by the death of the criminal.

Some of the minor offenses were punished by the colonial laws in very queer ways. For example, in Connecticut, if a man committed burglary, he was to be branded on the forehead with the letter B; but if the burglary was committed on Sunday, he was to have his ears cut off in addition to being branded. A man who stole corn from the Indians was punished by having to return to them twice as much as he had stolen. Henceforth, too, he was to be called by his first name instead of being addressed as *Mister* as he formerly had been.

In Virginia, if a person was convicted the second time for stealing a pig, he had to stand for two hours in the pillory and have both of his ears nailed to it. At the end of the two hours his ears were to be cut off and left nailed to the pillory.

In Massachusetts a man was sentenced to stand by

the court house with his tongue in a split stick as a punishment for swearing.

The pillory and the stocks. The pillory was a curious instrument which consisted of an upright post on top of which were placed two heavy planks, with holes made in them in such a way that the planks could be taken apart and a man's neck and wrists placed in the holes. These planks could then be locked together so that the man was securely fastened since he could not pull out either his hands or his head. The stocks were very similar except the holes were made to hold the man's ankles and wrists while his head was left free.

These instruments of punishment were

From an old print

An offender in the pillory

usually set up in the town square so that the offender would be held up to the ridicule of the townspeople. Often the younger and less respectable members of the crowd would pelt the offenders with decayed vegetables and other missiles which he found difficult to dodge.

Sometimes offenders were sentenced to appear before the congregation in the church. Here they had publicly to confess their faults and be reprimanded by the minister.

Schools and Colleges

Education in New England. Because of the large part the church played in the life of the people of New England, they felt it very important that their ministers and leaders should be well educated. For this reason schools were early established in every New England community.

Reading and simple arithmetic were taught in the home or in dame schools which the teacher kept in one of the rooms of her house. This usually was all the education received by the girls.

The boys, when they grew older, were taught by the minister of the church in the small community, but in the larger and more prosperous towns, regular schools were established and teachers were employed to conduct them.

Where a separate schoolhouse was built, it was generally of logs like the houses of the settlers. The seats were arranged around the sides, and a fireplace was near the door. Wood for the fire had to be provided by the parents of the pupils. The schoolmaster sat at a high bench at one end of the room. Back of him hung a large bundle of birch rods, which were used for the correction of the mischievous pupils. The master had also to cut pens from large goose quills and set the copies for the writing lessons. Later on, the more promising

A colonial schoolmaster making quill pens

pupils had their education continued in Latin, Greek, and even in Hebrew by the village minister.

Harvard and Yale colleges founded. In 1636 Harvard College was established in Cambridge, Massachusetts, for the training of ministers for the church; and not long afterward Yale College, in Connecticut, was founded for this same purpose.

Colonial schoolbooks. When children first began to read, they were provided with what was known as a *hornbook.* This consisted of a sort of wooden frame shaped like an oblong hand mirror on which was placed a paper covered by a thin sheet of clear horn. On this

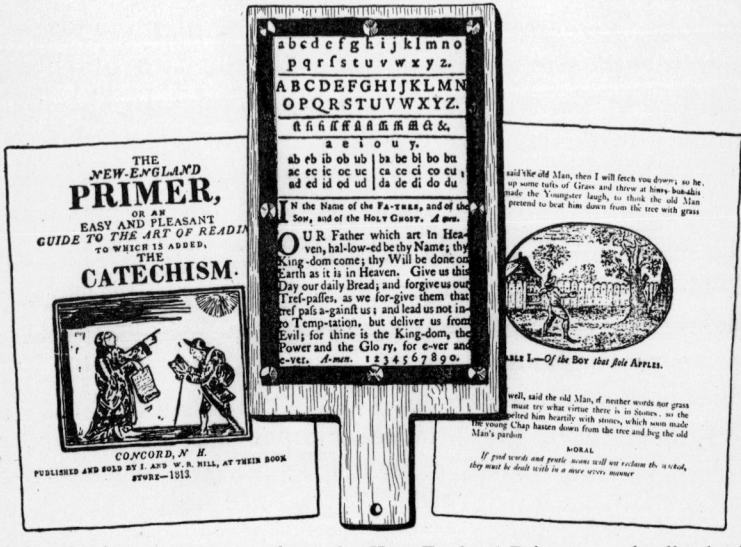

A hornbook and two pages from the New England Primer, a schoolbook of colonial times.

paper were printed the alphabet, the Lord's Prayer, and a number of syllables which were supposed to help the children to spell.

Another very popular book was what was known as the *New England Primer.* This was a small book about three by four inches in size. It had in it the alphabet with a picture for each letter, illustrating some person or incident. This was followed by part of the *Catechism* and a few stories.

Education in the Southern colonies. Since the people of the Southern colonies usually lived on widely separated plantations, instead of in towns as in New England, there was not the same opportunity to have schools. Generally a few of the wealthy planters would join together in hiring a tutor for the two or three families of the immediate neighborhood. In the few larger towns there were schools somewhat similar to those of New England. These were built in much the same fashion and used about the same sort of books as the schools of the Northern colonies.

There were few colleges and academies in the South. Before the Revolution most of the young men went either to England or to the New England colleges for their higher education.

Education in the Middle colonies. In the Middle colonies, lying between New England and the South, the schools resembled in part those of each of the other sections. In the towns and larger cities there were schools like the schools of New England. These were supported by the people who sent their children to the schools instead of everyone's paying a tax for the support of the school. Later on, however, the New England plan of paying for the support of the schools by taxes was followed.

In the more sparsely settled country districts there were few or no schools. Any education that the children received was given by the village pastor in schools connected with the churches.

The Scotch-Irish settlers were, however, very deeply interested in education. As soon as a town got to be any size at all, two or three people would get together

The buildings of the Academy and College of Philadelphia, which later became the University of Pennsylvania

and start what was called an academy. In the academies a few branches like Latin and Greek would be taught along with the study of the Bible. These schools were about the same as our high schools of to-day but with fewer studies.

The chief colleges in the Middle colonies were King's College, now Columbia University in New York, Princeton College in New Jersey, and the College of

Philadelphia, which became the University of Pennsylvania in 1791.

Colonial literature. The literature produced in the colonies was mostly religious. A few pamphlets on political matters, chiefly about the relations between

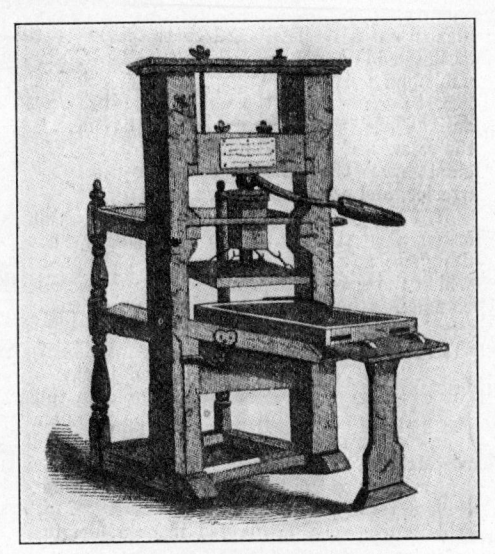

Benjamin Franklin's printing press
(A drawing made from the original in the Smithsonian Institution)

England and the colonies, were also printed. Almost all of the books that were read in the colonies were either imported from England or were the works of English authors that had been reprinted in the colonies. Even the few books for boys and girls that were to be had were almost all brought from England.

Colonial Life Compared with Life of To-day

Town life. You have already learned how few conveniences the townspeople of early times had. There were no automobiles or street cars to take the people about the towns, nor were there well-paved streets or rails for them to run on. There were no street lights and no police. People who went about by night would carry lanterns with them, as is sometimes done in the country to-day. Instead of police, a watchman or constable would go his rounds at night, crying out the hours and announcing any important news.

If a house got afire, an alarm would be sounded on the church bell. The neighbors would then run to the fire, each with a bucket. The buckets would be filled from wells or cisterns, and then passed from hand to hand until they reached the man nearest the fire, who emptied the bucket on it. Usually the best that could be done was to save neighboring houses from being burned.

Since there was no regular arrangement for removing waste, this was often thrown in the streets. This custom was probably the cause of the frequent outbreaks of serious diseases.

The business of the town was generally done in small shops, each selling a single kind of goods. These goods were generally made in the house or shop itself by the owner and his apprentices. There were no huge department stores or great factories such as exist to-day.

LIFE AND CUSTOMS IN THE COLONIES

Country life. Country homes in colonial days were even less comfortable than city houses. They had poorer methods of preparing food and of heating the house. Most of the farms could only be reached by

From an old fire certificate

Firemen at work in 1800. One set of men passed buckets of water from hand to hand and emptied the water into the engine. Others worked at the long handles to pump the water on the fire.

mud roads, which were even worse than the unpaved streets of the towns.

To-day almost every farmer has an automobile, can have his house lighted by electricity, has a good road almost if not quite reaching his door, and has a varied food supply, such as even townspeople did not have in olden times. He is protected from the attacks of wicked people by the state police, who constantly patrol the important roads.

On the farms themselves no effort was made to carry on scientific farming. The farmers knew nothing about suiting the crops to the kind of soil they had except what they learned by growing different crops and seeing which did the best. The farming tools and farming implements were nearly all of wood and did not last very long. There were no harvesters, reapers, mowing machines, or tractors to make the farmer's work easier. Market gardening, which to-day gives us such a fine supply of different sorts of vegetables for our table, was almost unknown.

Manufacturing. As you have already learned, very few industries were carried on in factories. The people in the homes spun the yarn and wove the coarse kinds of cloths that it was possible to produce in the colonies. Iron, lumber, leather, and paper could not be produced in the home. These were made in small mills or factories which were near where raw materials, such as timber, tanbark, or iron ore could be had. Hats were also made in fairly large factories from the furs which were obtained by trading with the Indians. It was usual to build all such factories near where water power could be obtained.

Transportation and communication. Transportation in colonial times started with pack horses. These were followed, as roads began to be built, by large wagons which needed six or eight horses to haul them along

LIFE AND CUSTOMS IN THE COLONIES 223

the poor roads. You have learned that it took several days to go from New York to Philadelphia and almost a week to go to Boston. The wagon road was first replaced by the railroad and steam locomotive. To-day one can go from Philadelphia to New York in

Old London Coffee House, Philadelphia

This inn was at Front and Market Streets during the Revolution. Note the coach and four, the watchman's box, and the group of Indians being shown the wonders of the city.

less than two hours in a train hauled by great electric locomotives. If one is willing to fly in an airplane, it need only take about one half of this time.

For thousands of years the common way of sending messages from one person to another, who were too far apart to talk together, was by writing a message or letter which would be carried by a messenger. This was the only method the colonists had of communicating with each other. About the time of the Revolution systems of signaling were invented, somewhat like the way Boy Scouts send messages to each other by using flags. When the Erie Canal was first opened, cannon were placed within sound of each other along the canal and the Hudson River from Buffalo to New York. When the boat started from Buffalo, the first cannon was shot off; then one after another was fired until at the end of about an hour the sound of the last one in line was heard in New York City. Then the people of New York knew that the boat had started.

Nowadays we have telegraphs, telephones, cables, and wireless. We can send not only human speech, but pictures by electric waves through the ether without the help of wires.

STUDY HELPS

Map Work

On a map of Europe mark all the countries from which you know settlers came to one or another of the American colonies.

Activities

Get pictures illustrating colonial life and times, such as houses, furniture, interiors, dresses, etc.

Make models of some things used in earlier days.

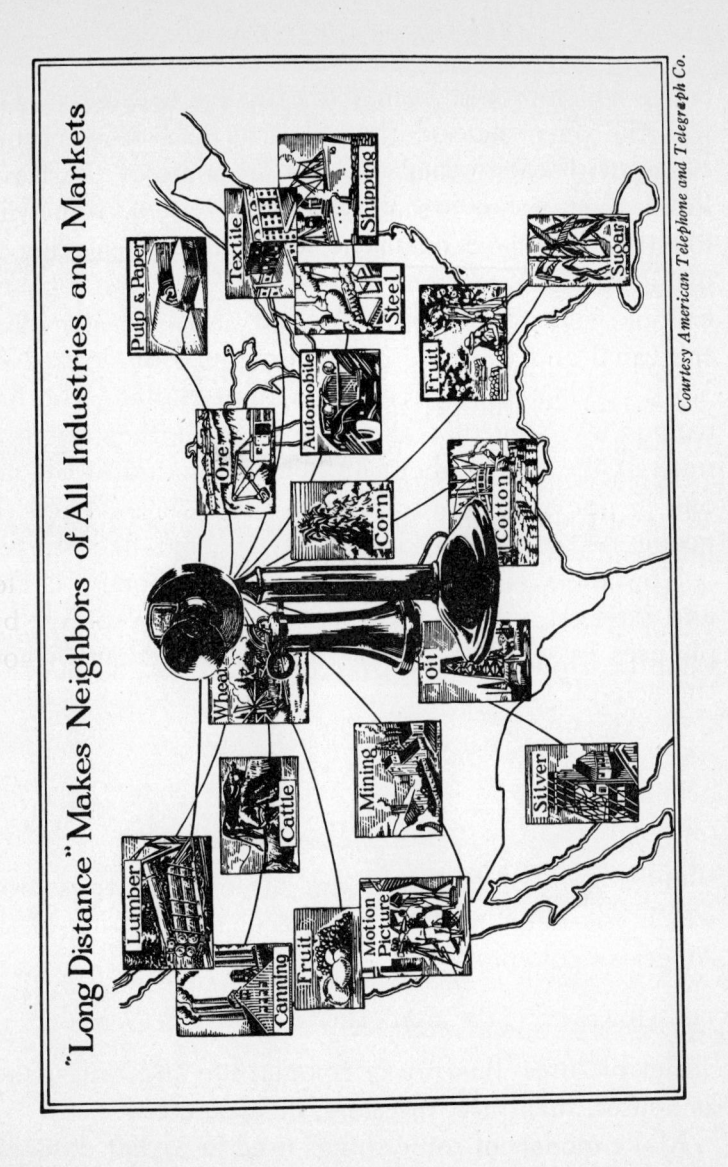

"Long Distance" Makes Neighbors of All Industries and Markets

Courtesy American Telephone and Telegraph Co.

Make a model of a stagecoach or of a Conestoga wagon.

Dramatize a New England town meeting.

Dramatize a meeting of the colonial assembly discussing English laws against colonial manufactures.

Special Work

In what colonies were the governor and representatives elected by the people?

What amusements or recreations do we have to-day that the colonists did not have?

What products did the colonies send to the West Indies and what did they receive in return?

Could all men vote in the colonies?

What are some of the reasons that pioneers followed Indian trails in traveling from one place to another?

Storybooks to Read

Bacheller, Irving A.: *In the Days of Poor Richard*
Coffin, Charles C.: *Old Times in the Colonies*
Gulliver, Lucile: *Daniel Boone*
Henderson, Daniel MacIntyre: *Boone of the Wilderness*
Power, E. and R.: *More Boys and Girls of History*
Pyle, Howard: *Jack Ballister's Fortunes* (Virginia)

UNIT III. THE STRUGGLE FOR THE CONTROL OF NORTH AMERICA

A colonial blockhouse

Note the loopholes and the projecting upper story. Of what use was this? How can you tell that it is built on high ground?

The Acadians driven from their homes by the English
(From a drawing by E. Bayard in Bryant's *Popular History of the United States*)

Courtesy Chas. Scribner's Sons

FORECAST OF UNIT III

In this part of the story of our country you will learn that the countries of Europe had long been struggling to see which would become the most powerful. As the people of these countries became interested in America and learned about the wealth of products from the New World, a new rivalry commenced. The nations of Europe believed that the country which possessed the riches of America would become the most powerful. As quarrels arose in Europe, they were taken up by the little groups of settlers in America.

Since we are especially interested in the English colonies, the wars in which they were involved are of the most importance to us. In the earlier wars the English colonists had little help from the mother country. In spite of this they were able to hold their own against the rival colonies of France. At last both England and France realized that one or the other would have to abandon its North American colonies. The struggle for the possession of the rich Mississippi Valley really began with the journey of Washington to demand that the French abandon the forts which they had built in lands claimed by the English.

The French and Indian War which followed resulted in the loss by France of almost all its possessions in the New World. One of the important reasons for the success of the English colonists in this war was that they were fighting for their homes and firesides while their opponents were largely interested in extending the French Empire by acquiring a vast territory in America. This war definitely determined that this country would be inhabited and governed by an English-speaking nation with Anglo-Saxon institutions and ideals of self-government.

UNIT III. THE STRUGGLE FOR THE CONTROL OF NORTH AMERICA

Quebec in 1690
From an old print
The citadel, or fort, is on the high ground at the left side of the picture.

1. THE INTERCOLONIAL WARS

European conditions. While the different nations of Europe were trying to get ahead of each other in exploring and settling America and in making rival claims to land in the New World, they were also struggling with each other in the continent of Europe.

During the time that the English colonies were being settled, it was generally agreed that France had become the strongest European nation. The other countries were not very well pleased with this and were constantly trying to lessen the power of France or, at least, to keep it from growing any greater.

When anything happened that the other countries thought would give France more power, they would join together in an alliance against that country. These disputes in Europe continued for several hundred years. Indeed our own Revolution was a part of one of these disputes.

King William's War (1690–1697). You will recall the quarrel in England between the king and Parliament (p. 117). This dispute became so bitter that a war took place in England between the followers of each. King Charles I was put off his throne and finally was put to death by command of Parliament.

Later on Charles II, his son, was called to the throne. He was followed by his brother James, who became as unpopular as his father had been. At last King James fled from the country and went to France. After this Parliament asked King James's daughter, Mary, and her husband William to come from Holland, where they had been rulers, and be king and queen of England.

The king of France, who had a powerful army and good generals, decided to make war on Holland. He thought that, if he could defeat Holland, he would be able to add it to France and also could put back his friend, King James, on the throne of England.

The war spreads to America. The first troubles in America as a result of this war between England and France were Indian raids on the New England settlements. These were followed by raids on the French by Indian friends of the English. The French commander of Canada then resolved to strike a heavy blow at the English. A large party of French Canadians and Indians, led by French officers, captured Schenectady and massacred nearly all the inhabitants. This was followed by the same kind of attacks all along the frontier.

The New Englanders conquer Acadia. French war vessels had given the New England shipowners a great deal of trouble by seizing their ships and carrying them off to French ports in Canada. The colonists decided to prepare an expedition against the French settlement of Port Royal, now Annapolis, in Nova Scotia. Seven ships and about 450 men under Sir William Phips entered Port Royal harbor, and the French commander yielded the fort almost without a struggle. A later attempt was made by the New Englanders to capture Quebec, but this plan did not succeed.

For six or seven years the war between the French and English colonies continued as a series of raids from time to time by one side or the other with the help of their Indian allies.

The result of King William's War in America. When the time came to make the treaty of peace, neither the French nor the English could claim to have been very successful in capturing lands or places belonging to the other. It was agreed that the possessions which they held at the beginning of the war would continue to be held by each. The question of the exact boundaries between the French and English claims was not settled.

Queen Anne's War (1701–1713). A few years after the close of King William's War another dispute arose in Europe. The king of Spain had died and had left no one to take his place on the throne. The king of France wished to have one of his relatives chosen king of Spain. This would have made France very much more powerful than it had been.

To prevent this, the other nations of Europe joined together to keep the relative of the king of France from becoming the king of Spain. Besides all this, France tried to put the son of King James on the English throne in place of Anne, a daughter younger than Mary. This was the principal reason that England joined in the war against France.

The French and English colonies take up the quarrel. This war like King William's War soon spread to America. Just as before, the trouble started with a series of raids, chiefly on the New England frontier, by parties of French and Indians. These caused much destruction and loss of life. There was also a great deal of colonial commerce destroyed. This time not only did the New England colonies suffer, but also the Middle colonies suffered. Penn's agent wrote that within four days three vessels from the Delaware had been sunk or burned by French war vessels.

New England again attacks Acadia. As the war went on and the attacks of the French continued, New England again resolved to organize an expedition

234 STRUGGLE FOR CONTROL OF NORTH AMERICA

against Acadia, which included what is now New Brunswick as well as Nova Scotia. Two regiments of New England troops and a ship of the royal navy made an attack on Port Royal, Nova Scotia, but did not succeed in capturing it. A few years later the attack on Port

The expedition against Acadia in 1707
Note the fort on the hill and the small size of the attacking fleet. (From a print in Des Barres' *Atlantic Neptune*, 1777)

Royal was renewed by a larger force, and after a siege of a week the French commander was obliged to surrender. An attempt was also made to capture Quebec. On the way several of the ships were wrecked in the St. Lawrence, several hundred soldiers were lost, and the expedition decided to return to Boston.

The New England forces under Sir William Pepperell landing to begin the siege of Louisburg in 1745
(From an engraving after a painting by Stevens)

and 1300 or 1400 farmers, fishermen, and others who could not be depended upon. Meantime other English warships had arrived, but no reënforcements had come to the French. One after the other of the French outposts was taken. Finally at the end of six weeks the fort was surrendered.

The colonists form plans to attack Canada. The colonists also planned for the third time to make an attack on Canada and to capture Montreal and Quebec with the assistance of English troops. The English government did not send the promised help, and the colonists heard that the French were going to try to recapture Acadia and Louisburg.

The colonial troops were hastily moved over to the coast for the defense of the English possessions in Acadia. The garrisons were reënforced before the French could raise sufficiently large armies to capture the strongholds. The English were able to hold them until the end of the war.

The treaty of peace. When the nations had become tired of fighting each other and had concluded to make peace, they agreed that all captures of lands and forts should be returned to the nations that held them at the beginning of the war.

The New England colonists were greatly angered at this decision. The fortress of Louisburg, which they had captured and held to the end of the war at great expense and danger, was returned to France. The colonists rightly believed that it would again serve as a rallying place for French attacks on their commerce and their settlements just as it had done before its capture by the colonists.

STUDY HELPS

Map Work

On a map of northeastern United States show all the places mentioned in the Intercolonial Wars.

Activities

Put into your book of pictures any you can get of people or places connected with the Intercolonial Wars, such as Port Royal (Annapolis, Nova Scotia), Louisburg, Cape Breton Island, Queen Anne, etc.

Dramatize the meeting of representatives of New York and New England planning for a united force against the French and Indians in King William's War.

Special Work

What were the names of the wars in Europe that correspond to King William's War, Queen Anne's War, and King George's War?

Is there anything that shows that these wars gave the colonists a feeling of unity among themselves?

Storybooks to Read

Gordon, W. J.: *Englishman's House* (Louisburg)
Oxley, J. Macdonald: *Fife and Drum at Louisburg*
Roberts, Charles G. D.: *A Sister to Evangeline* (Acadia)

2. THE FRENCH AND INDIAN WAR

Conditions in Europe. You have learned that King George's War was caused by the desire of the rulers of some of the European countries to take away from Empress Maria Theresa the Austrian possessions which her father had left her. When that war ended, all the captured lands were to be returned to the nation that had held them when the war broke out.

There was one case, however, where this did not happen. Frederick the Great, king of Prussia, was permitted to retain the province of Silesia which he had seized from Austria. This seemed to make Prussia so important that France decided to change sides and to join with Austria in trying to defeat Prussia. This left Prussia alone to fight almost all the rest of Europe. England now felt that, if Prussia were defeated, France would become much too powerful; so the English helped Prussia with money and supplies.

Colonial rivalry between England and France. Besides the companies that England had organized to trade and settle in America, other English companies were organized to trade in other parts of the world.

One of the most important of these companies was the East India Company, which had been given the right to trade between England and the countries of the East. This company had established a number of trading stations in India and at places on the way. France had established similar trading stations. It was

THE FRENCH AND INDIAN WAR 241

not long before the people in charge of these rival trading posts, in their desire to obtain all the trade of these rich lands, had serious encounters with each other. Usually these occurred when two native rulers engaged in war with each other. The British would side with one ruler and the French with the other.

In America the rivalry was somewhat similar. Two important sources of revenue for both the French and the English were the fur trade and the fisheries. Each nation encroached upon the other's fishing grounds. The English sailed far up into the Gulf of St. Lawrence, and the French went as far south as the Delaware capes on their fishing trips.

The two nations were also bitter rivals in their efforts to make friends with the Indians and to secure the bulk of the fur trade. In this effort the French were usually more successful. There were a great many more fur-bearing animals in the region that had been occupied by the French, and the French relations with the Indians were, in general, more friendly.

The French build forts to hold their claim. In order to make their possession of the country west and north of the English colonies still more secure, the French had built a line of forts from Canada along the Great Lakes and the Ohio and Mississippi Rivers.

Meanwhile the English had established no important posts in this region with the exception of a few which were built to protect the settlements from Indian raids. Besides, the English colonies were thirteen separate governments not accustomed to acting together. Sometimes there was just as much rivalry between two neighboring English colonies as if they had belonged to different nations.

On the other hand, the governor of New France, as Canada was called, was an almost absolute ruler who

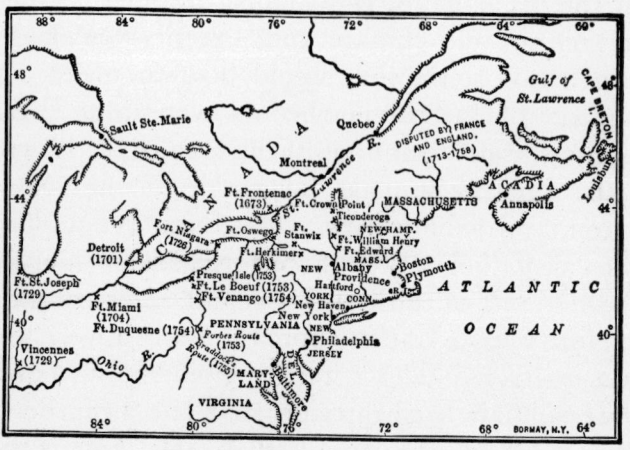

Scene of the last French war

was supplied with powerful military help and much money by his king. This enabled him to establish many forts and blockhouses to protect the claims of France in America.

New France compared with the English colonies. The harsh climate and the poor soil of New France made it almost impossible for the French colonists to do more than make a bare living from their little farms. Besides there was no special reason why they

THE FRENCH AND INDIAN WAR

should make any such efforts since the French government took good care of the settlers and sent most of their needed supplies over from France. In return France only asked that the settlers send back plenty of the natural products of the country, such as furs and fish.

On the other hand, the English colonies, being in a more comfortable climate and, except New England, having a far richer soil, found how to make a good living from the land. They could even produce surplus enough to make many of them wealthy. They had come to America to make homes for themselves where they could worship as they pleased and live under such laws as they themselves chose to make.

As the result of these two different ideas of colonization, New France had a population of not over 80,000 people, scattered over a territory extending from the Gulf of St. Lawrence through the valleys of the Great Lakes and the Mississippi River to New Orleans. England had thirteen colonies close together along the Atlantic coast, containing one and a quarter million people.

In all the English colonies considerable manufacturing was done. This was large enough in amount to cause the English Parliament to pass laws against the colonial manufactures. There were no manufactures in New France.

The French and English claims conflict. As you have just learned, the French claim included the valleys of the St. Lawrence, the Great Lakes, and the Mississippi River and its branches. The grants to the English colonies in nearly every case covered lands which lay to the west of the Appalachians and so overlapped the French claims. This did not cause much trouble so long as the English settlers stayed on the eastern side of the mountains.

The increase in population of the English colonies and the reduced amount of good land to be had east of the mountains led not only hunters and trappers but farmers and cattle raisers to move to the west. Here they took up lands which the French had always considered to be theirs, but which the English colonies believed were granted to them by the king.

Most of the people from the English colonies who occupied this frontier region were the Scotch-Irish, who have already been spoken of in connection with the settlement of Pennsylvania (p. 148). These people were almost always to be found in the outlying settlements. They were good fighters, independent, and self-reliant. They were not at all ready to retreat, when they found themselves ordered off their lands by French officials.

Relations of the French and the English with the Indians. You may recall that Champlain, the French explorer, had joined a war party of Algonquin Indians, who at that time were fighting the Iroquois (p. 52). As a result of the aid that the guns of the French soldiers brought to the Algonquins, the Iroquois were defeated.

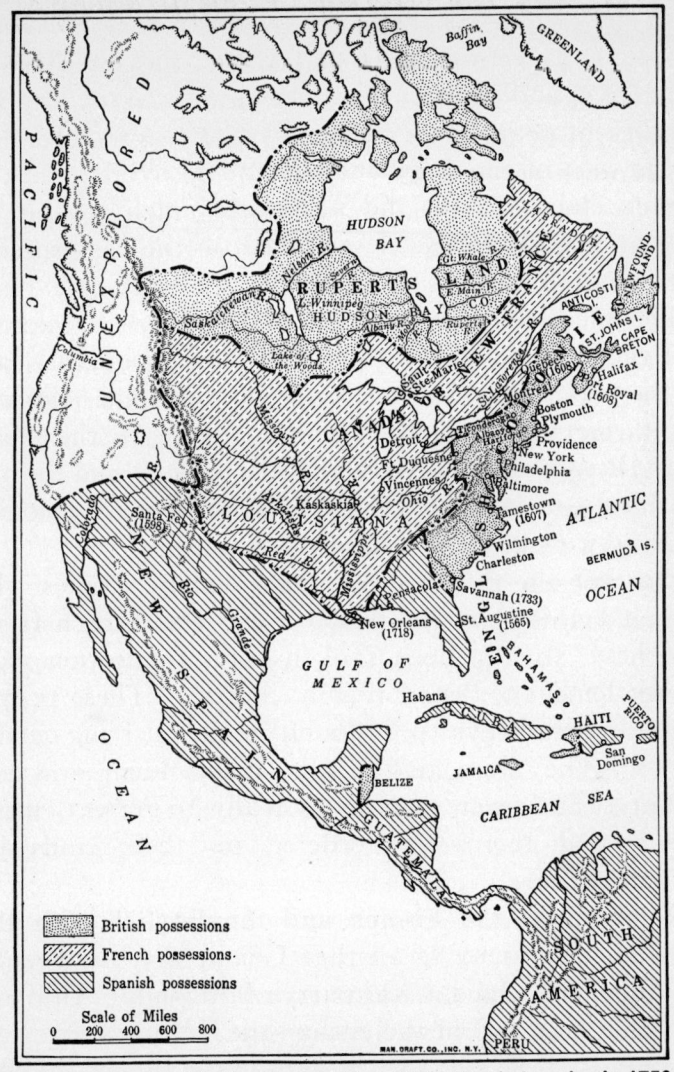

Claims of the British, French, and Spanish in North America in 1750

From that time on these Indians sided with the English. It is fortunate for the colonists that this was so since they occupied territory which was between the French and English settlements.

As the French fur traders traveled farther and farther westward in search of furs, they did not make the same mistake that had been made by Champlain. They made friends with the Indians, lived in their wigwams, ate the same kind of food, played their games, and often married into the tribes. This made the Indians of the Northwest very friendly to the French. When the final struggle came between the two nations, the French were always able to gather around them a greater number of Indian allies than the English.

The French forts in the Ohio Valley. When the French heard that the English settlers were making their way over the mountains from the English colonies on the coast, they tried to drive out the ones that had already come and to prevent the making of additional settlements. They built a fort, called Fort le Boeuf, not very far from what is now Erie, Pennsylvania. The English had built a fort a short distance away, called Fort Venango. This was soon captured by the French and the English were driven away. The French then decided to build another fort at the junction of the Allegheny and the Monongahela Rivers. This was land that was within the grant that had been given to Virginia. It also happened that some Virginians had formed a land company to buy some hundreds of thousands of acres in this neighborhood. This land they hoped to sell to the people of Virginia and others who wished to move to the West. When Governor Dinwiddie of Virginia heard about these French forts, he picked a young man named George Washington to go as a messenger to the French commander of this region. Washington was to carry a note from Governor Dinwiddie, protesting against the French occupation of land that rightfully belonged to Virginia.

Washington journeys to the French forts.

French forts in the West and Braddock's line of march

Washington had as his companion Christopher Gist, who lived in western Pennsylvania and was familiar with this region. Together they followed an old Indian trail from Cumberland in Maryland to the forks of the Ohio. Then they followed the Allegheny River until they reached the French forts in northwestern Pennsylvania. Here Washington was received with kindness by the French commander, who, however, told him that the French had no idea whatever of giving up this territory to the Eng-

From an old print
Washington and Gist crossing the Allegheny River on a raft

lish. He said that it had been discovered and explored by French people and that years before it had been claimed by them. Not only that, but the French had built forts and had settlements all over this territory and proposed to keep them.

Washington returns to Virginia. Having received the answer of the French commander, Washington and Gist started back after having gotten what information they could concerning the strength of the French forces. On the way home their horses had to be abandoned and they were forced to proceed on foot. Once an Indian tried to shoot Washington. Fortunately the gun missed fire; the Indian was seized and deprived of his weapons and was sent back to his tribe.

When Washington and Gist reached the Allegheny River, it was full of floating ice. They decided to make a raft to reach the opposite shore. On the way across, while poling the raft, Washington was knocked into the water by a large piece of ice striking the pole. He was saved by his friend Gist. They succeeded in landing on an island in the river, where they spent the night. The next morning they found the river frozen over and they could walk easily to the shore.

After many other difficulties, Washington reached Virginia and made his report to Governor Dinwiddie.

Fort Duquesne. Meanwhile the French had decided to make good their promise and had built a fort on the point of land where the Allegheny and Monongahela form the Ohio. When this became known, Washington was again sent to this region. This time he was sent with the object of driving the French away from the forks of the Ohio.

Washington's little band, after passing along the old trail, reached a place not far from Pittsburgh, called Great Meadows, where he built a stockade and named it Fort Necessity. Several skirmishes occurred with the French and Indians, which resulted in a number on each side being killed. It was not long before the French and Indians came in large numbers and besieged Fort Necessity. Washington was forced to surrender but was permitted to take his company back to Virginia.

Fort Pitt in 1758

Braddock's expedition against Fort Duquesne. Up to this time the struggle for America had been in the hands of the two groups of the French and English colonists. Now, however, England decided to send soldiers to aid the colonies in their struggle for the Mississippi Valley. General Braddock, a capable officer, and some regiments of British soldiers were sent from England to help the Virginians and other colonists

THE FRENCH AND INDIAN WAR

to drive the French from Fort Duquesne. George Washington, who was a colonel in the Virginia militia at this time, joined this army as an aide to General Braddock.

Braddock refuses the advice of colonial officers. With much difficulty a road was cut through the dense forest to permit the wagon trains to follow the army. When the army had reached within a short distance of Fort Duquesne, Braddock was warned by Washington and other colonial officers to send out scouts ahead of and on each side of the main body in order to guard against surprise. It was pointed out to him that the French and Indian method of fighting in the woods was not the same as might be followed in a battle in the open. Braddock, deaf to all the warnings, refused to take the advice of the colonial leaders, and the solid columns of the British regiments marched bravely on through the wilderness.

Braddock's army defeated. Suddenly Indian war cries were heard, and French and Indian enemies appeared on every side of them. The British soldiers, not knowing what else to do, bravely stood their ground and fired repeatedly at their unseen foes. It was not long before many of them had been killed with almost no loss to the enemy.

Washington's Virginia militia, more used to the ways of Indian fighting, slipped behind trees in Indian fashion and held back the enemy until the scattered remains of Braddock's army were able to retreat. Washington had several horses shot under him, and several bullets passed through his clothes, but he was not injured.

Braddock himself was fatally wounded in the battle. It is said that he was shot by one of the colonial riflemen whose brother had been struck with a sword by Braddock when he sought refuge behind a tree.

Death of General Braddock
(From an engraving after a painting by C. Schuessele)

Fort Duquesne finally captured by the English. Some years later, toward the end of the war, a second expedition against Fort Duquesne was organized under Colonel Forbes, a British officer. By this time the British regulars had learned how to fight in the Indian fashion, and the expedition was larger and better prepared.

At this time the French garrison at Fort Duquesne was not large enough to cope with so great a force. Before the arrival of the British the French abandoned the fort, which the British occupied. They named it Fort Pitt in honor of the English prime minister.

Early French successes in the war. After the defeat of Braddock the Indians joined themselves to the successful French, and all along the frontier, from New England south, settlement after settlement was raided, and the people were massacred by bands of the French and the Indians.

Attempts were made by the English to invade Canada by the way of Lake Champlain, and forts were built, but these were soon forced to surrender to the French.

Expedition against Acadia. Early in the war the British sent an expedition against Acadia. About eight thousand of the poor people who had made their homes in this part of Canada were seized, placed on ships, and distributed among the English colonies. This was a very cruel deed. The excuse was that Acadia had been a center for raids by land and sea on the New England settlements.

The removal of the French settlers gave an opportunity to send English colonists in their place. The story of this event is told in Longfellow's celebrated poem, " Evangeline."

The tide turns in favor of the English. William Pitt, prime minister of England, resolved to conduct the war more vigorously. General Jeffrey Amherst was sent to the colonies with the special object of recapturing Louisburg. Twenty thousand provincial troops were made ready, and an equal number of regular British troops were added to the English forces in America. In addition to these troops strong support was given by the vessels of the British navy.

Louisburg is recaptured by the English. You have already read about the capture of Fort Duquesne by the expedition under Colonel Forbes. About the same time General Amherst with 14,000 regular troops and the help of the British fleet laid siege to Louisburg. By degrees the French fortifications and outer defenses were shattered. The French warships in the harbor were destroyed, and Louisburg at last surrendered. With it all the French possessions in and around the Gulf of St. Lawrence came into the hands of the English.

Thus we see that the English had been successful at the two ends of the French line of forts. Up to this

Lord Jeffrey Amherst who led the British forces at the capture of Louisburg in 1758
(From a portrait by Sir Joshua Reynolds in the National Portrait Gallery, London)

time, however, their attacks on the French strongholds from Quebec to Fort Frontenac, near Buffalo, had been without success. Neither side had been able to advance into the other's territory.

The English plan to capture Quebec. It was finally decided to make an attack on the strong fortress of Quebec. Colonial and regular troops were to be taken up the St. Lawrence on English war vessels and transports. The expedition was to be under the leadership of General James Wolfe, who had aided General Amherst in the capture of Louisburg. With 10,000 soldiers and a fleet of vessels carrying twice as many sailors and marines, the English proceeded to Quebec.

The fort at Quebec is on top of a high, narrow rock rising over three hundred feet straight up from the river. The top of the cliff could only be reached by steep paths. On a plateau not far from the fort, called the Plains of Abraham, French soldiers continually patrolled the tops of the cliffs so that the English forces could not make a landing.

The British besiege Quebec. For several months the British forces besieged the town, and a few of the outlying defenses on lower ground were captured. Several attempts to take some of the other defenses by assault were successfully repulsed by the French. Finally Wolfe decided to try to reach the plateau at the top of the cliffs, with the object of forcing the French general, Montcalm, either to fight or to surrender.

Landing by night at a point about two miles above Quebec, the English followed a small winding path that Wolfe had discovered and reached the top of the cliff with little opposition from the French guards. The next morning 4500 British troops were drawn up in front of the fort.

From an old print

Fortifications of Quebec from the St. Lawrence River.

The battle for a continent. Montcalm, who was ten miles away when he learned of the daring feat of the British commander, hastily massed the French troops for the fight. After a short but furious battle the French were defeated. The garrison of the fort, left without support, surrendered. The British and the French generals were both killed in the battle.

Death of General Wolfe

(From an engraving after a painting by Alonzo Chappel)

The story is told that, when Montcalm was informed that he could not survive his wounds, he said that he was glad that he would not live to see the surrender of Quebec. General Wolfe, as he lay wounded and supported in the arms of some of his men, heard some one cry, "They fly, they fly." "Who fly?" asked Wolfe. "The French," was the reply. "Now," said Wolfe, "I can die happy." A single monument bearing both their names commemorates on the battlefield the death of these two brave soldiers.

From a contemporary print
General Montcalm

Importance of the surrender of Quebec. The battle at Quebec is generally considered to be one of the decisive battles of the world. As the result of the defeat of the French, their whole colonial empire in North America came into the hands of England and Spain.

THE FRENCH AND INDIAN WAR

England received the valley of the Great Lakes and the St. Lawrence and the French territory on the east side of the Mississippi River. The lands west of the Mississippi were granted by France to Spain. The English colonies along the Atlantic coast no longer lived in fear that some day they might be overpowered by large and populous French provinces in the Mississippi Valley.

STUDY HELPS

Map Work

On a map of northeastern United States indicate the French and English possessions in different colors; indicate all the important places of the French and Indian War. Trace on the map the road from Virginia to Fort Duquesne and from there to Fort le Boeuf.

Activities

Make a model of Fort Duquesne or of Fort le Boeuf.
Make a model of Quebec and its fortifications.
Dramatize the scene between George Washington and the French commander at Fort le Boeuf.
Get pictures of events and places connected with the French and Indian War, such as young George Washington, Fort Duquesne, Quebec, the line of Braddock's road, or of memorials of this war.

Special Work

Find out about George Washington's early life.
Make a list of old defenses against the French and Indians that were near where you now live.

Why was Christopher Gist selected to help Washington on his journey to Fort le Boeuf? Where had he lived?

What dispute was there between Virginia and Pennsylvania about the land in the neighborhood of Fort Duquesne?

Why did the English remove the French Acadians from their homes? Where were they taken? What poem has been written about them?

Storybooks to Read

Cooper, James Fenimore: *Red Rover* (French and Indian War)
Cooper, James Fenimore: *Last of the Mohicans*
Henty, G. A.: *With Wolfe in Canada*
Rideing, William H.: *George Washington*
Seawell, Molly Elliott: *The Virginia Cavalier* (Washington)

UNIT IV. THE AMERICAN REVOLUTION

Colonial resistance to the Stamp Act

The patriots are burning the stamps and stamped paper. Note the pillory in the foreground. (From a drawing by A. B. Frost in Bryant's *Popular History of the United States*)

Portrait of General Washington
(From a portrait by Charles Wilson Peale in the Metropolitan Museum of Art)

FORECAST OF UNIT IV

In this part of the story you will learn how the colonists in their brave struggles to establish new homes in America had developed a spirit of self-reliance and independence.

When Great Britain tried to tax them or to interfere with their commerce and manufactures, they defied the laws or evaded them. Efforts at enforcement brought about resistance on the part of the colonists and appeals to the English government for greater consideration for what the colonists believed to be their rights as Englishmen. Further attempts of England to force the colonies into subjection resulted in their armed opposition, their uniting for mutual aid in the struggle, and finally in the Declaration of Independence.

You will read how for seven years the ragged, ill-armed, and badly fed patriot armies, under the leadership of Washington, fought the highly trained and equipped soldiers of King George. In spite of defeats and such suffering as was endured at Valley Forge, the little army held together. The surrender of Burgoyne brought them the important help of the French fleet and army. With this help Washington and his army were finally able to besiege and capture the army of Cornwallis at Yorktown. You will also learn about the naval exploits of John Paul Jones and John Barry, as well as the story of the brave men of other lands who made great sacrifices to help the patriots in their struggle for freedom. You will be interested in the story of George Rogers Clark and how he and his Kentucky riflemen held the lands west of the mountains.

The account of the First and the Second Continental Congresses and their labors in bringing the struggle for independence to a successful end and many other important events of the war that centered in Pennsylvania are stories of especial interest to the boys and girls of this state.

UNIT IV. THE AMERICAN REVOLUTION

Stamps used under the Stamp Act

1. EVENTS LEADING TO THE AMERICAN REVOLUTION

Growing differences between England and the colonies. As the colonies grew in population and in trade and manufacturing, differences gradually arose between them and the mother country. In the first century after they were started, the colonies were not important enough to attract much attention from England. They were allowed to do pretty much as they pleased under their charters from the king.

Besides, as you have already learned, the king and Parliament had had a long quarrel with each other in which each one tried to become the stronger power in England. This also kept the home country from interfering very much with the colonies.

It finally happened that Parliament turned out to be the stronger and was able to say who was to be king or queen of England. This important matter having been settled, Parliament began to think about the colonies across the sea, which had been allowed to have their own way for so long. It attempted to regulate the government, the trade, and the taxation in the colonies by passing a number of laws that interfered with these matters. The king and Parliament together also interfered more and more with laws passed by the colonial assemblies.

Laws against colonial trade. As far back as 1651 Parliament had passed the Navigation Act, which provided that no goods should be taken into or out of the colonies except in English or colonial ships (p. 91). It also provided that no sugar, tobacco, cotton, indigo, or other products of America could be taken to any other port than those of Great Britain or its colonies.

Later on, other laws provided that no goods could be exported from one colony to another colony. For example, a great many hats were made in Pennsylvania, but under this new law not any of these could be exported to any other colony. They had first to be sent to England and pay an import tax. They then could be sent back to one of the other American colonies. Besides this the products of any other nation of Europe or its colonies had to be brought to America by way of England.

Laws against colonial manufactures. Besides these laws against colonial trade Parliament passed many laws interfering with manufactures in the colonies. Some of these laws forbade the forging or rolling of iron and steel smaller than certain sizes. The object of this was to force the colonies to send the unworked iron to England. There it would be rolled into bars or plates of smaller size or perhaps manufactured into wheel tires, axles, horseshoes, or other articles for daily use. The only excuse for these laws was to aid the English manufacturers by preventing the colonists from taking away their trade.

The colonists evade many of these laws. These trade and navigation laws were often very hard to enforce, especially the parts of them that forbade trade with other colonies. In spite of the law against intercolonial trade in hats these articles were sent in large quantities from one colony to another.

After the French had built Louisburg, a considerable illegal trade in all kinds of food and other supplies was carried on between the French of this place and the merchants of Boston and other ports of New England.

The Molasses Act, which put duties on molasses and sugar brought from the French and Spanish West Indies to the English colonies, was never actually enforced.

England encouraged some colonial products. At the same time that England passed these laws against trade and manufactures which interfered with the trade of England at home, other laws were passed which aided the production of goods which the homeland badly needed and which it could not easily get elsewhere.

Among these were masts and other great timbers for ships. A bounty of so much a ton was given for all that were produced in the colonies. A bounty also was given for what are known as *naval stores*. These are tar, pitch, turpentine, and rosin, which were used in large quantities by English shipbuilders.

It is interesting to know that Parliament forbade the farmers of Ireland to grow tobacco in order to prevent interference with the tobacco trade of Virginia.

Shipping tobacco from Virginia in 1751
(A part of a decoration on an old map of Virginia)

Unjust tax laws. The trade and navigation acts which were intended to force the colonists to trade only with England aided the British merchants. Another result was that England could tax these goods when they came into England or when they were sent to the colonies. This caused the price received for colonial products to be lower in England than they could be sold for in other countries.

The taxes on goods brought into the colonies were often evaded by the colonial merchants. They did not feel this to be wrong since they had come to believe that England had no right to put taxes on the colonies except what were necessary to pay the officials and defray the other expenses of carrying out the provisions of the navigation acts.

England imposes new taxes on the colonies. The wars which England had waged in Europe almost continuously for 100 years had cost a great deal of money. Besides England had sent over soldiers and supplies to aid in the wars which had taken place in America between the English and the French and Indians. This was especially true of the French and Indian War. England had sent many soldiers over and also had paid much of the expense of the colonial troops. England had also sent many of the ships of its navy over to help in the fighting. All this money England had spent chiefly for the benefit of the colonies and to protect them from attacks by the French and the Indians.

Naturally England thought that, under these circumstances, the colonies should be willing to bear some of the expense and proposed that the money should be collected by laying additional taxes on things used in the colonies.

The colonies argued that they had received nothing as the result of the war and that England had taken the disputed land west of the Alleghenies and north of the Ohio for a great reservation for the Indians, in which no colonists were to be permitted to settle; so they protested against paying any more taxes.

The Stamp Act. The English government carried out the new taxing plan by laying on the colonies what is known as the *Stamp Tax*. This meant that stamps had to be bought from the government and put on the thing to be taxed. It affected chiefly legal documents, newspapers, and other articles made of paper. Sometimes the paper could be bought already stamped.

The old City Hall, New York City, where the Stamp Act Congress met to oppose the objectionable stamp tax

This Stamp Act made the colonists very angry. They refused to use the stamps, or stamped paper, some of which were seized and burned. They threatened the government officials that had the stamps for sale. Many newspaper articles were written against this attempt to tax the people. In the different cities and colonies the people assembled and made agreements to import no more goods from England until the Stamp

Act was repealed, claiming that England had no right to lay a tax of this sort. Patrick Henry, a prominent young lawyer of Virginia, presented to the Virginia Assembly a resolution that "the General Assembly of this colony have the only and sole exclusive right and power to lay taxes on the inhabitants of this colony."

A congress of representatives from nine of the colonies met in New York. It resolved that the people in the colonies had the same rights as Englishmen who lived in England. It asserted that one of these rights was that the colonists could not be taxed without their own consent.

Colonial ideas of government. Nearly all the grants from the king permitting settlements in America provided that the settlers would have the rights of Englishmen at home.

It happened that for many years after the colonies were founded they really had all the rights which Englishmen in England had. In every colony the lower house of the assembly was elected by the people, even if the governor and council were appointed by the king. No money could be raised from the people by taxation unless the lower house agreed.

Because of this many quarrels arose between the royal governors and the people's assembly. The lower house would refuse to pass any tax bills for the salary of the governor or for the judges or for military supplies unless the governor would agree to other laws that the people wanted. In this way the colonies had their own way and laid what taxes they pleased and refused to admit that the English Parliament had any right to tax them. They claimed that since the colonists sent no representatives to the English Parliament that body had no right to tax them. "No taxation without representation," became the slogan of the colonists.

The English idea of Parliament. The people of England had a different idea of what Parliament could do. They believed that Parliament not only represented Great Britain but it also could pass laws for all the possessions of England, no matter where they were. They believed that the members of Parliament, though they were elected by the people of Great Britain, represented Englishmen everywhere and so could pass tax laws or any other kind of law for any part of the British Empire.

Taxation. When thinking of this quarrel between the colonies and the mother country, you should remember that taxation is the only way by which a government can get money to do the things that people cannot do so well for themselves.

In colonial days a single group of settlers or a single town could have protection from Indian or other attacks only if it could get the help of the soldiers quartered in some of the towns of the province. These soldiers had to be fed and provided with arms and other military supplies. These all cost money. The only way the colonies had of raising such money was by putting a tax on everybody. Then everybody could share in the protection furnished by the soldiers that this tax money supported. Money that was needed to pay the salaries of the governor, the judges, and the other officials who carried on the public business likewise had to be raised by taxation.

Why we pay taxes. Taxes are paid to-day by the people for much the same reasons. It would not be possible for a single homeowner to pay for all the things that our government provides for us through the taxes it collects. We all share in the help and protection that we get from the police, the firemen, and the public officials who take care of the general health and welfare. We can use the streets and have the benefit of having them lighted at nights. People could not afford to pay for the kind of schools that they would like to have for their children if each family had to provide them individually.

The only way that such benefits can be had at a reasonable cost is by everyone paying taxes to the government. The government then uses the money received for the benefit of everybody. Nobody likes to give out money unless he gets something in return for it, but we should remember that all the money we pay in taxes comes back to us in the form of benefits of one kind or another. The things that we should be careful about are to see that the money is not spent wastefully and to make sure that the benefits for which we pay taxes are those that we really want.

Causes of misunderstanding between England and the colonies. One of the important causes of the difference of opinion about taxation and other matters between the English and the colonies was that they did not know each other very well. Most of the people living in the colonies had been born here and knew very little of what was going on in England. They had been used to doing very much as they pleased for many years and objected to these new attempts of England to control them and make laws for them.

The Englishmen knew even less about affairs in the colonies. They could not understand why the colonies objected to helping to pay for a war which the Englishmen believed had been carried on mostly for the benefit of the colonists. They themselves were paying much heavier taxes than Parliament asked the colonists to pay.

There was almost no communication between the colonies and England, except through the captains and crews of the merchant vessels and the few government officials who came over here. Very few of the emigrants returned to the old country. Books written by Englishmen and others who traveled in America told mostly about the commerce and trade of the colonies and very little of how the people felt about matters of government.

There was no such thing in those times as fast ocean steamers that could cross the Atlantic in four days, carrying hundreds of people back and forth on each trip. Nor was there any means of quick communication by cable or by radio.

It is easy to see that, when there were so few chances of the Englishmen at home and the Englishmen in the

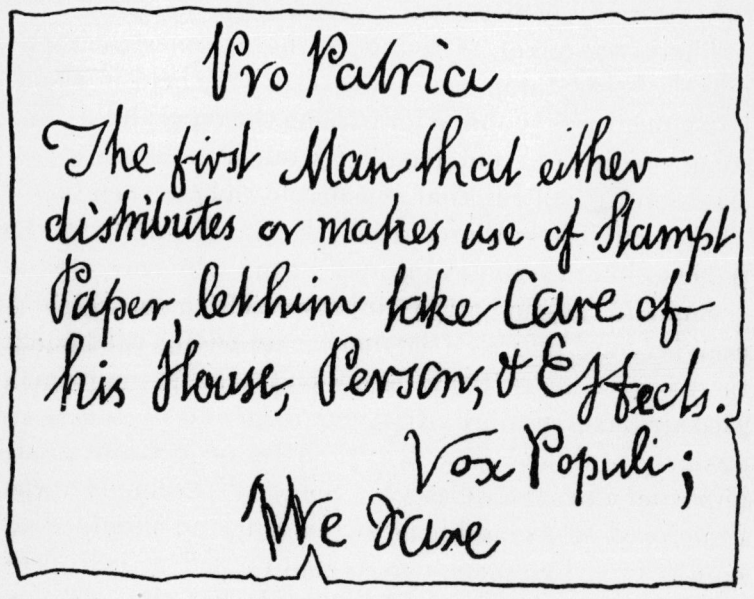

> Pro Patria
> The first Man that either distributes or makes use of Stampt Paper, let him take Care of his House, Person, & Effects.
> Vox Populi;
> We Dare

Warning against the use of stamps
This Stamp Act warning was posted on the doors of every public office and on corners of streets.

colonies to talk over things together, misunderstandings and even more serious difficulties were apt to arise.

The Stamp Act is repealed. As a result of the strong opposition by the colonies to the carrying out of the provisions of the Stamp Act and the great losses to English merchants on account of the nonimportation agreements, the English Parliament repealed the Stamp Act. At the same time Parliament declared that it had the right to tax the colonies in any way it wished and to pass any laws concerning them that it seemed wise for that body to pass.

There was great rejoicing in the colonies over the repeal of the Stamp Act. Meetings were held in which Parliament was thanked for passing the repeal bill. The colonists did not seem to pay very much attention to the claim of Parliament that it had the right to tax them. They were not bothered about England's right to tax them so long as no tax bill was being enforced.

England passes other objectionable acts. It was not very long before Parliament again passed acts which the colonists believed to be unjust. This series of acts provided for a more strict enforcement of the laws against trade and laid heavy duties on certain goods imported into the colonies. Some of the money was to be used to pay soldiers whom England intended to send over. These soldiers were supposed to help protect the colonies against Indian raids, but the colonists believed that they were to be used to force them to pay the taxes they thought were unjust.

The colonists oppose the new acts. At once the colonists resisted this new attempt to tax them without their consent. It was found impossible to collect the taxes, and the nonimportation agreements that had been done away with when the Stamp Act was repealed were again put into effect.

The result was almost the same as before. Parliament repealed almost all the acts. It kept the duty on tea in order to show its right to tax the colonies. The colonists then resolved to import no more tea.

Progress toward revolution. The quarrel over all of these laws between the colonies and the mother country had grown more and more bitter. A number of incidents that happened within the next few years made matters even worse. Some of the troops sent to America had been quartered in Boston. Since the colonists believed that the English government planned to use these soldiers to enforce the laws and so interfere with the trade of Boston, frequent quarrels arose between them and the inhabitants of the city.

The Boston Massacre. One day a small company of these soldiers was surrounded by a group of the rougher element of the city, who threw stones and otherwise abused the soldiers by calling them names. The soldiers, fearing that they were about to be attacked, fired on the crowd, killed one, and wounded a number of others.

Prominent citizens of Boston, aroused by this incident, which is called the *Boston Massacre*, went to the governor and forced him to have the troops removed to a fort in the harbor, where they would no longer annoy the citizens. The people of Boston then organized a Committee of Correspondence which was to send letters to prominent people in the other colonies, asking them to join with the people of Massachusetts in opposition to the English laws.

The Boston Massacre
The old Massachusetts State House is at the head of the street. (From an engraving by Paul Revere)

The tax on tea. England now determined to try another method of forcing taxation on the colonies. Parliament permitted the company that brought tea from the East Indies to take it to the colonies without having to pay any tax in England. This would make it possible to sell tea in the colonies, even after the colonial tax had been paid, cheaper than it could be sold in England. The colonists saw that this was merely a trick to get them to pay the tax in order to have cheap tea.

Again opposition arose in all the colonies where ships bringing the tea were expected. In Charleston, South Carolina, the tea was stored in damp cellars, where it soon spoiled. In Philadelphia the committee of citizens sent a letter to the captain of the tea ship, telling him not to dare bring his ship into port and threatening that, if he did so, he would be given a coat of tar and feathers. In Boston the ship was brought to the wharf. A meeting of the citizens was held, and it was resolved to ask the governor to forbid the landing of the tea. The governor refused to issue such an order. That night a company of men dressed as Indians made their way aboard the tea ship and threw all the tea into Boston Harbor.

Boston is punished for destroying the tea. When the news of the destruction of the tea reached England, Parliament and the chief government officials resolved to punish the people of Boston for their rebellious act. Parliament passed an act which closed the port of Boston to all commerce and other acts which took away from the people all the rights of governing themselves which they had had up to this time.

EVENTS LEADING TO AMERICAN REVOLUTION 279

It was even provided that certain offenders could be taken to England for trial and punishment.

These acts brought the quarrel to a head. Massachusetts, through its Committee of Correspondence, asked the aid of the assemblies in the different colonies.

From an old print

Throwing the tea overboard in Boston Harbor, December 16, 1773

The other colonies responded by sending provisions and other help to Boston and offered to permit the Boston merchants to bring their goods in through other colonial ports without paying duty or other charges.

Governor Dunmore of Virginia dissolved the colonial assembly for offering sympathy to Boston. Two days later the assembly met on its own account and adopted a resolution recommending that a congress of all the

Patrick Henry's speech before the First Continental Congress

"The distinctions between Virginians, Pennsylvanians, New Yorkers, and New Englanders are no more. I am not a Virginian but an American."

Courtesy American Telephone and Telegraph Company

colonies be called to consider what should be done for the best interests of America.

The First Continental Congress. In response to the suggestion of the Virginia assembly, delegates from all the colonies except Georgia met at Carpenters' Hall,

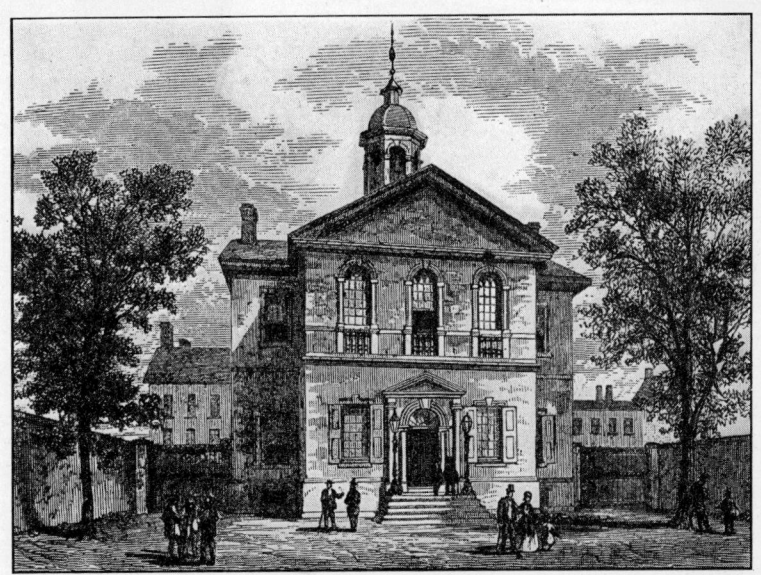

From an old print

Carpenters' Hall where the First Continental Congress met

Philadelphia, on September 5, 1774. This Congress declared that the colonies should tax and govern themselves in accordance with the laws of England. They sent a petition to the king and an address to the people of England asking that the colonies be treated differently. They also entered into an "Association," by which all the colonies agreed not to trade with England until these oppressive laws were repealed.

STUDY HELPS

Map Work

On a map of eastern United States show the boundaries of the colonies at the close of the French and Indian War. Indicate the part of the former French lands that England had reserved for the use of the Indians. Locate the principal commercial cities of the colonies.

Activities

Get some pictures for your book connected with the events of this chapter, such as pictures of English stamped paper or of the Boston Tea Party.

Dramatize the scene when the men of Boston demanded that the governor of Massachusetts should forbid the landing of the tea.

Make a model of the old South Church in Boston.

Special Work

Make a list of colonial products, trade in which was interfered with by English laws.

What excuse did England give for prohibiting the colonies from trading with other countries after they had adopted a nonimportation agreement?

What happened to the Philadelphia tea ship?

How would it help Boston for the merchants of that city to bring goods in through other colonies?

Storybooks to Read

Barr, Amelia E.: *The Strawberry Handkerchief* (Stamp Act)
Barton, William E.: *When Boston Braved the King* (Tea Party)
Davis, William Stearns: *Gilman of Redford*
Hart, William Surrey: *A Lighter of Flames* (Patrick Henry)
Kaler, James Otis: *The Charming Sally* (Stamp Act)

2. THE COLONIES AT WAR

Great Britain attempts to force obedience to its laws. When the news of the action of the First Continental Congress reached England, the British government at once decided to force the colonies to submit to the acts of Parliament. Parliament presented an address to the king, saying that the colony of Massachusetts had rebelled, and offered their aid in putting down the rebellion.

Acts were passed forbidding the people of New England to trade with any other nation. They were also forbidden to carry on their fishery trade, which was one of their chief means of support.

When Patrick Henry, who had been a leader in opposing Great Britain, learned of these new oppressive acts, he made a famous speech to a convention of Virginia patriots. He urged that the colonies should fight, if necessary, to rid themselves of control by England and ended his speech by saying, "I know not what course others may take but, as for me, give me liberty or give me death."

Later, when news arrived that other colonies had joined New England in a petition to the king and had approved the other acts of the First Continental Congress, the rest of the colonies were also forbidden to trade with any foreign nation.

Generals Howe, Clinton, and Burgoyne were sent from England with a large body of soldiers to reënforce General Gage, who at that time was in command of the British regiments around Boston.

The War in New England

The first fighting; Lexington and Concord. When the Massachusetts Assembly was dissolved by Governor Hutchinson, the people chose representatives to another assembly whose business it was to conduct the affairs of the colony without reference to the governor and his council. This body appointed a committee of safety, the chief members of which were John Hancock and Joseph Warren.

The committee immediately set about gathering stores that might be used in defending the people of the colony against attacks by the British soldiers. It was also provided that the patriots should organize bands of *minute men,* who were pledged to assemble, at a minute's notice, to defend the colony against British attacks.

A quantity of arms, provisions, and military stores were gathered, some of which were placed in storehouses at Concord. General Gage now determined to seize these stores and destroy them. News reached the committee of safety that this attempt was to be made on April 19, 1775. The committee laid plans to warn the colonists, and Paul Revere and William Dawes were sent out the night before to give the alarm.

About daylight the British troops reached Lexington on the way to Concord. As the

Photo from Ewing Galloway
The minute man leaving his plow to fight for liberty

result of the warning given by Paul Revere, a group of sixty or seventy minute men had come together to oppose the British and were drawn up on the village green under the command of Captain Parker. The

English commander ordered the patriots to lay down their arms and disperse. When the order was not quickly obeyed, Major Pitcairn, the British commander,

Paul Revere warning the men of Massachusetts of the coming of the British troops
(From a Copley Print of a painting by Robert Reid, copyrighted by Curtis & Cameron, Inc.)

ordered his men to fire. Eight were killed and a number of others were wounded.

The British then proceeded to Concord, where a similar group of minute men were drawn up at the old bridge at the north end of the town. The minute men returned the fire of the British, and a number on each side were killed or wounded.

The British then destroyed all the stores they could find and began the march back to Boston.

The fight at Concord bridge
(From an engraving after a painting by Alonzo Chappel)

The retreat to Boston. Meanwhile the warnings that had been carried to the near-by towns by Paul Revere had been spread over the countryside. Thousands of minute men, learning of the march of the British, made their way along the country roads toward Boston. These men in small bands from each village and town took positions all along the six miles of road between

Lexington and Concord. Concealed behind stone walls, bowlders, and trees, they poured a deadly fire on the retreating British. The British troops were as badly off as Braddock's army had been on its march through the woods on the way to Fort Duquesne. At Lexington a strong force sent out by General Gage met them; otherwise it is very likely they would have had to surrender.

When the combined British forces started again for Boston, the minute men renewed the fight. Exhausted and with the loss of about three hundred soldiers, the British were glad to reach Boston, where the guns of the fleet protected them.

The Battle of Bunker Hill. Within a few weeks twenty thousand patriot farmers were encamped in the neighborhood of Boston, determined that the British were to be prevented from carrying on any further warlike expeditions. The news of the resistance of the Massachusetts men had reached northern Vermont, where a body of colonial militia under Ethan Allan surprised and captured Fort Ticonderoga, getting a large quantity of provisions and some cannon, which were hauled to Boston for the use of the patriot army.

THE COLONIES AT WAR

In the meantime the leaders of the army around Boston, in order to strengthen their position, decided to fortify Bunker Hill, across the Charles River from Boston. However, on account of the darkness or because it had a better command of Boston and the

The Battle of Bunker Hill
(From an engraving after the painting of John Trumbull)

harbor, they fortified Breed's Hill instead of Bunker Hill, but the name of the latter has been given to the battle. Since the colonial troops could bombard Boston and the British ships from this position, General Gage determined to drive them from the hill.

With the help of boats from the ships, he ferried his soldiers across the river. Marching up the hill, they attacked the Americans. The minute men withheld their fire until the British approached so close that the whites of their eyes could be seen. A burst of flames came from the American trenches and the British regulars were driven down the slope. A second charge was also repulsed with severe loss to the British. On the third assault by the British, the Americans slowly retreated, having used up all of their powder and shot.

The British had succeeded in capturing Breed's Hill, but only at a loss of one third of their forces, a number twice as great as the loss of the Americans.

This defeat by the British was for the Americans as good as a victory. They knew now that they were capable of standing up before the British regulars and of giving a good account of themselves.

The Second Continental Congress. On May 10, 1775, the Second Continental Congress met in the State House, at Philadelphia. At first it only gave suggestions to the different colonies as to what seemed to be the best things to do in opposing the British attempts to enforce their laws.

When it learned of the thousands of minute men and other militia that had taken upon themselves the siege of Boston, it saw at once that some central authority was needed. It therefore adopted the forces around Boston as a colonial, or Continental, army, and, at the suggestion of the delegates from Massachusetts, appointed George Washington of Virginia as commander in chief. It also adopted a national flag.

As time went on, the Second Continental Congress was forced to take on more and more the responsibility of carrying the war to a successful finish. It raised armies and money, arranged for provisions, appointed generals, made treaties with foreign countries, and did many other things.

The different colonies had not agreed to give the Congress the right to do these things, but the Congress was the only group of men that represented all of them in the fight for independence.

The British are compelled to withdraw from Boston. When General Washington reached Boston, he took command of the colonial troops under an old elm tree in Cambridge. He surrounded himself with officers representing the different bodies of troops that had been independently besieging the city, and he organized the troops into an army. He decided where batteries were to be placed to command the land approaches of the city so that all the supplies had to come in by sea.

He next seized Dorchester Heights, which is now South Boston, and fortified it. General Howe, the British commander, saw that he would have to capture the American fortifications or else leave the city, since the guns on Dorchester Heights commanded the channel leading to the city from the sea. The size of the colonial army prevented him from risking an attack. The British therefore decided to leave the city. General Howe loaded his men on the ships of Admiral Howe, his brother, and sailed away to Halifax in Nova Scotia.

Recruits from Delaware

Commanded by Caesar Rodney, one of the signers of the Declaration of Independence, they are on their way to join Washington's army. (From a painting by Stanley M. Arthurs in St. Andrew's School, Middletown, Delaware)

The desire for independence grows. For more than a year after the Battles of Lexington and Concord and even after Washington had succeeded in driving the

The elm tree under which Washington took command of the Continental army at Cambridge, near Boston
This tree was destroyed by a storm only a few years ago.

British army out of Boston, most of the people in the colonies still believed it possible for them to become again good subjects of King George. Unfortunately every advance made by the colonies toward the healing of the differences between themselves and the mother country was answered by an act of the British government which still further angered the colonists and made them more than ever determined to resist.

From an old print

General Howe and his army leaving Boston for Halifax
This evacuation was the result of the fortifying of Dorchester Heights by General Washington.

After the British had sailed away from Boston, the question of independence came to be more and more discussed. The delegates to the Congress from Massachusetts and New England, together with the Virginians, were at first the strongest for independence. The other colonies were less anxious since they saw great losses to their trade if war should come. Finally, in the spring of 1776, the colonies were asked to give their delegates in Congress instructions regarding independence.

Courtesy Title Guarantee and Trust Company, New York
An interview between Lord Howe and a committee of the Continental Congress headed by Benjamin Franklin, in which any terms except complete independence were refused by the Americans

The Declaration of Independence. By the end of June a majority of the colonies had instructed their delegates to approve any action that might be taken that aimed at the independence of the colonies. On July 2, 1776, Richard Henry Lee of Virginia offered a resolution that " these colonies are, and of right ought to be, free and independent states." The resolution

Photo from Halliday Historic Photograph Co.

Reading the Declaration of Independence to the people of Boston
(From a reconstruction based on contemporary accounts)

was adopted, and a committee was appointed to draw up a suitable declaration.

Two days later, on July 4, 1776, Thomas Jefferson,

chairman of the committee, presented to Congress the *Declaration of Independence*, which was adopted unanimously.

The War in the Middle Colonies

New York captured by the British. When General Howe and his brother, the admiral, sailed off to Halifax from Boston, it was not their idea to give up the attempt to regain the colonies for England. Plans were soon set on foot for an attack on New York. It was felt that the desire for independence was less strong there than it was in New England. It was easily reached from Halifax, and General Howe thought that, if he could once get a footing in New York, he would separate Massachusetts from Virginia, the two colonies that were strongest for independence.

Washington moved the greater part of his army to New York and constructed some forts at the upper end of the city. He also fortified some low hills in Brooklyn, overlooking New York Bay, and waited the expected attack by the British.

Events proved that Washington was right in guessing where the next attack was to be made. The British arrived, landed their forces on Long Island, and attacked the American fortifications with a large and well-equipped army. The Continentals were driven from their intrenchments and barely escaped capture. That night the American forces were ferried across the river to New York by Massachusetts fishermen who

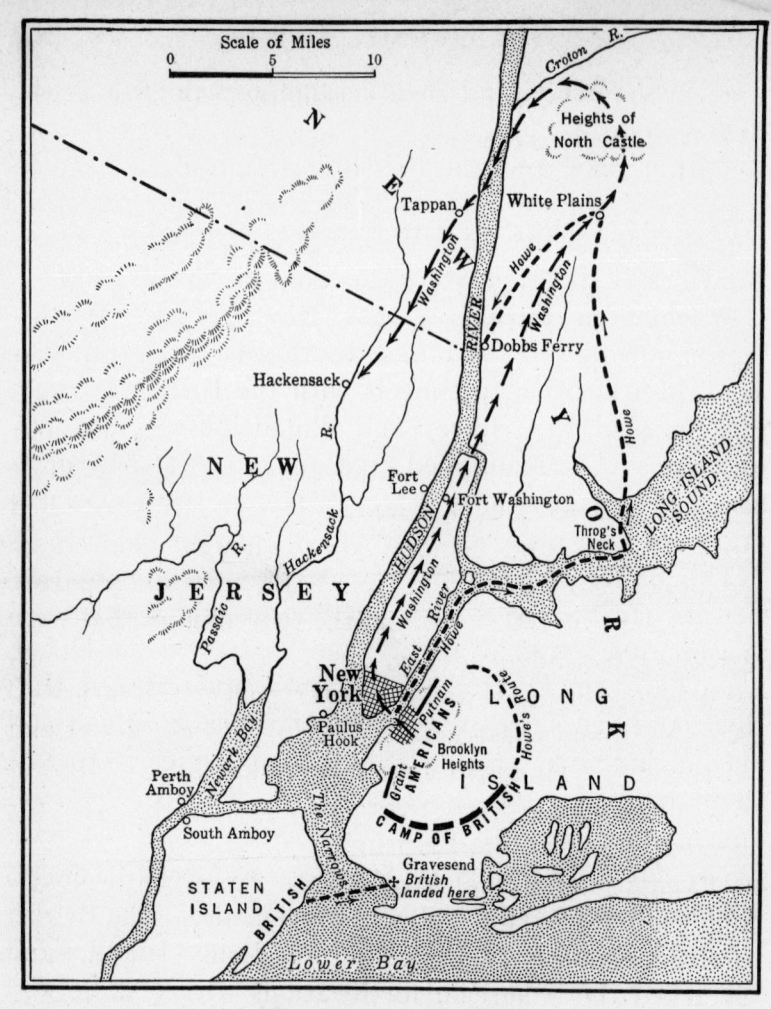

The campaign in New York

General Howe landed at Staten Island, June 28, 1776; crossed to Gravesend, August 22; battle of Long Island, August 27; Washington retreated across the East River, August 29, and proceeded up the Hudson; Howe took possession of New York, September 15; attacked Washington at White Plains, October 28; Washington retreated to North Castle and then into New Jersey.

were in the army, and thus Washington and his army were saved.

Within a few days the British moved into New York City. Washington and his troops were driven up the Hudson and the two forts, Washington and Lee, on opposite sides of the river, were captured by the British.

Washington retreats across New Jersey. Washington now moved south in order that he might put his army in a position to contest with the British for the possession of New Jersey and Philadelphia. Pursued by large and well-equipped divisions of General Howe's army, Washington later retreated across the Delaware into Pennsylvania.

The Battle of Trenton. Large detachments of the British had been stationed at Trenton and Princeton. Washington seized all the available boats on the Delaware between Trenton and Easton and crossed the river into New Jersey with part of his army, on Christmas night, 1776. After a nine-hour march through snow and sleet, the American army entered Trenton and captured almost the entire British force. A few weeks later Washington brought additional troops across the river and occupied the city.

General Cornwallis, who had been given command of the forces opposing Washington's army, now determined to punish the Americans for their daring exploit.

The Battle of Princeton. Taking most of the troops that had been encamped in Princeton, Cornwallis attempted to surround the American army.

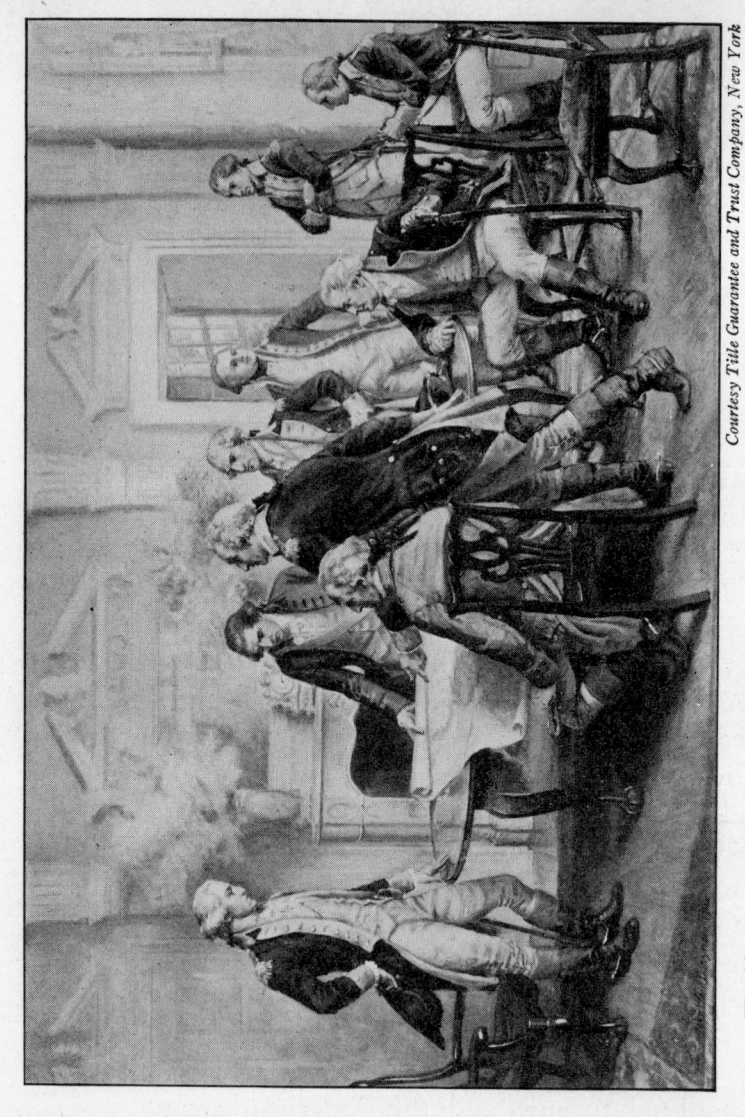

Courtesy Title Guarantee and Trust Company, New York

Washington and his generals holding a council of war after the Battle of Long Island, 1776

Washington, knowing that he could not successfully fight such a large army, decided to make a surprise attack on the regiments which had been left at Princeton. Leaving his camp fires burning to deceive the enemy, he marched around the British forces by back roads. Suddenly falling upon three British regiments

Courtesy Metropolitan Museum of Art

Washington crossing the Delaware with his army, to surprise the British at Trenton

(From a painting by Emanuel Leutze)

at Princeton, he defeated them and then retired to winter quarters at Morristown, New Jersey, where he could watch Howe in New York.

The British plan to capture Philadelphia; the Battle of Brandywine. Having failed in his attempt to reach Philadelphia by the way of New Jersey, General Howe decided to attack Philadelphia from the south. His army was taken on ships up to the head of Chesapeake Bay. Washington, meanwhile, had moved his army south through Philadelphia. The two armies met at Brandywine Creek, not far from the present city of Wilmington, Delaware. For several days the armies

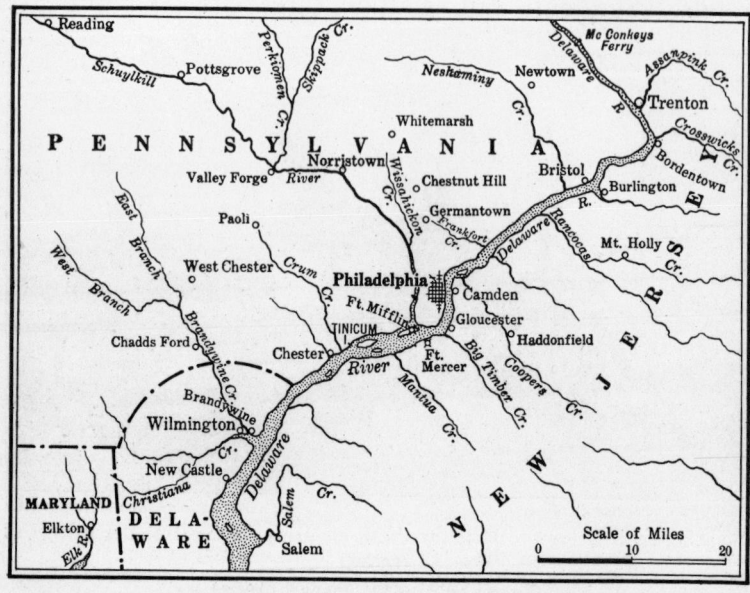

Valley Forge, Philadelphia, and Brandywine

confronted each other. Then General Howe learned that a ford some distance up the creek had been left unguarded by the Americans. He detached part of his army, which crossed the Brandywine at this ford, while the British in front of Washington's force made a pretended attack. Washington, unable to hold his ground under this double attack, retreated through Chester to Philadelphia and was followed by Howe. The British in a few days occupied the city. Washington encamped to the north and the west of the city.

The attack on the Chew House, Battle of Germantown
This house is still standing and shows many marks of the battle. (From a painting by Alonzo Chappel)

The Battle of Germantown. Some of the British troops had been sent back to act as a guard for the supplies that were being brought from the ships at the head of Chesapeake Bay. Washington determined to attack the main body of the British, which was encamped at Germantown. Careful plans were made, and the American army advanced upon the British from several directions. The British were slowly but surely being driven into a retreat when one of the American detachments, not being able to see clearly on account of a heavy fog, mistook another American force for a detachment of the British and fired upon them. In the confusion that followed, the American troops became disorganized and withdrew from the field.

The Chew house, an old colonial mansion that is still standing, was at the center of the British lines. When the British troops near this house were driven back, the house itself was used as a fort by a strong body of British soldiers, and the Americans were unable to dislodge them. The constant and heavy firing upon the Americans from this house added to the confusion and had much to do with the American defeat. After the defeat at Germantown Washington withdrew to the hills of Valley Forge north of Norristown.

Valley Forge. The winter at Valley Forge probably marks the lowest point of the American hopes during the war. The chief cities of the Middle colonies had been occupied by the British. The Continental Congress had been driven from the city of Philadelphia. Many of the people of the Middle colonies who were not in favor of independence welcomed the success of the British. Meanwhile Washington's ragged army, with insufficient shelter, food, and clothing, spent the winter amid the snows of Valley Forge.

Their shelters were log cabins hastily constructed

Baron von Steuben drilling the patriot troops at Valley Forge

Note Washington's headquarters and the soldiers' huts in the background. (From a Copley Print of a painting by Edwin A. Abbey in the State Capitol at Harrisburg)

© Curtis & Cameron

and with almost no provision for warmth. Few of the soldiers had warm clothing or blankets. Their shoes in many cases were merely bundles of rags wrapped around their feet.

Often during this terrible winter the army was without sufficient food, and, even when it was obtained, there would be only enough for two or three days at a time. Still Washington did not despair. He held the little army together and, with the help of Lafayette, Steuben, and other foreign officers who had joined the patriot army, drilled them in the art of war.

Surrender of Burgoyne at Saratoga. Part of the plan of the British was to separate New England from the rest of the colonies. They believed that New England was the hotbed of the Revolution. While they knew that Virginia was strong for independence, they believed that it would be easy to conquer the Southern colonies and then take up the question of subduing New England.

About the time that Howe decided to attack Philadelphia, a plan was also made that General Burgoyne would bring a British army down from Canada along Lake Champlain and the Hudson River. Burgoyne soon captured Fort Ticonderoga and other defenses on Lake Champlain and made his way south to Saratoga. Here he ran short of supplies and sent out two detachments, one to the east and one to the west, to obtain food from the country. Both of these detachments were defeated by New York and New England militia.

Part of Washington's army which had been left along the Hudson River now moved to the north, joined the

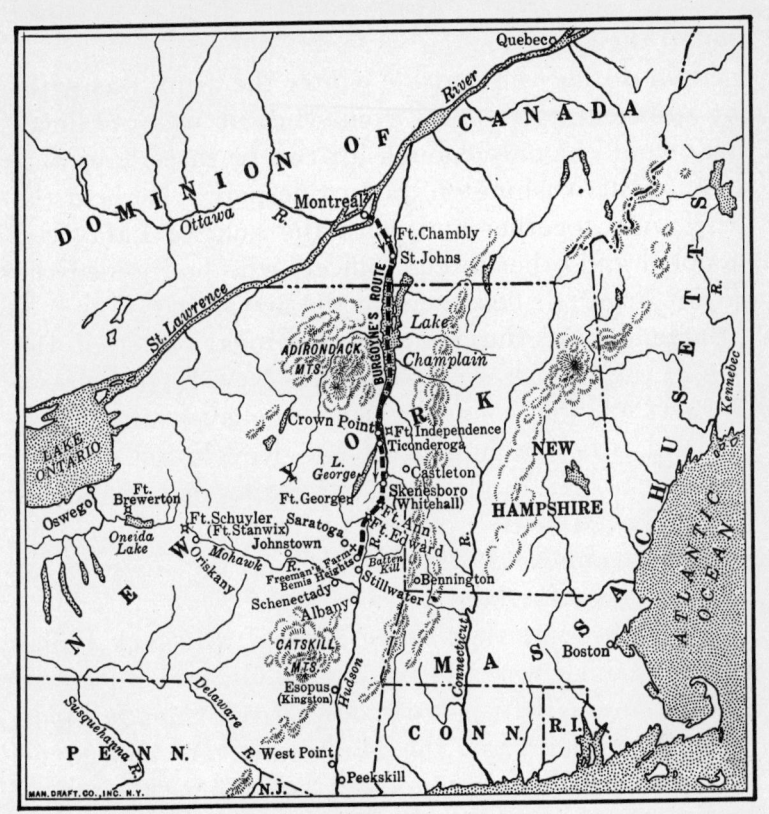

Burgoyne's expedition which was intended to cut off New England from the rest of the states

militia which had been attacking Burgoyne, and surrounded him near Saratoga. It had been planned that Howe would send a strong force under Sir Henry Clin-

The Surrender of Burgoyne at Bemis Heights, near Saratoga
(From a painting by John Trumbull in the Gallery of Fine Arts, Yale University)

ton up the Hudson to meet Burgoyne. This army was never sent. Later General Howe did decide to help Burgoyne, but it was too late.

Burgoyne said that no matter which way he fronted his army there were thousands of Americans in front of him. After vainly trying to force himself out of the trap in which he found himself, Burgoyne took a position on Bemis Heights, near Saratoga, to await the expected help from Howe. Several assaults by American troops under General Benedict Arnold resulted in so much loss that Burgoyne finally surrendered on October 14, 1777.

The effect of Burgoyne's surrender. Burgoyne's surrender had a number of important results. First, the British now realized that the rebellion in America was really a revolution and that different measures would have to be taken if the colonies were to be brought back to their loyalty to the mother country.

Another result was that France, which had secretly been helping the Americans for some time with money and supplies, was induced to come openly to the aid of the colonies. Other nations of Europe also came to the aid of America.

England, finding that it would be opposed from now on by a group of strong nations allied with the Americans, offered to the colonies even more than the rights they had asked for before the war began. It was now too late for England to make this offer. The colonies would not be satisfied with anything but complete independence.

The British and Indians attack the Western settlements. You have already learned that the colonists, after occupying most of the river valleys along the coast, pushed over the mountains and settled in the rich lands of the Mississippi Valley. You also recall that the French and Indian War was undertaken for the purpose of keeping this region free for settlement of the English. At the end of the war Great Britain decided to keep settlers out of this region and planned to make it a great hunting ground for the Indians.

The British commander at Detroit at the beginning of the Revolution had organized bands of Indians and English which he sent through Ohio with the object of destroying any settlements that had been made there. These raids reached even to Kentucky, and soon there were only a few hundred settlers left west of the mountains.

The War in the Northwest

George Rogers Clark captures the Northwest from the British. George Rogers Clark, a daring Virginia hunter, saw that whatever country had control of the West at the end of the war would be able to keep it by the treaty of peace. He also saw that one way to stop these Indian raids was to take possession of some of the old French towns and forts which had come into the possession of the British. These towns the British had used as rallying places for the Indians that raided the settlements.

Setting out from Redstone, now Bedford, in Pennsylvania, Clark went down the Ohio River with about one hundred and fifty Virginians. When he reached Illinois, he left the boats and marched across the country until he reached the old French fort at Kaskaskia.

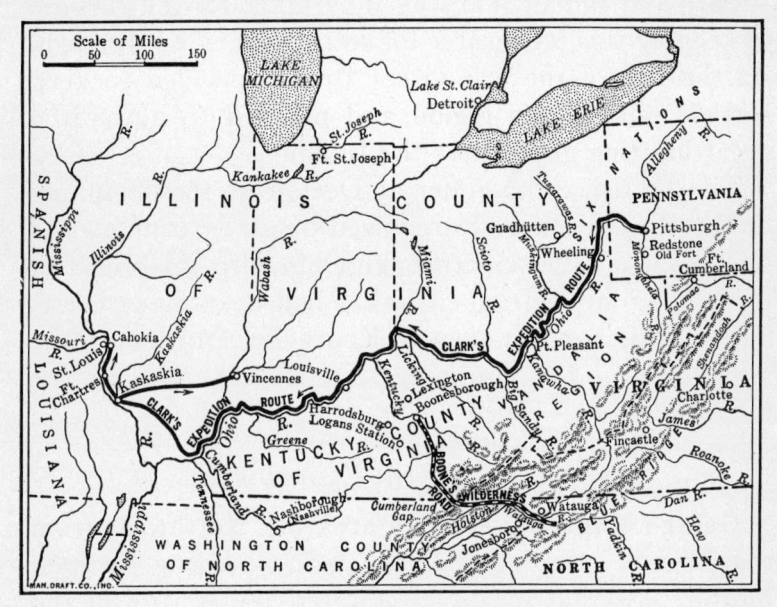

The expedition of George Rogers Clark

Clark's attack was such a surprise that he found the door of the fort open. Rushing in, his men seized the English commandant and overawed the garrison. The French people of the town were glad to side with Clark, especially when they learned that France had made an alliance with the United States.

Clark's influence soon spread far and wide among the Indians as well as among the French of this region. Later old Fort Vincennes was induced to surrender to the Americans.

When the British commander at Detroit heard of Clark's success, he sent a strong detachment which recaptured Vincennes.

© *Caufield & Shook, Inc.*
George Rogers Clark leading his men in the attack on Vincennes
(From a painting by T. Gilbert White in the Seelbach Hotel, Louisville)

Clark now resolved to drive the British back to Detroit. He marched for over two hundred miles from Kaskaskia to Vincennes with a few hundred men. Almost the whole distance was through flooded country. Often the soldiers marched through water as high as their breasts and had to carry their guns and powder horns above their heads.

Vincennes is captured by the Americans. When Clark and his band reached the town, he marched his men back and forth so as to give the impression that he had a large army. He also persuaded the French inhabitants to remain neutral. He then attacked the fort and the British commander was soon forced to surrender. Only the want of sufficient men and provisions kept Clark from seizing Detroit.

Clark was able to hold the places that he had captured until the end of the war. When the treaty of peace was made, the fact that Americans held possession of this region resulted in the United States' receiving it from England as part of the gains of the war.

Enmity between England and France. Because France had been unsuccessful in its recent war with England, many Frenchmen had almost from the very beginning given aid to the colonies in their fight for independence. A number of prominent Frenchmen came over to help them. The French government through secret agents advanced the Continental Congress large sums of money as well as furnished them with cannon, powder, and other supplies.

The surrender of Burgoyne convinced the French that the Americans were likely to succeed in their struggle and that there would be little danger in more openly helping the new nation across the ocean.

France makes a treaty of alliance with the United States. Very early in the struggle Congress had sent Benjamin Franklin to France in order to arrange for the secret help. He was received by the French court and nobility with great honor and respect. He soon persuaded the government that it was to the advantage of France to join with America in helping to defeat England. As a result of Franklin's efforts, France agreed to sign a treaty with America to give each other aid against the English. In return France agreed not to make peace with England until America had been granted independence.

The results of the French alliance. This alliance with France helped the Americans in several ways: first, the strong French navy would be able to protect American commerce and fishing from the English navy and enable the colonial armies to get supplies from their friends in Europe. At the same time the French fleet would prevent the British army from freely bringing in reënforcements and supplies. A second result was that France also furnished a French army, which was brought to America as an aid to the colonial troops. The British forces now had two large armies to contend against.

A third result was that England had to divide its forces and keep large portions of them in the West Indies and other British possessions in order to protect them against seizure by the French.

The British abandon Philadelphia. General Howe, who was afraid that the large French fleet might make an attack on New York, resolved to leave Philadelphia and collect all his army at New York. There were not ships enough for all who wished to leave the city; so General Clinton, who succeeded Howe, decided to

Franklin at a reception at the court of France

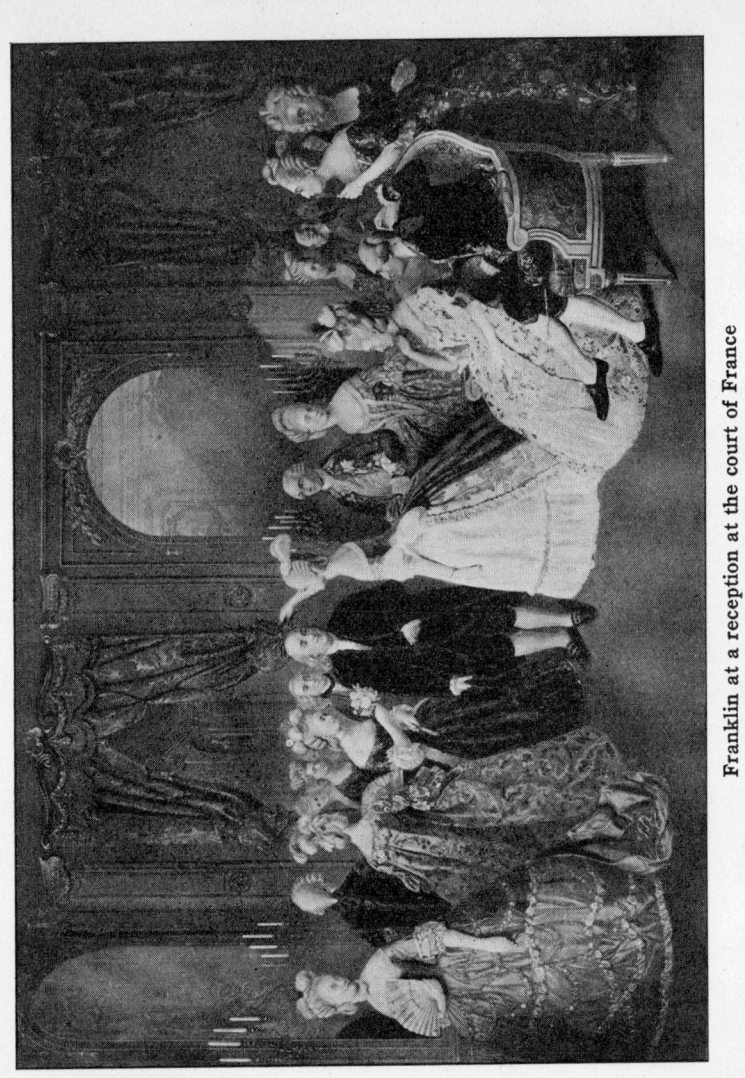

Note the contrast between the plain attire of Franklin and the rich clothes of the courtiers. (From a painting by Baron Jolly)

take his army across New Jersey. Washington and his army entered the city as the last of the British left. He then resolved to follow Clinton toward New York.

The Battle of Monmouth. Washington caught up with the British at Monmouth, in New Jersey, where he attacked them. During the fight General Charles Lee, who was to lead an attack on a British column, delayed doing so and almost threw the American army into a disorderly retreat. Only the presence of Washington saved the American army. The British, however, were able to gather their forces together and finally reach New York.

Washington slowly followed and took up his position at White Plains, a few miles east of the Hudson, where he could watch General Clinton's army in New York.

The treason of Benedict Arnold. General Benedict Arnold had shown much skill and bravery in many of the battles of the Revolution. In an attempt to capture Quebec during the war he led his troops through the Maine wilderness and displayed much bravery in battle. Later on he was conspicuous for his daring in the events at Saratoga and was largely responsible for Burgoyne's decision to surrender.

When stationed in Philadelphia, he had married Peggy Shippen, daughter of a wealthy loyalist, or *Tory*. He soon found that he was living beyond his means and was heavily in debt. He was also accused of having misused some military funds and was sentenced to be reprimanded by Washington. Arnold had felt for a long time that he had not been given the promotion in the army that his services to the American cause had justified. All these things seem to have preyed on his mind to such an extent that he decided to betray the patriot cause for a large sum of money.

West Point in 1780
The plans for the fortifications were made by Baron Kosciuszko.

Arnold offers to surrender West Point to the British. Washington thought highly of Arnold and, when he asked for the command of West Point, a key position of the American lines, Washington gave it to him. Arnold then entered into correspondence with Sir

Henry Clinton, Military Governor of New York for the British, offering to surrender West Point for about $30,000 and a generalship in the British army.

Major André, a young British officer, was sent to make the arrangements. On his way back to New York

From an old print
Major André captured while returning to New York after his negotiations with Benedict Arnold at West Point

he was seized and his papers, proving him to be a spy, were taken from him. Arnold learned of the capture and managed to escape to the British lines.

When Washington received the dispatch informing him of Arnold's treason, he turned sadly to General Knox and said, "Whom can we trust now?"

At Schuylerville, New York, there is a monument commemorating the surrender of Burgoyne, with places for four statues of the generals who brought victory to the patriot cause at Saratoga. Three places are occupied by the statues of General Gates, General Schuyler, and General Morgan, but the place where Arnold's statue would have been is left vacant.

The War in the South

The capture of Charleston, South Carolina. The British, having been unsuccessful in conquering New England and the Middle colonies, decided to make an effort to bring the South under their control. Part of the British fleet sailed from New York with 8000 soldiers for Charleston, South Carolina. Slipping past the French vessels, the expedition under General Cornwallis reached Charleston. General Lincoln, who commanded the patriot army, had only about one third as many troops as Cornwallis. Instead of leaving the city, he let himself be shut up in the fort and surrounded by the British troops. Since he was not able to fight his way out, he soon had to surrender. Other British forces had succeeded in overrunning Georgia, and soon both Georgia and South Carolina were in the hands of the British.

Cornwallis moves into North Carolina and Virginia. Congress now sent General Gates, the hero of Saratoga, with a small army to try to hold the British in check. Cornwallis, part of whose army had left Charleston and was marching to the north, met the army of Gates at Camden, where Gates was defeated and his army

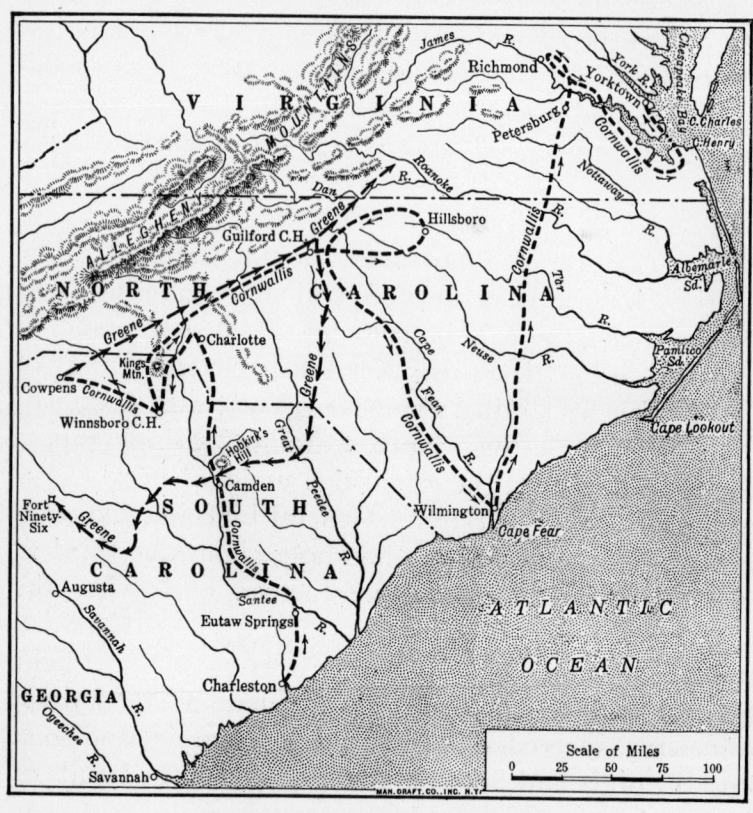

The Revolutionary War in the South

broken up. Cornwallis steadily pursued the retreating forces of General Gates through North Carolina. On the way he sent Colonel Ferguson to try to enlist

THE COLONIES AT WAR

settlers in the British army. The patriot backwoodsmen gathered in such numbers from the mountains of Kentucky and the Carolinas that Ferguson was soon surrounded at Kings Mountain. After a fight, in which the frontiersmen fought in true backwoods

Charleston, South Carolina, in 1780 *From an old print*

fashion, Ferguson was compelled to surrender. Cornwallis now received additional troops from Clinton and was able to continue his march to the north in pursuit of the Americans. The American army had also received reënforcements and was now under the command of General Greene. The Americans were not strong enough to risk a battle, but Greene managed to delay the British advance through North Carolina. The result of this

The surrender of General Cornwallis at Yorktown
(From a painting by John Trumbull in the School of Fine Arts, Yale University)

delay was that Washington and the French commanders, Admiral de Grasse and Count Rochambeau, were able to make plans to capture Cornwallis's army.

The siege of Yorktown. Cornwallis succeeded finally in making his way to Virginia, where he camped at Yorktown, and waited for the arrival of further help from General Clinton.

Meanwhile Washington had deceived Clinton into thinking that he intended to stay near New York. Instead he marched his army rapidly south until he faced the army of Cornwallis. Here he was joined by a French army which had been brought by the ships of Admiral de Grasse. The French fleet also prevented the British from bringing aid to Cornwallis.

The surrender of Cornwallis. The French and American forces worked harmoniously together. Plans were made for the attack on the British forces, intrenchments were built up, and large guns were borrowed from the fleet in order to batter down the British defenses.

Cornwallis could not obtain supplies or reënforcements, nor was he able to escape from the armies which surrounded him. After a desperate resistance he surrendered the 7000 men of his army to the American and French forces on October 19, 1781.

THE WAR ON THE SEA

The beginning of the American navy. When the Revolution first broke out, there was no Continental

"I have not yet begun to fight"
Paul Jones in the fight between the *Bon Homme Richard* and the *Serapis*
(From a group by Dwight Franklin)

navy. Congress made several attempts to provide one but without success. Fast colonial sailing vessels were armed with a few guns, and their captains were given permission to act as privateers for the purpose of capturing British trading vessels.

At first these ships did much damage to English commerce, but they were soon driven into port by the strong English navy. A few vessels had been armed and stationed in the Delaware River in the effort to prevent the British from reaching Philadelphia, but when the city was captured, this little fleet was destroyed.

John Paul Jones. The first man to raise the American flag over an American man-of-war was John Paul Jones. In 1777 Congress gave him command of a ship called the *Ranger*. Jones decided that the place to attack English commerce was near England. After crossing the Atlantic, he captured the British man-of-war *Drake*, which he took into a French port. He then succeeded in getting the French government to give him four old vessels, the largest being the famous *Bon Homme Richard*.

Benjamin Franklin, who was at this time the American representative in France, had printed a number of books of wise sayings, which he called "The Sayings of Poor Richard." Paul Jones admired these books and in honor of Franklin named his vessel *Bon Homme Richard*, which means "Good Man Richard."

Jones spent the summer cruising around the English

coast. He took many prizes and raided a number of the seaport towns. Although England had at this time probably the largest fleet in the world, it seemed as though it was not able to protect its own coast against the daring American commander.

In September he encountered a British merchant fleet guarded by several British war vessels. After a fight which lasted three hours, Jones captured the *Serapis* and the *Countess of Scarborough* and took his prizes to Holland. The British demanded that he be given up. Holland refused the demand, and Jones later escaped to France.

John Barry. John Barry came to America from Ireland when he was fifteen years old. By the time of the Revolution he had become a well-known ship captain. When he offered his services to the Congress, they were at once accepted. He was first given command of the *Lexington* and, later, of a larger vessel known as the *Effingham* and was placed in charge of the Continental naval vessels on the Delaware River and Bay. He helped to keep the British from coming up the Delaware and later kept supplies from reaching them in Philadelphia.

After the Revolution he was in charge of the building of a new navy for the United States. Barry was put in command of the *United States*, the first built of six frigates. In 1797 this vessel under Barry's command took part in the short naval war with France and captured a number of French ships.

Courtesy "The Philadelphia Evening Bulletin"

The statue of Commodore John Barry in Independence Square, Philadelphia
Exercises conducted by the Fleet Reserve Association of Philadelphia on Navy Day

The Close of the War

England decides to grant independence to the colonies. When Cornwallis surrendered, the English government realized that it was time to grant independence to America. France had succeeded in bringing Spain into the fight on its side. Other nations of Europe were almost ready to join with America.

The surrender of Cornwallis caused the British officials who had been in favor of the war to resign, and the new government was ready to make peace with America. After long discussions between the English and American peace commissioners, a treaty between England and America was signed finally on September 3, 1783. The colonies were granted their independence, the right to fish on the Newfoundland fishing banks, and the control of the Northwest, which had been gained for the Americans by the victories of George Rogers Clark.

The effect of the treaty in England and in America. When the Revolutionary War broke out, the English government was chiefly in the hands of the king. The king controlled Parliament through his friends and so was able to get it to pass any laws that he wished. When the British armies failed to force the Americans to obey the acts of Parliament, the British people lost confidence in the government of the king and his friends and sent members to Parliament who were ready to oppose the king's wishes. In this way Parliament became able to pass laws for the government of

THE COLONIES AT WAR

the colonies that England still held, which were better than the ones it had tried to force on the American colonies.

In America the treaty was with thirteen united colonies and not with thirteen separate colonies. A great territory between the Alleghenies and the Mississippi had been added to the colonies along the coast. Some of the colonies thought they had special claims to parts of this region. It was generally thought, however, that these lands belonged to the colonies as a whole. In order to get the benefits of this region and of the other rights which England had granted, it was necessary for the colonies to maintain the union which had brought them their freedom.

The condition of the colonies at the end of the war. The close of the war brought many hard problems to the new nation. The people who had remained loyal to England and who during the war were called Tories by the patriots were among the best citizens of the colonies. They were often people who were connected with the upper classes of English society and were supposed to be in sympathy with England's treatment of its colonies. Others among them were manufacturers and business men who had large dealings with England and whose business would be destroyed as a result of war. At the close of the war these people were forced to leave the colonies and had their estates and properties seized and sold by the new state officials under severe laws.

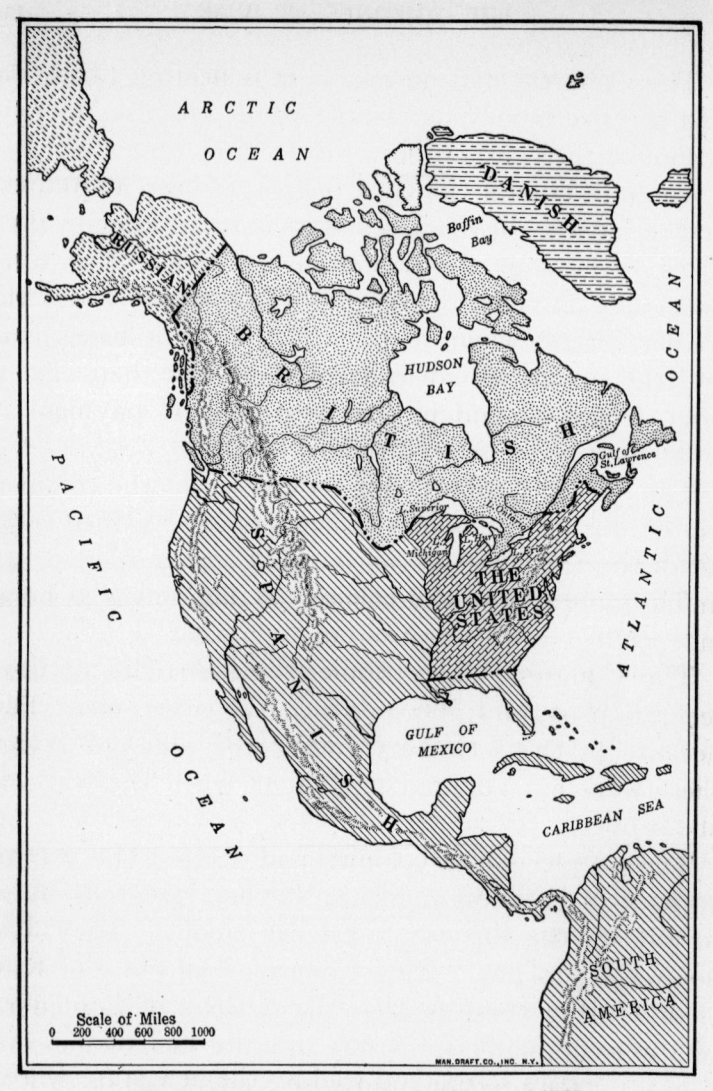

North America according to the Treaty of 1783

The Congress had no means of collecting taxes and had to raise money by issuing paper promises to pay. Although the war had been won, nobody knew whether it would be possible for the Congress to keep its promise and to redeem these notes and issue real money in their place. Many of the poorer people owed large sums of money but had no means of paying. Even the soldiers of the Continental army had not been paid, and the Congress had to grant them and their officers large tracts of land in the West in part payment of what the Congress owed them.

The necessity for sticking together held the colonists united during the war. When they had gained independence, the states began to think less and less of the union under Congress and more of themselves as being independent and separate from each other.

The Congress had submitted the Articles of Confederation to the states as a frame of government, but, because of the jealousies among the different states, these were not adopted until 1781 when the war was about over.

The people of the colonies had started the war on account of taxation and because they resented having to pay for the support of English troops. They were not willing to put " King Congress " in place of King George. For these reasons the Articles of Confederation were not sufficient firmly to unite the colonies into a single strong nation, and wise leaders began to plan a stronger form of government.

Soldiers from Europe Helped America to Win Independence

Marquis de Lafayette. After the United States had declared its independence, many foreign soldiers of high rank came to America to join Washington's army. Although some of these were of noble families, they were desirous of helping America to become free from England.

The best known of these foreign officers was Marquis de Lafayette, a young French nobleman, who was much taken with the idea of helping the United States become independent. He came to this country when he was only nineteen years old. Washington gave him a place on his personal staff. His bravery and his military knowledge soon made him a general. Lafayette was wounded at the Battle of Brandywine. He afterward accompanied Washington's army to Valley Forge and sub-

The Marquis de Lafayette
(From a mezzotint by P. L. de Bucourt)

mitted to all the privations of that terrible winter when he might have been living at home in France in comfort and in the brilliant society of the French court.

From time to time Lafayette made raids on the British outposts near Philadelphia in order to prevent them from obtaining supplies too easily. At Barren Hill, near Philadelphia, a large force of British nearly captured Lafayette and his soldiers. The young general skillfully got out of the trap and took his men safely back to Valley Forge. Later he was sent south to Virginia, where, with the help of General Wayne, he caused Cornwallis to shut himself up in Yorktown. There Cornwallis was kept until Washington and Rochambeau came and forced him to surrender.

Soon after Lafayette returned to France, he helped his French fellow citizens to get rid of their despotic king.

Many years later, in 1824, he returned to the United States as a guest of the nation. He visited every one of the twenty-four states in the Union and was astonished at the wonderful growth of the country.

Since he had sacrificed much of his fortune in coming to the help of the colonies during the Revolution, Congress made him a gift of $200,000 in appreciation of his services.

Baron von Steuben. Baron von Steuben was a skillful German soldier and nobleman who came to America about the time that Philadelphia was captured by the British. Up to this time the American troops, while skilled in the use of guns and rifles, had little idea of military discipline or of fighting against large bodies of trained troops.

When the army went into camp at Valley Forge, Washington appointed Steuben drillmaster of the army. All through the winter Steuben and American officers under his direction trained the Continental soldiers in the art of warfare against regular troops. The training received under Steuben had much to do with the later success of the American army.

Kosciuszko, Pulaski, and De Kalb. Barons Kosciuszko and Pulaski, from Poland, and De Kalb, a German, who had been in the service of France for thirty years, reached Washington's headquarters at Morristown, New Jersey, just before the British left New York to attack Philadelphia. They, like Lafayette and Von Steuben, were of great help in training the American army in European methods of warfare against skilled troops.

Kosciuszko came with a letter of introduction from Benjamin Franklin to Washington. He was a trained engineer, and Washington placed him in charge of constructing the defenses at West Point. This was only one of the important services that he rendered in the patriot cause.

Count Pulaski, who had fought for years to prevent his native land, Poland, from being divided among other countries, was put in charge of the Continental cavalry by General Washington. After two years of service for America, he died for the cause of liberty in an attack by the British at Savannah, Georgia.

Baron de Kalb came over with Lafayette and was made a major general in the Continental army. He served the colonies bravely and well. He was killed at the Battle of Camden, South Carolina, where Gates and his army were so badly defeated by the British. Many other foreign officers, less well-known, came from various countries to help the colonies win their independence. We should always keep gratefully in mind the important aid they gave us.

STUDY HELPS

Map Work

On a map of the United States east of the Mississippi indicate all the places mentioned in the story of the Revolutionary War. Outline in red the boundary of the United States as settled by the treaty with Great Britain.

Activities

Make a model of the encampment at Valley Forge or of the old State House in Philadelphia or of the Liberty Bell.

Put into your book pictures of places, people, or events connected with the Revolution, especially those associated with your own neighborhood.

Dramatize such scenes as the adoption of the Declaration of Independence or the surrender of

General Burgoyne. Many instances easily dramatized occurred during the war.

Special Work

What were the reasons that caused the Massachusetts men to propose George Washington, a Virginian, as commander in chief?

What is the story of the surrender of Fort Ticonderoga to Ethan Allen?

Why did General Howe approach Philadelphia by way of Chesapeake Bay instead of coming up the Delaware?

What is the story of the "Battle of the Kegs"?

Storybooks to Read

Canavan, M. J.: *Ben Comee: A Tale of Rogers' Rangers* (Lexington and Concord)
Cooper, James Fenimore: *The Spy* (New York)
Cooper, James Fenimore: *The Pilot* (Paul Jones)
Kaler, James Otis: *With the Swamp Fox* (the Carolinas)
Kaler, James Otis: *With Washington at Monmouth*
Kauffman, Reginald W.: *Mad Anthony's Drummer*
Knipe, E. B. and A. A.: *A Maid of '76*
Knipe, E. B. and A. A.: *Polly Trotter, Patriot*
Skinner, Constance Lindsay: *Silent Scot, Frontier Scout*
Thompson, Maurice: *Alice of Old Vincennes*
Tooker, L. Frank: *John Paul Jones*

3. PENNSYLVANIA'S PART IN THE REVOLUTION

Prominent Men

Benjamin Franklin. For many years Benjamin Franklin had been the most prominent man in Pennsylvania. He had taken a large part in the affairs of the province. You already know much that he did.

When the First Continental Congress met, Franklin was in France as the agent of Pennsylvania. The petition to the king that was adopted by the Congress was sent to Franklin to be presented to the king, but the king refused to receive it.

Franklin came back to the United States in time to be elected to the Second Continental Congress. He was made a member of the committee which prepared the Declaration of Independence. He constantly urged the need for united action. When another member of Congress said, "We must all

Benjamin Franklin at the time of the Constitutional Convention in 1787

(From a painting by Charles Wilson Peale in the Metropolitan Museum of Art)

hang together," Franklin said, " Yes, if we don't hang together, we will certainly all hang separately."

Franklin was well-known abroad, especially in France, on account of his studies about electricity. When the Congress decided to send an envoy to France, Franklin was chosen. It was largely due to his efforts that France made the treaty of alliance with us. He also was one of the commissioners that made the final treaty of peace with England.

Robert Morris. Robert Morris was a Philadelphia banker, who for a long time refused to believe that we should declare ourselves independent of Great Britain. He later changed his mind, however, and became a devoted patriot. Many times when the Congress had trouble in getting money from the states to pay the expenses of the war, Morris raised the money on his personal word that it would be repaid.

When Washington needed money to send the American troops to Yorktown against Cornwallis, Robert Morris was able to borrow $500,000 from the French to help Washington out. After the victory, when the unpaid soldiers threatened to march to Philadelphia to demand their pay from Congress, Morris went from house to house among his friends and so raised money to pay the troops part of what was owed to them. He was also very influential in persuading the people of Pennsylvania to ratify the new Constitution in 1787.

Later, Morris became bankrupt through speculation

Robert Morris in his office
(From a painting by Stanley M. Arthurs)

in land and had to go to prison for not paying his debts. He was later released and died in 1806.

Anthony Wayne. General Anthony Wayne was a Pennsylvanian who joined the Continental army in 1776. He was soon made a general and put in command of the Pennsylvania regiments. He fought at Brandywine and at Germantown. He spent the winter at Valley Forge with the rest of the Continental army and accompanied Washington across New Jersey in pursuit of the British.

At this time the British held Stony Point, a strong position on the Hudson not far from New York. Washington decided that, for the safety of his army, this British outpost had to be taken, and selected General Wayne to do the work. With a small body of picked men, Wayne silently approached the fort. He had ordered the soldiers to remove the powder from their guns, so

The equestrian statue of General Anthony Wayne at Valley Forge

This statue was erected by the Commonwealth of Pennsylvania.

that the British might not be warned by an accidental shot. By a sudden rush the Americans succeeded in capturing the fort with five hundred prisoners.

After the war England delayed the giving up of the posts that were held in the West because Congress had failed to pay the loyalists for property they had lost as was agreed upon by the treaty.

Some of the commanders of these forts kept the Indians stirred up against the Americans. General Wayne was sent out to the Ohio country, where he tried to make peace with the Indians, but the raids continued. Wayne now decided to use his army and pursued the Indians until he had most of them surrounded at a place called Fallen Timbers. In the battle which followed, the Indians were so badly beaten that no serious attempt afterward was made by them to interfere with the settlers. The Indians said, " The whites now have a chief that never sleeps." Wayne died at Fort Erie in Pennsylvania, and in 1809 his remains were removed to Radnor, near Philadelphia, where they now rest in St. David's churchyard.

Important Events

First Continental Congress. Among the important events that occurred in Pennsylvania during the Revolutionary War was the meeting of the First Continental Congress. You have already learned (p. 281) that this body met in Carpenters' Hall in Philadelphia. Its most important act was the adoption of the

Declaration of Rights which presented the colonial side of the dispute to the king and to the people of England. It sent also a petition to the king and agreed to carry on no trade with England until England recognized the rights of the colonists. The Congress also tried to bring in Canada and the West India colonies on the American side.

The Second Continental Congress. The Second Continental Congress met in Philadelphia in the old State House (pp. 290–291). You have read about many of its activities. The most important things that this Congress did was to adopt the Declaration of Independence and the Articles of Confederation, a form of government for the new nation. These articles put into exact form what Congress was actually doing in carrying on the war. It was found that the articles had many defects. It was later necessary to make a strong constitution in order that the states might really become a united nation. The Congress also made Washington commander in chief of the Continental army and adopted a national flag.

The Congress did many other things during the war that it had no real authority to do, but the people were willing that this should be so since there was no other way by which the war could possibly be won.

On several occasions, when the British threatened Philadelphia and later actually occupied the city, the Congress packed up its papers and moved out of danger. The first time it went to Baltimore. Later, when the British occupied Philadelphia, the Congress moved first to Lancaster, and then to York, Pennsylvania.

The Congress held its sessions at York from September 30, 1777, to June 27, 1778. While here the Congress framed the Articles of Confederation and offered them to the states for adoption. The Congress also received word from Benjamin Franklin at this time that the French government was ready to aid the Americans in their struggle for liberty, and it received the first money aid from France in June, 1778. Much of the Continental money ordered by Congress was printed in a house situated at Market and Beaver Streets on a press owned by Benjamin Franklin.

General Lafayette, at a dinner given by General Gates at York during this period, offered a toast to General Washington with the sentiment that he should remain commander in chief until the war was over. This indicated to the members of the Conway cabal that their plan for replacing Washington with General Gates had been discovered, and the plan itself immediately collapsed.

After the surrender of Cornwallis when some of the soldiers proposed to march to Philadelphia to demand their pay, Congress moved to Princeton, New Jersey, for a short time until the trouble was over.

The Liberty Bell. When the old State House was built in Philadelphia, many years before the Revolution, it was decided to place a bell in the tower, and one was ordered from England. When the bell arrived, it was found to be damaged, and Philadelphia workmen were engaged to recast it. The following words were molded around the top of the bell, as a motto: " Proclaim liberty throughout all the land and to all the inhabitants thereof."

Years later, when independence was declared (p. 296), the bell fulfilled this motto by joyfully ringing out the news of the birth of the United States. Since then the bell has been known as the *Liberty Bell*.

About fifty years after the Revolution the bell was badly cracked while being tolled for the death of John Marshall, Chief Justice of the Supreme Court, and ever since it has been preserved as a special object of veneration by the people.

Photo from Ewing Galloway
The Liberty Bell, now in Independence Hall on Chestnut Street in Philadelphia

When Congress moved to Lancaster at the time of the British occupation of Philadelphia, it was ordered that the Liberty Bell and the church bells should be removed in order to prevent them from falling into the hands of the British. The Liberty Bell was taken to Allentown by the way of Bethlehem, where it was buried in the cellar of the Zion Reformed Church in that city. After the Revolution it was brought back in triumph to Philadelphia.

The first American flag. At the beginning of the Revolution and for several years thereafter there was no American flag. A few of the troops of the different states had state flags. Most of the companies of soldiers had adopted special flags for their own group. A favorite design was that of a rattlesnake, ready to strike, with the motto, " Don't tread on me! "

Later what was known as the Grand Union flag was used, which consisted of thirteen red and white stripes for the thirteen colonies. The flag of Great Britain was placed where the stars are in our present American flag. This was to show that the colonies still felt themselves to be subjects of Great Britain.

Soon after independence was declared, it was thought necessary to have a different flag. On June 14, 1777, the Congress resolved that the flag of the United States should have thirteen stripes, alternately red and white, with thirteen stars arranged in a circle on a blue field.

General Washington, Robert Morris, and Colonel Ross, the committee in charge, called upon Mrs. Betsy Ross at her home to get her to make a sample flag. Under their direction she made the first United States

The flag committee calling on Betsy Ross to have her make the first American flag
This house is still standing on Arch Street near Second in Philadelphia. (From a painting by Stanley M. Arthurs)

PENNSYLVANIA'S PART IN THE REVOLUTION

flag. Her work was well done, and later she was authorized to make other flags for the use of the army.

The first place where the flag was flown was probably over Fort Stanwix in New York in 1777. It was first used in battle at the Battle of Brandywine. It was first saluted by a foreign nation when John Paul Jones sailed his ship into a French port. June 14 is now celebrated as Flag Day all over our land.

Important Places

Events near Philadelphia. At the time of the Revolution Philadelphia was not only the chief city of the state but was the largest city in all the colonies. Because the Congress met there, it became a special object of attack by the British since they thought that, if they could capture the capital where the Congress met, the Revolution would soon be over.

Many important events of the Revolution, therefore, happened in or near Philadelphia. Perhaps the most important was the day-to-day work of the Continental Congress in carrying on the war. Philadelphia was also the scene of the first reading of the Declaration of Independence and of its announcement to the people by the ringing of the old Liberty Bell.

Forts Mercer and Mifflin, on opposite sides of the Delaware, just below Philadelphia, were successfully held against the attempts of the British to reach Philadelphia by way of the Delaware River. They were afterward captured after a stubborn defense when the British occupied the city. The Battles of Brandywine and Germantown were part of the Philadelphia campaign. What is known as the *Paoli Massacre*, in which part of Wayne's troops were destroyed by the British, took place not far from the city. Frequent skirmishes also took place along the northern edge of the city when British troops, sent out from time to time to obtain supplies, encountered scouting parties from Washington's army.

Other places where important incidents of the Revolution occurred, such as Valley Forge, Lancaster, York, and Allentown, have already been mentioned at their appropriate places in the story.

Contrast in Warfare

Differences in methods of fighting in 1776 and to-day. In 1776 war was carried on very differently from the way it is carried on to-day. In those days the soldiers were usually dressed in bright colors with plenty of shining metal in the form of buttons and belt buckles on their clothing. The guns they used had to be loaded by pouring powder down the muzzles and then ramming the bullet down on top of it. These guns could not shoot very far, and most of them not very straight. Some of the Western hunters had succeeded in making guns with very long barrels and with grooves on the inside of the barrel. These could shoot farther and straighter than the ordinary muskets.

The cannon were mostly made of cast iron and were not very large or strong. It would have been dangerous to put a large quantity of powder in them; so the best of them could not throw the shot much over a mile.

On account of the bad roads transportation of supplies and food to the armies was very difficult. The soldiers generally had to depend upon getting their supplies from the people who lived in the neighborhood of the camp. For this reason armies did not stay very long in one place.

There were no such things as airships or airplanes to discover the position of the enemy or to destroy the enemy's camps and fortifications by bombs. Radio and the telegraph had not been invented. The only way the officers could learn what was going on or send orders to their soldiers was by messengers on horseback or on foot.

Battles in which large numbers of men or many separated bodies of troops were used could not be fought. On the other hand, because there was no easy and quick way of sending information, it often was easy to surprise the enemy by sudden attacks.

Warfare to-day. To-day war is carried on very differently. Soldiers are dressed in dull-colored uniforms so that at a little distance the color of their clothes blends with the color of the ground. Shining metal is forbidden on their uniforms since the enemy might see the glint of the sun on the metal and so discover their position.

The guns are made of special kinds of strong steel so that heavier charges of powder can be used that will carry a bullet for several miles. The powder and the bullet are put together in a copper or brass case, called a *cartridge*, which can easily be slipped in at the rear

U. S. Signal Corps

American machine gunners in the thick of the fight near Château-Thierry in the World War

end of the gun barrel. Machine guns have been invented which use cartridges about the size of the ordinary rifle cartridge, and which, by means of special machinery, can be fired several hundred times a minute.

The cannon are even more powerful. During the World War Germany invented a cannon that could

Photo from Ewing Galloway

A United States submarine equipped with a long-range wireless

fire a shot weighing several hundred pounds a distance of 65 miles, or two thirds of the distance from Philadelphia to New York.

The radio and telegraph have made it possible for a single commanding general to direct the movements of

Photo by U. S. Army Signal Corps
The terror of the submarines — a U. S. destroyer

a million men in order to bring about the capture of a single section of the enemy's defenses.

Information of the position of the enemy's forces is brought to him through observations made by airplanes. These flying machines can also carry destructive bombs and drop them on the enemy's camps, intrenchments, or supply depots. By the use of bombs containing poisonous gases, it is possible to render large bodies of troops unfit for fighting for a considerable time, if not permanently.

Just as important changes have been made in methods of warfare at sea. Instead of wooden sailing ships, with a large number of small guns that were only useful when the ships were very close together, warships are now huge fortresses of steel, driven through the water at high speed by powerful engines. These ships can move in any direction they wish, no matter which way the wind is blowing. Their huge guns can fire a shot weighing a ton a distance of fifteen or twenty miles. It is possible for a naval battle to take place without the gunners' being able to see the ships they are trying to hit. Another important modern invention is the submarine. This underwater boat can approach an enemy vessel without being seen and so can get close enough to destroy it with a powerful torpedo. War has now become so terrible and so destructive that the victor in a war is almost as badly off as the loser.

STUDY HELPS

Map Work

On a map of the Middle States indicate all the places in Pennsylvania or in campaigns near Philadelphia where events of the Revolution took place.

Activities

Collect for your book pictures of places or events connected with the Revolution in Pennsylvania, such as the State House, Liberty Bell, Washington's headquarters at Valley Forge, etc.

Dramatize the scene in which the committee of Congress visits Betsy Ross to have her make the first flag.

Dramatize the visits of Robert Morris to his friends for the purpose of collecting money for Washington's army.

Make a copy of the first American flag.

Special Work

What is the story of the Meschianza?

Learn the story of Lydia Darrah, and tell it to the class.

What is the story of General Sullivan's expedition against the Indians?

Learn the story of the Wyoming Massacre.

Storybooks to Read

Altsheler, Joseph A.: *In Hostile Red* (Philadelphia and Monmouth Campaign)
Mitchell, S. Weir: *Hugh Wynne*
Skinner, Constance Lindsay: *Debby Barnes, Trader*
Tomlinson, Everett T.: *Mad Anthony's Young Scout*
Tomlinson, Everett T.: *Marching Against the Iroquois* (Sullivan's Expedition)

UNIT V. THE DEVELOPMENT OF THE CONSTITUTION

Drafting the Declaration of Independence

The members of the committee were Franklin, Jefferson, Adams, Livingston, and Sherman. (From an engraving after a painting by Alonzo Chappel)

Washington as president of the Constitutional Convention of 1787
(From a mural by Violet A. Oakley, copyrighted by Curtis & Cameron, Inc.)

FORECAST OF UNIT V

In this unit you will learn how the English colonies gradually developed from small settlements dependent on the home country into strong colonies which were self-supporting; how they were able to defend themselves against their French rivals and hostile Indians; and how their desire for freedom led to the development of a new form of government unlike any that had ever before existed in the world.

You will be interested in the growth of the idea of united action on the part of the colonists. This idea finally led to the Stamp Act Congress which sought some united way of resisting the increasing efforts of the British government to bring the colonies under closer control.

The two Continental Congresses show that the colonists had learned the lesson that in union there is strength. You will also be interested in learning why the Articles of Confederation, which were intended to weld the thirteen colonies into a strong union, were not even so successful as the Continental Congress had been in holding the colonies together.

You will learn the stories of the wise leaders who saw that only by sacrifices of some of their rights would the states be able to form a nation that would be recognized by other countries and how their thoughts and plans resulted in the formation and adoption of our Constitution. Finally you will learn how the whole nation turned to Washington as the one who, as our first President, could wisely start the new country on its march to the power and importance it holds to-day in the world. When you have finished this unit, you should be able to appreciate the wisdom and foresight of the makers of the Constitution who were able to devise a system of government that worked effectually for a population of less than four million people and yet is to-day effectual in governing one hundred and twenty million.

UNIT V. THE DEVELOPMENT OF THE CONSTITUTION

The preamble to the Constitution as it appears on the original document

STEPS LEADING TO A NEW GOVERNMENT

Growth of the Idea of Union

Why the idea of union was slow in growth. When the king from time to time gave land in America to companies or individuals, it was felt to be important that these grants should not conflict with each other. For this reason it was the custom at first to leave between two grants large tracts of land which would be left to future settlement.

As the demand for land in America grew, these intervening stretches of territory were given to other companies or individuals. Sometimes the same piece of land was given to two or three different groups. As the result there was much jealousy and many disputes among the different claimants. Since the settlers had to buy their land from the ones who had the grant from the king, it was important for them to know just who was the real owner. Often, after a colonist had paid for his land, he would be asked to pay for it a second time by a new claimant under a grant from the king.

In this way the disputes over the boundaries of the different grants were taken up by the settlers themselves. This would tend to keep the colonies separate on account of the bad feelings that arose between neighboring colonies.

Another reason for the slow growth of the idea of union was that the different settlements in the various colonies were far apart and the difficulties of travel were great. It was nearly as easy to take a ship and sail to England as it was to travel by land from Pennsylvania to Virginia.

Besides there were differences in religion and in the general customs of the different colonies which also tended toward keeping them apart.

In spite of these differences there were many reasons why the colonies should be joined together. In the first place, they had all been settled by people from England. Later on, people from other countries of Europe and speaking other languages made their way to America and settled. Yet in general these formed a very small part of the total population. While there were differences in manners and customs among the different colonies, yet after all these were English manners and customs.

Early attempts at union. There were a number of early attempts at union suggested during the first one hundred years of the colonial period. The first of these was the New England Confederation which was formed in 1643. The New England colonies were worried for fear the Dutch settlers in New York might attack some of their outlying settlements. The Pequot Indians, whose lands lay between the English and the Dutch, were also inclined to be hostile. To protect themselves against the possibility of attack from these groups, the colonies of Massachusetts Bay, Connecticut, New Haven, and Hartford joined together in a confederation for mutual protection. There were to be two representatives from each colony, and the votes of six representatives could decide any question. This union worked very well for about ten years (p. 126).

In 1697 William Penn made the suggestion that all the colonies should unite in the appointment of a congress composed of two representatives from each colony. This congress was to provide for the common defense of all the colonies and for other matters of general benefit.

A few years before this the English government had made an attempt at a union of the Northern colonies. According to this plan all of New England, New York, and the two Jerseys were united under Governor Andros. This plan would have still left the colonies with their different kinds of governments, and, unless the English government had given them new charters, there would have been no real union.

In 1690 New York, Massachusetts, Plymouth, and Connecticut sent representatives to meet at New York for the purpose of making plans for an attack on Montreal during King William's War. Some of the colonies failed to furnish their quota of troops; so the proposed plan fell through.

The Albany congress. About the time that the French and Indian War broke out, delegates of all the colonies north of Virginia, except New Jersey and Delaware, met at Albany. It was intended that this congress should make plans for the general protection of all the colonies against the French and Indians. At this congress Franklin presented a plan for the union of all the colonies. After some changes this plan was adopted. However, both the king and the colonies rejected it. The king did not like it because it provided that the colonial assemblies should appoint the representatives to the colonial congress. The colonies did not like it because it provided that Parliament could change the form of their government, and many of the colonies felt that they would not be changed for the better.

There were several good results, however, that came from this congress. First, the colonists got the idea of coming together to settle matters of general importance to the colonies as a whole. Besides, it brought many of the most prominent men in the colonies together and gave them a chance to find out that many of the troubles that were thought to belong to a single colony were really difficulties that were common to all of them.

The Stamp Act Congress. After the passage of the Stamp Act, nine colonies sent representatives to a congress held in New York, called the *Stamp Act Congress*. This has sometimes been called the first congress of the Revolution. For several weeks the delegates debated the right of England to tax the colonies. There was not much said about the charters of the colonies since some of these were more liberal than others. The members talked about their rights as Englishmen and the need for standing together to protect those rights. One member said that there should be "No New Yorker or New Englander, but all of us Americans."

This congress adopted a Declaration of Rights and Grievances and declared that there was no way of taxing the colonies except by representatives chosen by themselves. For this reason the Stamp Act and other new acts violated the rights and liberties of the colonists.

The First and Second Continental Congress. Up to this time the colonies were more and more becoming accustomed to the idea of joining together for mutual support and combined resistance to England's oppressive laws.

So when Parliament attempted to punish Boston and Massachusetts for the destruction of the tea, it was to be expected that the Massachusetts Committee of Correspondence would send letters to the other colonies asking that something be done to help them.

As you have already learned, many of the colonies sent help, and all of them supported the resistance of Massachusetts. Virginia suggested the calling of a Congress to consider the grievances, not only of Massachusetts, but of all the colonies.

To this Congress delegates came from all the colonies except Georgia. They promised aid to Massachusetts and presented an address to the people of England, and also to other English colonies, explaining their side of the story. Their petition to the king was refused acceptance when it was presented to him by Benjamin Franklin.

With the outbreak of the Revolution the Second Congress came together with representatives from all the colonies, and, as you already know, it took care of the government during the war. The colonies simply had to act together; otherwise the war could not have been won. We can see to-day how they might have joined together in a much better fashion. We must remember, however, that it was a great thing for these different colonies, which considered themselves independent of each other, to stick together as well as they did.

Growth of the Idea of Independence

Beginnings of the idea of independence. It is very hard to say just when the idea of independence arose among the colonies. It is likely that some people thought of separation from the mother country very early in the history of the colonies. It began to be generally talked about at the time of the French and Indian War. The name, "Sons of Liberty," had been given in New York even before that time to those who opposed the power of the royal governor. It was easy for this name to be applied to those who were opposed to any form of English rule in the colony. A traveler who visited the colonies in 1760 said, "The Pennsylvanians are great republicans and have fallen into the same ideas of independency as most of the other colonies."

In Massachusetts Samuel Adams, who was the clerk of the Boston town meeting, wrote to the other colonial assemblies, suggesting that they all act together in their opposition to the unjust English acts. He continued to stir up opposition to England in his correspondence with the other colonies.

As clerk of the town meeting he understood very well the feelings of the people of Massachusetts and was one of the first to realize that there was a strong feeling for independence in that colony.

Desire for independence increased by English reprisals. The addresses, petitions, and other papers adopted by the different assemblies and Congresses were sent out with the idea of finding a plan or arrangement by which the colonies and the English government could in some way smooth over their differences. If this could have been done, the colonists would have been content to remain subjects of the king and Parliament. Unfortunately every time this attempt was made, the English government either passed an act or made some regulation that made the colonists angrier that they were before.

Although the right to petition the king for a redress

Photo from Ewing Galloway

An early New England town meeting

Note the men casting their votes into a hat held by one of them and the blockhouse behind the trees on the left. (From a painting by Max Bohm in the Law Library of the Cuyahoga County Court House, Cleveland)

of grievances is one of the strongly held rights of Englishmen, the king refused to accept the petition of the Congress. Parliament declared the Americans rebels, and it sent warships and soldiers to make war on them and force them into obedience. It was determined to make the colonists pay the expenses of the soldiers that were to keep them in subjection.

The thing that especially angered the colonists was that King George had hired, from one of the little countries which is now included in Germany, foreign soldiers who were to beat down the opposition of the Americans.

Building up independence in the Congress. Six months before the Declaration of Independence was passed, probably only the delegates from Massachusetts to the Second Continental Congress were in favor of independence. The five Middle colonies had gone so far as to instruct their delegates against independence.

Virginia probably sided with Massachusetts, and in May, 1776, it instructed its delegates to propose that the colonies be declared free and independent states.

When John Adams reached Pennsylvania on his way to the Continental Congress, he said that he was met by some of the Sons of Liberty in Philadelphia. These men told him that he must not utter the word *independence* either in Congress or out of it. He was not careful to follow this advice, and it soon became known that he was in favor of independence. Consequently, the Quakers and other important people of the community thought him one of the worst of men.

As news came from time to time of the determination of the English government to force obedience to its unjust laws, one after another became convinced of the necessity for independence.

The Declaration of Independence. As you have learned (p. 295), in May, 1776, the Congress requested the various states to send instructions to their delegates regarding independence. When it was found that most of the instructions were in favor of separation, Richard Henry Lee of Virginia, on July 2, proposed a resolution that the colonies were free and independent states. The resolution was seconded by John Adams of Massachusetts, and a committee was appointed to draw up a declaration to that effect. The committee consisted of Thomas Jefferson, John Adams, Benjamin Franklin, Roger Sherman, and Robert R. Livingston. Thomas Jefferson did the actual writing of the declaration.

Contents of the Declaration. The contents of the Declaration of Independence may be divided into a number of different sections. The first is the preamble, in which it is stated that, when a country decides to separate from another, the reasons which lead to the separation should be set forth. The second section gives the reasons why governments are necessary and reasons which might lead to a change. The third group is a series of statements which set forth the tyrannical acts of the king and Parliament of England. This is

Congress voting independence

Benjamin Franklin is seated in the chair near the middle of the picture. Robert Morris is prominent at the left. Jefferson stands in front of the table. (This painting which belongs to the Historical Society of Pennsylvania was begun by Robert Edge Pine and finished by Edward Savage.)

followed by a statement of the unsuccessful efforts of the colonies to secure a hearing and the redress of their grievances. Finally, there is the declaration that " these united colonies are of right and ought to be free and independent states; that they are absolved from all allegiance to the British crown; and that all political connection between them and the state of Great Britain is and ought to be totally dissolved."

The Articles of Confederation. At the same time that the Congress appointed a committee to draw up the Declaration of Independence, it also appointed a committee to draw up a form of government for the United States. After the committee worked on this for a year, Congress approved the Articles of Confederation and sent them to the states for adoption.

Although these articles did not provide for anything very different from that which the Congress was actually doing in holding the colonies together and conducting the war, there was considerable opposition to them. The last colony did not adopt the Articles until 1781, only six months before Cornwallis surrendered.

Difficulties of the Congress during the Revolution. Without any real authority the Congress had great difficulty in managing a successful war. There was still a great amount of jealousy among the different states. The people of the states were sometimes not very much interested in the success of the war when their own state seemed not to be in danger.

Because of the absence of a strong central authority

the Congress was not able to enforce its orders. The different states often refused to furnish the Congress with their fair share of the money, supplies, and troops necessary to carry on the war.

Difficulties of the Congress under the Confederation. The Confederation was stated to be a firm league of friendship among the several states. There was only one house of Congress to which each state sent from two to seven delegates. Each state had only one vote no matter how many delegates represented it. There was no president but only a committee of the states, which was composed of one member from each state. There were no judges, and any question concerning the Articles had to be decided by a vote of the Congress. Matters concerning war, money, and taxes, international affairs, and disputes between the states were in charge of the Congress, but that body had no power to enforce its decisions. The Articles could only be amended by the unanimous vote of all the states.

The defects of the Articles of Confederation. The defects of the Articles of Confederation lay chiefly in the fact that the Congress had no means of compelling the states to furnish the money necessary to run the government nor to furnish the men for the army that was under the control of the Congress. It did not have any power over commerce and trade. As soon as the Revolution was over, the different states proceeded to impose taxes and duties on the commerce with other colonies as well as with foreign nations. These matters were the very same ones about which the Revolution had been fought. The states were all afraid that, if they gave the Congress too much power, they would be in exactly the same situation they were in before the Revolution with regard to taxes and trade laws.

Many of the states issued paper money in violation of the Articles, and there were many bitter disputes over boundaries between some of the colonies, so that the Union was in danger of falling apart. This would give England the chance of reconquering the colonies one at a time.

The Articles of Confederation were useful in getting the colonies used to a central government and in showing the need for a stronger government. They also enabled the Congress to act for the whole country in dealing with other nations.

Important acts under the Confederation. The Congress succeeded in doing two important things under the Articles of Confederation: first, it succeeded in persuading the various states to give up their claims to lands beyond the Appalachians, which were included in the western territory that England had given to the United States at the end of the Revolution. It also adjusted a number of disputed claims between the different states, such as the claim of Connecticut to a large part of Pennsylvania.

Another important act was the passage of the Northwest Ordinance of 1787. This ordinance provided for the organization of the territory north of the Ohio and west of Pennsylvania. It contained three notable provisions: First, it provided that a certain part of the land should be set aside for the support of public schools. Second, slavery was forever prohibited in this territory. Finally, it provided that five states could be organized in this territory and could be admitted to the Union whenever they had a large enough population.

All the laws providing for the government of territories which the United States has passed since that time have been based on the Ordinance of 1787.

The Annapolis Convention. The states of Virginia and Maryland found it necessary to make some arrangement about navigation on the Potomac River. After several attempts it was decided to invite the other states to send delegates to a convention at Annapolis which should provide some uniform system of trade regulations in all the colonies. When the convention met, only five states had sent delegations. The convention, therefore, decided to ask the appointment of delegates from all the states to meet at Philadelphia in May, 1787.

This new convention was to propose such changes in the Articles of Confederation as would make them better adapted to the needs of the new nation. A copy of this resolution was sent to the Congress, which called for a convention at the time and place suggested.

A Demand for a Stronger Government

The Constitutional Convention. As a result of the resolution of the Annapolis Convention which had been approved by the Congress, all the states except one sent delegates to the convention which met in Philadelphia in 1787. Rhode Island was the only state that failed to send representatives.

The convention was composed of fifty-five members, most of whom were the strongest and best minds in the colonies. George Washington was chosen president of the convention. It was resolved that all the meetings should be in secret. Consequently the only information that we have about what happened in the debates on the different questions that arose is taken from the notes made by members of the convention. The notes made by James Madison of Virginia, afterward President of the United States, are the most complete.

Prominent members of the convention. Among the important members of the convention there are some names that stand out above all the others. George Washington, who acted as president of the convention, has already been mentioned. As president he could not take sides in the open debate, but, from what we know of his later actions when he became President, we may be sure that he lent his great influence to the establishment of a strong, united government that would be powerful enough to be recognized as a nation by all the world.

Another prominent member was the aged Benjamin Franklin, whose many public services, both before and during the Revolution, you already know something about. During the convention Franklin's most important services were rendered in bringing people with different opinions together and wisely persuading each one to give up part of his beliefs for the sake of harmony.

Alexander Hamilton, the young friend of Washington, rendered important help as one of those in the convention who stood for a strong central government. His chief services were, however, rendered after the convention had finished its work and the Constitution was offered to the states for adoption. Many of the states felt that the new form of government gave the central government too much power. Hamilton, Madison, and John Jay published a series of papers called *The Federalist*, urging the adoption of the Constitution. These men by means of these papers had much to do with the adoption of the Constitution in some of the doubtful states.

> In the PRESS,
> and speedily will be published,
> THE
> FEDERALIST,
> A Collection of Essays written in favor of the New Constitution.
> By a Citizen of New-York.
> Corrected by the Author, with Additions and Alterations.
>
> *This work will be printed on a fine Paper and good Type, in one handsome Volume duodecimo, and delivered to subscribers at the moderate price of one dollar. A few copies will be printed on superfine royal writing paper, price ten shillings.*
> *No money required till delivery.*
>
> *To render this work more complete, will be added, without any additional expence,*
>
> PHILO-PUBLIUS,
> AND THE
> *Articles of the Convention,*
> *As agreed upon at Philadelphia, September 17th, 1787.*

An advertisement of *The Federalist* published in the Philadelphia *Independent Gazetteer*

James Madison, whose notes tell us almost all we know about the work of the convention, had with the help of others from Virginia prepared beforehand a plan which contained almost all the important provisions of the Constitution.

James Wilson, a delegate from Pennsylvania, ably backed Madison, Hamilton, and the others in the convention who saw clearly that the need of the United States was a strong, central government.

Work of the convention. While the convention was called to revise the Articles of Confederation, it was soon found that to make these articles a satisfactory basis for government would require so many changes that all the states would probably not adopt them. The convention then decided to build up a new plan of union which would go into effect among those states which were willing to accept it.

The greatest difficulty was in bringing the large and small states together. The small states desired that each state should have only one vote, as in the Continental Congress. The large states wished to have representation and voting according to the population of the various states. This difficulty was settled by providing two houses of Congress. In the one, the states were to be equally represented; in the other, representation and votes were in proportion to the population.

Another difficulty arose over counting the slaves in the population. The Northern States, where there

The signing of the Constitution

Washington is sitting in the "rising-sun" chair at the desk. Franklin is standing at the left side of the picture. (From a painting by Albert Herter in the Supreme Court at the State Capitol, Madison, Wisconsin)

Photo from Ewing Galloway

were few slaves, thought the slaves should not be counted. The Southern States thought that they should be included in the population on which representation was based. This dispute was settled by providing that three fifths of the slaves should be counted. The Northern and Southern States also differed over the question of importing slaves. It was finally agreed that this should not be forbidden until 1808.

The Constitution is sent to the states for adoption. After the convention had finished the Constitution, a committee, of which Gouverneur Morris of Pennsylvania was chairman, wrote the Constitution in its final form. It was then sent to the states for ratification. Delaware, a small state, was the first to ratify the Constitution. Pennsylvania was the second.

In many of the states much opposition developed. Most of this opposition arose because the leaders in those states felt that the central government had been given entirely too much power and the rights of the people had not been protected.

In time, however, a majority of the people in all states adopted the view of Benjamin Franklin who had said, "I consent, sir, to this Constitution because I expect no better, and because I am not sure that it is not the best."

Opinions of the Constitution. The Constitution has come to be looked upon as one of the greatest documents of the world. It is the fundamental law of the oldest republic on earth. As other republics have from time to time been established, they have written into their constitutions many of the provisions of ours.

Gladstone, a great English statesman, called it "the greatest work ever struck off at any time by the mind and purpose of man."

On the back of the chair on which Washington, as president of the convention, sat, a picture of a rising

The Ninth PILLAR erected ?
"The Ratification of the Conventions of nine States, shall be sufficient for the establishment of this Constitution, between the States so ratifying the same." *Art.* vii.
INCIPIENT MAGNI PROCEDERE MENSES.

If it is not up it will rife. The Attraction muft be irrefiftible

DEL. PEN. N-JER. GEOR. CON. MASSA. MARY. S°CARO. N.HAMP. VIRG. N. YORK

The adoption of the Constitution
The artist indicates that nine states have already ratified, which puts the Constitution into effect. Virginia is on its way while New York will be unable to hold out.

sun was painted. While the last members were signing, Benjamin Franklin said that he had often in the course of the sessions looked at the design on the president's chair, without knowing whether the sun was rising or setting; "but now," he said, "I have the happiness to know that it is a rising, and not a setting, sun."

The Constitution goes into effect. The Constitution provided that, when it had been ratified by nine states, it was to go into effect among those nine. When the Congress was informed that nine states had ratified the

Mount Vernon — the home of George Washington

Constitution, arrangements were made for the new government to go into effect by providing for the election of a President and the Congress. Meanwhile

Photo from Brown Bros.
Washington taking the oath of office as first President of the United States

two other states ratified it. Rhode Island and North Carolina declined to ratify at first, but both later joined the Union.

George Washington elected the first President. After the electors were chosen by the people of the several states in accordance with the Constitution,

STEPS LEADING TO A NEW GOVERNMENT

they met together to elect the President. George Washington of Virginia was unanimously chosen President, and John Adams of Massachusetts was chosen Vice President.

Washington once again heeded the call of his country and started for New York, which had been made the first capital. His journey was a procession through the different towns and cities along the way. Parades and receptions in honor of the new President greeted him everywhere. On account of the difficulties of travel and communication the electoral returns were not counted until April 6, and Washington did not reach New York until April 30. There on the balcony of Federal Hall Washington was publicly inaugurated the first President of the United States.

STUDY HELPS

Map Work

On a map of eastern United States show the Northwest Territory. Show also the states that ratified the Constitution prior to the election of George Washington as President.

Activities

Get pictures for your book that show men or events connected with the Constitutional Convention.

Dramatize a scene in the Constitutional Convention in which the question of equal or proportional representation is debated.

Try to obtain reproductions of the Declaration of Independence or of the first or last pages of the Constitution.

Special Work

What were some of the quarrels over trade among the states under the Confederation?

What was Shays' Rebellion in Massachusetts?

With what nations did we make treaties under the Confederation?

How many states had adopted the Constitution when Washington was elected President?

What states did not choose electors because they had not adopted the Constitution?

Books to Read

Cooke, Grace MacGowan: *The Fortunes of John Hawk* (Old New York)

Gerwig, George William: *The Declaration of Independence for Young Americans*

Nicolay, H.: *The Boys' Life of Alexander Hamilton*

Sparks, E. E.: *The Men Who Made the Nation*

UNIT VI. LAWS AND LAW ENFORCEMENT

Justice

She holds in one hand the scales as a token of impartiality and in the other hand a globe to symbolize the world. Condemnation and Acquittal are represented by two children, one of whom holds a sword and the other the dove of peace. (From a mural painting by Edward Simmons in the New York Criminal Court House, copyright by Curtis & Cameron, Inc.)

Good Administration

In her right hand she holds evenly the scales of justice; on her lap is the book of the law; at her feet, on either side, is an urn; into one of these a maiden is winnowing wheat; into the other urn an eager youth, with books of knowledge under his arm is casting his ballot. (From a mural painting by Elihu Vedder in the Library of Congress, copyright by Curtis & Cameron, Inc.)

FORECAST OF UNIT VI

By the study of this unit you will learn how a great deal of the material wealth of Pennsylvania has been used up since the time of William Penn. Not only have the forests been cut down and the products of our mines used without regard for the future, but the flowers, the birds, and the other wild life that were important natural attractions of the state when it was founded have rapidly disappeared. Some have been already exterminated from the state. Through carelessness and disregard for the rights of others some people have been able to profit for themselves at the expense of the rest of the people. Some wicked persons have even gone so far as to adulterate the food that goes on our tables and the medicine that the doctor gives sick people to make them well.

You will be interested in learning that through wise laws Pennsylvania is trying to repair as far as is possible the damage that has been done and to prevent a continuation of such unsocial practices by selfish people. New forests are being planted that will in time supply our needs for lumber. Conservation laws have resulted in better practices in dealing with the mineral resources of the state so that there will be less waste and therefore greater reserves for future generations. Laws controlling hunting and fishing have resulted in a large increase in the wild life of the state and have made it possible for the people to gain greater pleasure from its recreational resources. You will learn also that the successful enforcement of these laws is not a matter for public officials alone but is the duty of every citizen, whether man or woman, boy or girl, in the state.

UNIT VI. LAWS AND LAW ENFORCEMENT

Government

In this picture the artist depicts the outstanding marks of a successful free government — strength, fairness, democracy, restraint, security, and justice. (From a mural painting by Elihu Vedder in the Library of Congress, copyright by Curtis & Cameron, Inc.)

THE GOOD OF ALL IS THE GOAL OF WISE LAWMAKERS

The Need for Laws

Why laws are necessary. A law is only another name for a regulation or rule that tells us how to behave or what to do under certain circumstances. The principal difference is that laws are made by some public authority that has the right to make them and represents, therefore, the opinion or will of the people as a whole. A rule or a regulation usually applies to a smaller part of the population and is privately made by agreement of those concerned.

All of us have played games of one kind or another, and we all know the need for rules if the games are to be played properly. If the players on a baseball team would refuse to abide by the rules, there simply could be no baseball game.

Sometimes in school it is necessary to have rules governing the movements of the pupils through the corridors and on the stairways as well as their behavior on the playground. These rules are different in purpose from those for playing a game. In the first place, they make it easier for boys and girls to make their way about the school building. They also make it safer since they help avoid crowding in the halls and stairways and prevent rough play that might cause injury in the schoolyard.

Sometimes there are other rules that are intended to protect the health of pupils, such as those requiring pupils not to use one another's pencils, and others to prevent the destruction of school property.

Laws are made to help us. You can see then that laws made by our government are very much the same as rules for a game or the rules that govern behavior in school. Some of these laws, like the traffic regulations, laws relating to health, and laws against crimes, are made to protect us in our daily lives.

Other laws are sometimes made in order that we may get more enjoyment out of life. The United States

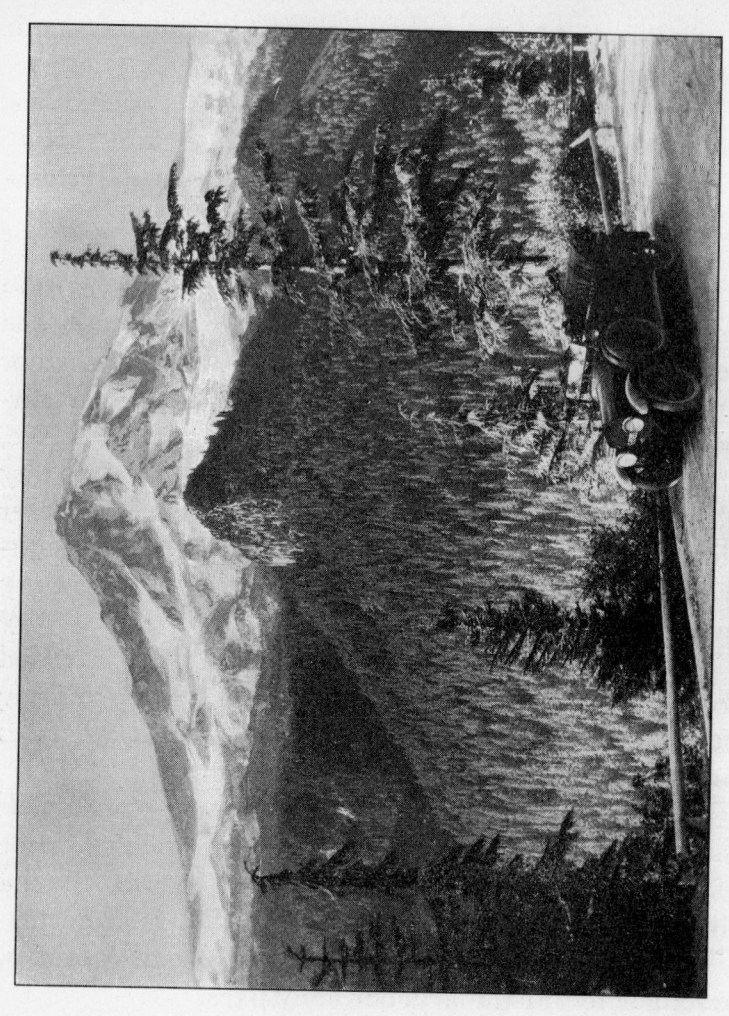

Mt. Rainier in Rainier National Park

Government has set apart, at different places in our country, what are known as *national parks*. These are places often of great natural beauty. People visit them in order to enjoy the wonderful scenery they contain. Others of these national parks include spots

Courtesy Pennsylvania Department of Forests and Waters
Enjoying life in the woods
Campers in Caledonia State Forest Park, Franklin County, Pennsylvania

of historic or scientific interest, such as the homes of the cliff dwellers in Arizona or the giant trees of California.

Still other laws are those which have been made in order to prevent the unnecessary destruction, or waste, of the resources of the country. These laws apply especially to the prevention of forest destruction through the careless use of fire in forest lands. In this case destruction of life or property may also be prevented, but the chief aim is to keep our forests from being destroyed so that future citizens of our country will have sufficient lumber for their needs. These laws are known as *Conservation Laws.* Sometimes they are concerned with the preservation of wild flowers, wild birds, animals, or fish. By this means our food supply is increased, and at the same time people derive much pleasure and recreation through the opportunity to hunt and fish in the woods and streams.

Laws against bad foods. It has also been found necessary for our government to pass laws against the sale of food which is unwholesome, which has been preserved by the use of dangerous or poisonous chemicals, or has been adulterated by the use of substances that are cheaper or less wholesome. These are known as *Pure Food Laws.*

The Result of the Absence of Laws

Many species of birds, animals, and fish almost extinct. As the result of absence of laws in the past many species of beautiful birds, wild animals, and eatable fish have almost or entirely disappeared although they were once plentiful. Only a few hundred buffaloes remain in protected herds, where once there were millions. The passenger pigeon was once so numerous and traveled in such enormous flocks that their weight broke down the branches of the trees on

Courtesy Pennsylvania Game Commission

Some of the wild animals and birds of Pennsylvania

which they rested. The naturalist Audubon said that the flocks darkened the skies and that men with clubs could beat them to the ground. Not one of these birds has been seen for years. The same story is true with regard to the wild turkey, which was at one time so numerous and so easily obtained that a little over one hundred years ago twelve-pound turkeys could be bought at the rate of five for a dollar.

The Carolina parakeet, a small parrot that looks very much like the little green love birds that are often trained by pretended fortune tellers to pick cards out of a box, has almost entirely disappeared.

Flowers and shrubs exterminated. A like story may be told regarding many species of flowers and shrubs. It is true that these are more difficult to exterminate completely than birds and animals, but flowers and shrubs add very much to the natural beauties of our country. When these are destroyed in a given neighborhood by ruthlessly tearing them up by the roots, much of the beauty of that neighborhood is gone.

Adulterated and unwholesome foods sold. It is sometimes difficult to tell whether certain foods are wholesome or not by the inspection the buyer is able to give them in the store. Meats that have come from diseased animals look exactly like good meats. Others that have been made unwholesome by preserving them with poisonous chemicals cannot be told from fresh meats. Dishonest dealers can cheat the public by adulterating food, or other articles, with cheaper substances that are hard to detect. For example, it is possible to mix a large quantity of cheap cottonseed oil with expensive olive oil without its being possible to know that this has been done.

Unless these practices are forbidden by wise laws the amount of illness and disease among the people would be increased.

The Present Situation in Pennsylvania

Scarcity instead of plenty. What you have just read about the increasing scarcity of wild life, both plant and animal, and the wasting of forests in the nation, is just as true with regard to Pennsylvania.

Many animals that once were found in Pennsylvania in considerable numbers are now only found in remote parts of the United States and have disappeared entirely from this state. Among these may be mentioned the buffalo, the mountain lion, and the wolf. The passenger pigeon and the heath hen, which were mentioned by William Penn as being plentiful in the colony, have not only disappeared from Pennsylvania but appear to be completely extinct.

The growth of manufacturing industries and of mining has resulted in our streams' becoming so polluted with waste products that fish can no longer survive in them. Where our people were formerly able to get a large part of their food supply from these streams, little or none can be obtained to-day. Another reason for the scarcity of food fishes in our streams is the illegal methods of fishing that were carried on in

Courtesy Pennsylvania Department of Forests and Waters

A result of carelessness and neglect

A burned-over area in which the useful trees have been replaced by a growth of almost worthless scrub oak and pitch pine

past years, which stripped the streams of fish, leaving none to carry on the species.

The destruction of the forests. When Penn founded his colony, the forests of Pennsylvania were as large and valuable as those of New England. William Penn aimed at conserving these forest lands by introducing into his Frame of Laws a regulation that one acre in six of the trees should be left standing so as to leave a timber supply for the future. These extensive forest lands were drawn on so heavily and were so much neglected that there is now little timber left. In 1860 Pennsylvania was first among the states of the Union in the

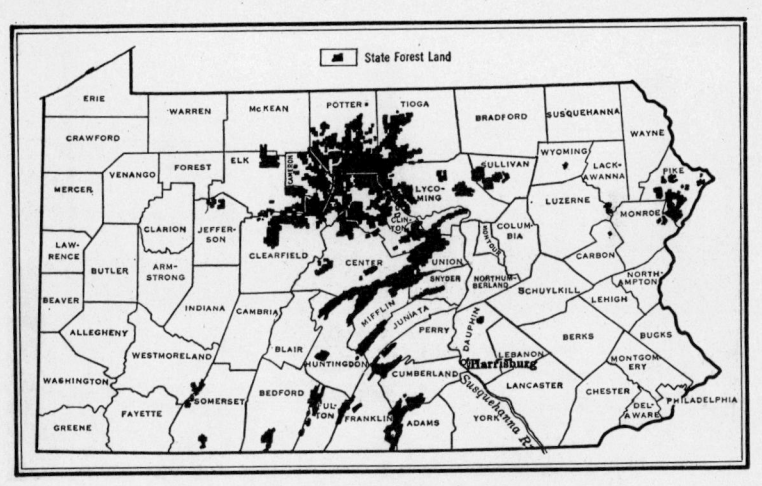

The location of the state forest lands in Pennsylvania

value of forest products; now it is eighteenth. The forests do not produce more than one sixth of the needs of the state.

About one third of the original forest area is still forest land, but the replanting was either neglected, or badly done, with the result that our forests are producing only about one tenth of the lumber and wood that they should produce.

Courtesy Pennsylvania Department of Forests and Waters
A stand of big trees in Snyder-Middlesworth State Park
Pennsylvania was almost covered with forests like this in the time of William Penn.

Protective Laws Made

Game laws. In recent years the state has made efforts to undo the damage of past years as far as that is possible. In the first place, many laws have been passed for the replacement of wild life. With the help of the Department of Forests and Waters, much progress has been made toward increasing the numbers of wild birds and animals that had almost disappeared. Streams from which the important food fishes disappeared years ago have been restocked with fish that are hatched out and protected in their early life in state fish hatcheries.

Regulation of hunting and fishing. In addition to laws that provide for the restocking of our woods and streams with wild animals, birds, and food fish, additional protection has been given to our wild life by having closed seasons for most of the year during which certain animals, birds, or fish cannot be hunted or caught. These closed seasons vary for the different species. As a result our forest regions are once again beginning to support wild life to an amount which compares very well with that of colonial days. Some of the damage that was done through unregulated hunting and fishing can never be repaired, but at least it need not become worse. There is hope that, through the wise regulations of our forest and game laws, there will be a continued increase in the wild life of the state.

Other laws which have been passed, such as those forbidding the destruction of wild flowers, should in time bring our woods and countrysides back to the natural beauty that they had in the days of Penn.

Courtesy Pennsylvania Department of Forests and Waters
The wild creatures are returning to our forests.
A beaver dam in Fulton County, Pennsylvania

In a letter to the Free Society of Traders in London Penn wrote, "The woods are adorned with lovely flowers for color, greatness, and variety. I have seen the gardens of London best stored with that sort of beauty but think they may be improved by our woods."

Laws protect the buyers of food. Another important group of laws seeks to protect the buyers of food. Food that has been kept so long in storage that it is likely to be unwholesome may not be sold for human food. In case it has been properly stored and is wholesome, it still may not be sold as fresh food. Preservatives that are poisonous or that may cause illness are forbidden to be used.

Other laws which provide for the frequent testing of scales and measures protect the buyer from being cheated in the quantity of goods that he pays for. Still other laws forbid the substitution of one product for another without the knowledge of the buyer and prohibit the adulteration of a product with a cheaper substance even though the adulterant used may not be harmful to the body.

Thus you see that a great many of our laws have been passed for the safety and protection of the people as well as to preserve for them the resources and beauties of our great state.

Law enforcement. If you were asked, " Who makes these laws? " you would probably answer, " The Congress," or " The legislature of the state." If a second question were asked, " Who gives these bodies the right to make these laws? " there is only one answer, " All of us."

Since all of us have a share in the making of these laws, and because we live in a republic, we must agree that the majority shall rule. We should be willing to obey the laws because they have all been made for our protection and to help make our lives more pleasant and comfortable. These laws protect the community

Courtesy Pennsylvania Department of Forests and Waters
A camp site in a state forest
Note the shelters and the fireplaces.

from those people who are cruel, careless, or selfish and who only want to have their own way regardless of the rights of others.

Since everybody is responsible for making the laws and everybody is equally responsible for obeying them, let us see that enforcement and obedience start with ourselves.

If we all do this, we will, like the Greeks of old, pass

our country on to our descendants greater, better, and more beautiful than we received it.

STUDY HELPS

Map Work

On a map of Pennsylvania show the extent of the present forest regions. Outline the extent of the original forest regions.

Activities

Get pictures showing forested areas and cut-over areas; pictures of washed-out lands and floods caused by deforestation.

Get pictures of animals, flowers, and birds that are extinct or nearly so in Pennsylvania.

Make bird boxes for use about the house or garden.

Plant a tree or shrub on Arbor Day.

Special Work

Make lists of animals and of birds that used to be plentiful in Pennsylvania but which have disappeared now. In what part of the state were they formerly found?

What is the law against picking wild flowers?

What animals and birds are not protected by law? Why not?

How is Pennsylvania trying to remedy the destruction of its forests?

What are the duties of game wardens and fire wardens?

What should a person do who sees a willful violation of the law?

Books to Read

Blanchan, Neltje: *Bird Neighbors*

Burroughs, John: *Squirrels and Other Fur Bearers*

Gress, Ernest Milton: *Preservation of Wild Flowers in Pennsylvania*

Pennsylvania Department of Forests and Waters: *Lessons in Forest Protection*

PLACES OF HISTORIC INTEREST IN PENNSYLVANIA

Below will be found a list of places of historic interest in Pennsylvania arranged by counties. It is not pretended to be complete but to suggest the development of a new interest in local and county history.

The wealth of known historic places is illustrated by the fact that over two hundred and fifty forts and blockhouses were constructed in the state under the direction of the provincial assembly. This does not take into account the probably greater number that were constructed by the efforts of individuals and communities.

Much of the material here presented was obtained from books printed before some of the counties were divided. Every effort was made to list each place under its proper county, but it is possible that, under the circumstances, a few regrettable errors have been made.

ADAMS

Battlefield of Gettysburg
Sites of old ironworks — Caledonia furnace, on the Chambersburg road; Maria furnace, in Hamiltonban township
Site of Indian massacre, at Marshall's Mill

ALLEGHENY

Old blockhouse, Pittsburgh
Major Grant's camp, at the Hump, or Grant's Hill, Pittsburgh
Forbes' road, East Liberty
Braddock's last camp, near McKeesport
Point where Washington crossed the Allegheny River on his return from the French forts
Site of Braddock's defeat, in Braddock

ARMSTRONG

Site of old Indian town, Kittanning
Battle with Indians, Blanket Hill, five miles east of Kittanning
Scene of Captain Brady's affair with Indians, near mouth of Mahoning Creek

BEAVER

Site of early Moravian mission, near Darlington
Site of Logstown, near Ambridge
Site of Indian village, Mingo Town, near the Crosscreeks
Site of Fort McIntosh, Beaver, foot of Market Street
Site of blockhouse, at New Brighton
Sites of early ironworks, at Brighton
Site of early paper mill, on Little Beaver Creek
Buildings of the Harmony Society, at Economy
Indian picture rocks, near Smith's Ferry

BEDFORD

Line of Forbes' road, through the county
Site of Rystown fort, Bedford, between Richard and Juliana Streets
Sites of Martin's fort and Piper's fort
Site of Indian massacre at Tull's Hill, six miles west of Bedford
Site of Indian fight, on Bloody Run
Washington's headquarters, Pitt Street, Bedford
Site of burial place of Captain Phillips' Rangers, near Saxton
Line of underground railroad, through the county

BERKS

Site of Pilgrim Spring, a few miles north of Bethel, on top of Kittatinny Mountain
House and burial place of Conrad Weiser, a quarter mile east of Womelsdorf
Site of Hessian camp, on the hill east of Reading
Homestead of the Boone family, at Exeter, seven miles east of Reading
Site of Fort Henry, near Bethel
Site of Fort Northkill, near Strausstown
Homestead of the Lincoln family, near the Boone house
Washington stopped at Federal Inn, site now occupied by Farmers' Bank, Reading
Mayberry's forge, near Huff's Church, Hereford township, where first iron stove in America was made

i

APPENDIX

BLAIR

Site of old fort, at Hollidaysburg
Line of Indian trail through Kittanning Gap — chief trail from the West
Old portage tunnel, Hollidaysburg
Sinking Spring lead mines, Tyrone township — much lead from here was used by patriot armies during the Revolution
Fountain Inn, historic hotel, near Altoona
Old Portage Railroad, planes No. 6 to No. 10
Site of Logan House, at Altoona, where Northern governors met during the Civil War, now occupied by the post office
Site of Fort Roberdeau, 1778
Site of Fort Lowry, 1779

BRADFORD

Moravian mission to the Indians, at "Friedenshutten," Wyalusing
General Sullivan's camp, at Wyalusing
General Sullivan's camp, at Wysox
Fort Sullivan, at Tioga Point, now Athens
Spanish Hill, where Stephen Brule first entered limits of Pennsylvania in 1615
Route of General Sullivan on his expedition against the Indians in 1779 — from Wilkes-Barre to state line
Battle on Indian Hill — Colonel Hartley's expedition
"Ogehage," "Oscaline," or "Newtychanning," a noted Indian village, at the mouth of Sugar Creek
Site of old French fortifications, on Tioga Creek above Athens
Old French settlement, at Asylum
Home of Queen Esther, Athens
Home of David Wilmot (Wilmot Proviso), Towanda
Miciscum, or Great Indian Meadows, used by early Moravian settlers as hayfields
Mt. Pisgah, inclined plane for railroad; also beautiful view from summit

BUCKS

Washington's Crossing, Taylorsville
Site of building of John Fitch's steamboat, Warminster
Washington's headquarters, Neshaminy
Starting point of Indian Walk, at Wrightstown
First stopping place on Indian Walk, Ottsville
Grave of Tamanend (Tammany), near Chalfont
Keith House, Upper Wakefield, on road from Brownsburg to the Eagle Tavern — Washington's headquarters, 1776
Battle of Crooked Billet, at Hatboro
Headquarters of Hamilton, Knox, and Merricks, near Buckmanville
Site of Washington's camp, at Thomson's Woods near Bowman's Hill
Headquarters of General Greene, at Buckingham
Headquarters of Lord Sterling and De Fermoy, at New Hope
Washington's headquarters, at Newtown
Site of Log College, Warminster, on Neshaminy Creek
Camp of Washington's army, Doylestown
Camp of General Lee's division, on way from Valley Forge to the Jerseys, at house of Benjamin Paxson, Aquetong Spring
House of Fries, leader of Fries' rebellion, in Lower Milford township
Remains of old Durham furnace at Kintnersville, where cannon balls for the Revolution were made

BUTLER

Site of Murdering Town mentioned in Washington's *Journal*, on the southeast fork of Beaver Creek
Site of Reed's blockhouse, one and a half miles northeast of Butler
Harmony, first town of the Harmony Society
Monument in commemoration of Washington's escape from death on his return from Fort le Boeuf, Butler

CAMBRIA

Site of ancient fort about one and a half miles above forks of Beaver Dam and Slatelick Creeks
Site of early Welsh settlement at Beulah, two miles southwest of Ebensburg

APPENDIX

Inclined planes of old Portage Railroad, No. 1 to No. 5
Site of South Fork Dam — cause of Johnstown flood
Colonel Hart's sleeping place, near Carrollton, signer of the Declaration of Independence
Site of mission of Father Gallitzen, at Loretto

CAMERON

Site of early salt-manufacturing plant, Driftwood
Site of Indian town, at Sinnemahoning — includes much of present site of the village
Site of Indian cemetery, near Miller's or Bennett's Branch
Scene of fight with Indians, on Sinnemahoning Creek at mouth of Grove's Run
Site of historic Pine Street Log Church, two miles east of Sterling Run — graves of early settlers here

CARBON

Site of Moravian Indian mission, a half mile above mouth of Mahoning Creek
Old Indian trail, Warrior's Path, over Nescopeck Mountain
Site of Moravian mission, at Weissport
Site of first anthracite mine, at Summit Hill
Switchback railway that brought coal from Summit Hill to Mauch Chunk
Site of Fort Allen, at Weissport
Site of fort, Lehigh Gap

CENTER

Home of Count Leon, leader of Harmony Society, Philipsburg
Sites of many early iron furnaces, such as Harmony forge, near Bellefonte
Site of old blockhouse, Bald Eagle township
Site of cabin of Logan, the celebrated Indian chief, about six miles from Lewistown
Bellefonte, home of three governors of Pennsylvania — Curtin, Beaver, and Hastings

CHESTER

Point where Lafayette received wound, Brandywine Battlefield
Stargazer's stone, near Embreeville, erected by Mason and Dixon
Grave of Indian Hannah, County Home, near Embreeville
Early iron industries — Lukens Iron and Steel Co., Coatesville; Warwick furnace; Coventry forge
Birthplace of Bayard Taylor, Kennett Square
Birthplace of Thomas Buchanan Read, north of Downingtown
Birthplace of Humphrey Marshall, botanist, at Northbrook
Battlefield of Brandywine
Battlefield of Paoli
Chester Springs hospital, used in the Revolution
Old meeting houses and churches
Jeffrey's ford, where British crossed Brandywine Creek

CLARION

Site of home of Samuel Brady, the first settler, near East Brady
Place of battle with Indians, at Brady's Bend, near the mouth of Red Bank
Site of Indian town, opposite mouth of Tom's Run
Old Indian trails; Clough's Riffle, near Strattanville, and Bullock's ford, near Callensburg

CLEARFIELD

Lines of important Indian trails, through the county
Site of old Indian village, Clearfield
Site of ancient Indian fort, near Mount Pleasant
Site of early French settlement, below mouth of Trout Run
Indian millstone, one mile east of Clearfield

CLINTON

Site of Fort Reid, Lock Haven
Site of Horn's fort, on the West Branch below Chatham's Run at McElhattan

Place of Pine Creek Declaration of Independence near Horn's fort, Wayne township, above Jersey shore
Council place of Indians, at Chatham's Run

COLUMBIA

Site of Indian village, near mouth of Fishing Creek
Site of Fort Jenkins — Revolutionary defense against the Indians, at Briar Creek
Site of Fort Wheeler, Bloomsburg, used by Major Van Campen
Graves of first white settlers killed by the Indians, on the south side of the Susquehanna River near Catawissa
First grist mill in this part of the state, at Millville
First Quaker meeting house, at Catawissa, 1787
Site of Fort McClure, near Bloomsburg

CRAWFORD

Site of old blockhouse, Water Street, Meadville
Site of Drake's oil well, at Watson's Flats, Titusville
Farm of John Brown at Harper's Ferry, southeast of Cambridge Springs
Mound builders' fort, halfway between Waterford and Cambridge Springs

CUMBERLAND

Site of Fort Louther, at Carlisle, northwest corner of the public square
Sites of Forts Morris and Franklin, at Shippensburg
Site of Washington's headquarters during the Whisky insurrection, Carlisle
Site of Fort Croghan, home of Croghan, the Indian trader
Northern limit of Confederate invasion of Pennsylvania, north of Carlisle
Dickinson College, Carlisle, founded 1783
Old Presbyterian churches in the Cumberland Valley — Silver's Spring, Meeting House Springs (church destroyed), Big Spring, Middle Spring, Falling Springs, Rocky Springs

Old iron furnaces at Boiling Springs, Mt. Holly Springs, Pine Grove Furnace, and Newville where cannon for the Revolutionary army were made
State monument to Molly Pitcher of Revolutionary fame, at Carlisle

DAUPHIN

Site of Fort Halifax, at mouth of Armstrong's Creek, at Halifax
Site of Fort Hunter, at mouth of Fishing Creek
Site of Indian town, on Duncan's Island, at mouth of the Juniata
Site of the Paxton settlement, three miles east of Harrisburg
Site of John Harris's house and his grave, on the river bank at Harrisburg
Scene of Indian attack at Wiconisco Creek
Site of Camp Curtin, near Harrisburg

DELAWARE

Grave of John Morton, the signer, at Chester
Grave of General Wayne, old St. David's churchyard, Radnor
Birthplace of John Morton, Essington
Site of home of the Swedish Governor Printz, at Essington
Site of Washington's headquarters, Battle of Brandywine
Lafayette's headquarters, Battle of Brandywine
Old City Hall, Chester
Sandelands house at Chester — place of first lawmaking assembly of the Commonwealth
Home of Benjamin West, Swarthmore College campus
Log cabins of Virginia trappers, at Addingham and Oakview, on Darby Creek — these are earlier than those of either the Swedes or William Penn
Pusey House, Upland, built 1681 — William Penn was a guest there
First landing of Penn in Pennsylvania, Penn Street, Chester
Site of blockhouse, Edgemont Avenue and Second Street, Chester

APPENDIX

Friends Meeting House, Eagle Road, Haverford township — one of two remaining buildings where Penn worshiped

Washington Hotel, Chester, where Washington wrote his report of the Battle of Brandywine to the Congress

Radnor Meeting House, Sproul and Conestoga Roads, used as officers' quarters and hospital during encampment at Valley Forge

Hendricks House, about 1640; oldest building standing in Pennsylvania; erected by Swedes on the east side of Crum Creek, near Delaware River, Eddystone

Site of Leiper Railroad, 1806 — the first in the United States, Crum Creek near Sproul Road to Ridley Creek

ELK

Typical old sawmill
Site of early mill at Kersey
Site of early settlement, at Burned Mill, near Centerville

ERIE

Niagara, Perry's flagship, State Street, Erie
Site of old French fort, at Erie
Site of Fort le Boeuf, at Waterford
Site of General Wayne's fort, at Erie
Site where Perry built his fleet, on Lake Erie
Place of Battle of Presque Isle, Pontiac's War, Parade Street, Erie

FAYETTE

Indian picture rock
Fort Necessity where Washington was defeated by the French
Grave of General Braddock, near Chalk Hill
Grave of Jumonville, near Fort Necessity
Plantation of Christopher Gist, companion of Washington, near Mt. Braddock
Stewart's Crossings, near Connellsville, where Braddock's army crossed the Youghiogheny

Home of Colonel William Crawford, who was burned at the stake by Indians

Washington's mill at Perryopolis, owned and operated by George Washington, twelve miles north of Uniontown

Course of Braddock's Road, through the county

Redstone old fort (Fort Burd), at Brownsville

Sites of a number of blockhouses, in various parts of the county

Home of Albert Gallatin, near New Geneva

Washington's spring, one mile west of Jumonville

Fort Mason, Masontown

FOREST

Cook Forest Park, 6500 acres of virgin timber
Site of first settlement, Holeman Ferry

FRANKLIN

Site of inn where Washington and Hamilton stopped on the way to quell the Whisky rebellion, Main Street near Queen, Chambersburg
Site of Fort Loudon, near Loudon
Site of Dunkard settlement, at Snowhill on Antietam Creek
Site of old fort, at Chambersburg
Scene of Indian fight, at mouth of Conococheague Creek
Scene of Indian raid, at Great Cove
Site of Fort McDowell, McDowell's Mill — scene of Indian raid
Birthplace of President Buchanan, near Mercersburg
Mason and Dixon marker, east of Pen Mar station

FULTON

Site of Fort Littleton, near Sugar Cabins, Dublin
Place of Indian massacre, Big Cove, Ayr township
Line of Forbes' Road, in Brush Creek township
Site of blockhouse, near McConnellsburg
Place of Indian raid, Burnt Cabins

APPENDIX

GREENE

Site of Garard's or Jarret's fort, on Whiteley Creek, about seven miles west of Greensboro
Site of Fort Jackson, near Waynesburg
Old covered wooden bridge, one mile east of Waynesburg
Old Indian mounds, at Crow's Mills
Site of Fort Ryerson, western end of county

HUNTINGDON

Sites of many old iron furnaces
Site of Fort Shirley, near Aughwick Creek at Shirleysburg
Old Indian village, at Frankstown at Beaver Dam
Site of Indian town, Standing Stone
Site of Fort Standing Stone, at Huntingdon

INDIANA

Site of Indian village, near Saltsburg
Cherry Tree Point, junction of Cambria, Clearfield, and Indiana Counties — northern boundary of Stanwix purchase from the Indians, Cherry Tree
Site of Fort Wallace, near Blairsville
Site of Fort Moorehead, near Indiana
Clark's blockhouse, two miles west of Kittanning

JEFFERSON

Cave of Captain Hunt, an Indian, at the Sand Spring, Brookville
Site of Indian town, at Punxatawney
Ancient stump fence, near Brookville
Site of Fort Barnett, one mile east of Brookville

JUNIATA

Scene of Indian massacre, on the Juniata near Thompsontown
Site of Fort Patterson, Tuscarora Valley near Mexico
Site of Pomfret Castle, fort built in French and Indian War at Richfield
Site of Fort Bigham, Beale township

LACKAWANNA

Site of first house in Scranton, in yards of Lackawanna Iron and Coal Company
Old Indian trail from Indian town of Cocheaton, crossed Roaring Brook a little below Scranton
Warrior trail, Pittston to the Delaware
Site of first grist mill, at Roaring Brook
Site of Indian town, at junction of Susquehanna and Lackawanna Rivers
Site of Indian town, Capoose Meadow, between Scranton and Providence at old Scranton race track
Site of old Connecticut settlement, at Taylor
Site of early settlement, mouth of Tuscarora Creek
Site of General Sullivan's camp, Black Walnut Bottom
Site of first sawmill, north of Tuscarora Creek

LANCASTER

Home of George Ross, signer of the Declaration of Independence
Robert Fulton's birthplace, Little Britain
Home of Hans Herr and site of Mennonite settlement
Christiana slavery riot and treason trials
Home of General Edward Hand, aide-de-camp of Washington, at Rockford, on the Conestoga, near Lancaster
Memorial to Revolutionary soldiers who died at Ephrata at the Battle of Brandywine, Mt. Zion
Home of Baron Stiegel, at Manheim
Site of Stiegel's glassworks, at Manheim
Pequea Church where Whitefield preached
Old Cloisters at Ephrata, used as hospitals during the Revolution
Old ironworks, on the Conewago and Octoraro Creeks
Home of President James Buchanan, at Wheatland near Lancaster
Indian picture rock, Susquehanna River near Safe Harbor

LAWRENCE

Sites of Indian mounds and villages, near Edenburg
Scene of Indian attack, near Edenburg
Site of Moravian mission, at Friedenstadt, at junction of Shenango and Mahoning Creeks, opposite Moravia

APPENDIX

Line of old Indian trail along the Mahoning River
Site of old fort, at Newcastle, Washington Street, between Mercer Street and Apple Alley

LEBANON

Lick Monument, at Fredericksburg
Stover House, at Cleona — used as refuge in the French and Indian War
Old Jewish cemetery, at Schaefferstown — containing graves of first settlers in Lebanon County
Fort Swatara, close to Swatara Gap
The Zeller refuge for settlers during the French and Indian War, near Newmanstown
Meadow Bank, home of George Steitz, founder of Lebanon
Lei homestead, where George Washington stopped
Old charcoal furnace and cannon foundry, at Cornwall, 1742 — used during the Revolution
The old tunnel of the Union Canal, between Swatara and Tulpehocken — oldest tunnel in America
The residences of Governor Shulze, at Myerstown and Lebanon
The old Ulrich refuge during the French and Indian War, opposite Reading station at Annville
The old Lehigh refuge during the French and Indian War, in north Lebanon, on the banks of the canal
Oldest incorporated waterworks in the United States, at Schaefferstown

LEHIGH

Zion Reformed Church, where the Liberty Bell was concealed during the Revolution
Place of massacre by the Indians, Whitehall township
Site of Fort Everett, near the northwest corner of the county
Fort Deshler, near Egypt
Home of Judge Rhoads, Revolutionary patriot — oldest house in Allentown
Site of Moravian Indian village, Nain
Site of Revolutionary Wagon Brigade
Graves of Revolutionary soldiers, West Bethlehem, and Geisinger Farm, Salisbury
Sites of Revolutionary hospitals, Allentown

LUZERNE

Site of Fort Wilkes-Barre, public square, Wilkes-Barre
Site of Fort Durkee, foot of South Street, Wilkes-Barre
Site of Fort Ogden
Site of Forty Fort, at Kingston
Site of Fort Wintersmoot, one mile below Fort Jenkins
Sites of three blockhouses, at Pittston
Place of Sugar Loaf massacre, Captain Klader
Site of fort, at Nanticoke Falls
Queen Esther's Rock, near Fort Wintersmoot
Site of Fort Wyoming, foot of Northampton Street, Wilkes-Barre
Scene of Wyoming massacre, Exeter
Tract of land at West Nanticoke, still belonging to the Penn heirs

LYCOMING

Site of Fort Muncy, near Hall's station
Site of Fort Antes, opposite Jersey shore
Spot where Captain Simon Cool, Colonel Hunter's scout, was killed
Site of massacre of settlers by Indians, 1778, Williamsport
Indian paintings of their history, at Picture Rocks, Big Muncy Creek
Ostonwakin, Indian village, at mouth of Loyalsock Creek
Sheshequin Trail, Fourth Street, Williamsport
Friends Meeting House built in 1799 and still in use, at Pennsdale
Muncy Manor, Samuel Wallis's house built in 1769 — probably oldest house in county
French Margaret's, Indian village, Williamsport, seventh ward
Home of Madame Montour, at Montoursville on Loyalsock Creek
Site of Fort Wallis, at Muncy

MCKEAN

Site of first settlement in county, two miles south of Ceres, New York
Site of settlement, Potato Creek, about three miles north of Smethport
Route of General Brodhead's expedition, near Lafayette
Home of Jim Jacobs, great Indian hunter, at Lewis Run
Site of Norwich settlement, on Potato Creek, about three miles southeast of Smethport
Site of early salt-making plant, southeast part of Sergeant township
Site of early German community settlement, on Stanton Creek about five miles southwest of Smethport

MERCER

Site of Indian village, Centertown, Worth township
Site of Indian village, Big Bend, Shenango Creek
Site of Indian fort, West Salem township near Booth Run
Site of home of first settler, Greenville, northwest corner Main and First Streets
First settlement, at Mercer
Site of Indian village, Sandy Lake

MIFFLIN

Site of Fort Granville, about one mile northwest of Lewistown
Site of home of Logan, famous Indian chief on Kishacoquillas Creek, about one mile above the Narrows, near Reedsville
Site of Indian mounds, junction of Aughwick Creek and the Juniata, and on Kishacoquillas Creek, near Lewistown

MONROE

Sites of Forts Hamilton and Penn, at Stroudsburg
Site of Fort Norris, near Greensweig
Site of Dupuy's fort, at Shawnee
Site of Fort Hyndshaw, mouth of Bushkill Creek
Scene of Indian attack, at Wichetunk
Site of early Dutch settlement from New York, at Minisink Flats near Shawnee

MONTGOMERY

Site of General Sullivan's bridge, Fatland Ford
Washington's headquarters, Valley Forge
Wayne's headquarters, near Valley Forge
Lafayette's headquarters, near Valley Forge
Valley Forge Park
Powder mills, Sumneytown, where powder was manufactured for the Continental forces
Pennypacker mills, Schwenksville, and old mill, near Fatland Ford, where flour was made for Continental army
Fort Hill and Lafayette's retreat, Whitemarsh township
Washington's headquarters on Knapp Farm, Montgomery Square, and on Isaac Schultz's farm, near Center Point
General Wayne's headquarters, near Fagleysville
Towamencin Mennonite burial grounds, where General Nash and three other officers wounded in Battle of Germantown are buried — General Washington attended funeral of Nash
Old Lutheran Church, Trappe (still standing), scene of labors of the Muhlenbergs; also burial place
Norriton Presbyterian Church, probably two years older than Trappe
Lutheran Church, Fairview village
Friends Meeting Houses — Abington, Plymouth Meeting, Horsham
Trappe school — older than the church at Trappe
Old school in Frederick township, where General Muhlenberg taught at same time as at Trappe; established same year or year later
Old schools in Upper Merion township
Marker for Christopher Dock, Skippack township, in Lower Mennonite Church
Hope Lodge, Whitemarsh; Keith Manor, Horsham; Van Bebber estate, Skippack

APPENDIX

Home of David Rittenhouse, astronomer, Worcester and Lower Providence townships
Home of John James Audubon, ornithologist, Audubon
Birthplace of General Hancock, Montgomery Square; later used as a school and now abandoned

MONTOUR

First steel rail made in America at Danville in 1843
Site of Fort Bosley, Washingtonville
Site of Fort Mead, Washingtonville
Site of Boyle's (Brady's) Fort, Washingtonville
Site of Indian village, mouth of Mahoning Creek, Danville
Home of General William Montgomery, Revolutionary War, corner of Mill and Bloom Streets, Danville
Home of Christopher Sholes, inventor of the typewriter, at Mooresburg

NORTHAMPTON

Site of Teed's Fort, near Windgap
Site of Brown's Fort, at Balston
Site of Nazareth stockades
Site of old fort, near Slatington
Site of first Connecticut settlement, on Mill Creek
Place of many Indian treaties, junction of Delaware and Lehigh Rivers

NORTHUMBERLAND

Site of Fort Augusta; magazine and well extant, Sunbury
Grave of Colonel Hunter, Sunbury
Indian village of Shamokin, Sunbury
Grave of Shikellimy, Sunbury, at Fort Augusta
Indian trail to Harrisburg, Wyoming Valley, etc.
Home of Dr. Joseph Priestley, discoverer of oxygen, Northumberland
Site of Fort Freeland, two miles above McEwensville
Site of Fort Rice, or Fort Montgomery, in Lewis township
Site of Fort Boone, one mile above Milton

Site of home of Captain John Brady, East Lewisburg
Sodom schoolhouse (octagonal), near Milton

PERRY

Site of home of Simon Girty, noted Indian trader, on Sherman's Creek
Site of Fort Robinson, Sherman's Valley
Locks of old Pennsylvania Canal, near Liverpool
Old Indian village, Shermans Dale

PHILADELPHIA

The historic places in Philadelphia are too numerous to list. A few are, however, given —
Independence Hall and Liberty Bell
Carpenter's Hall, where the Continental Congress met
Site of house in which Jefferson wrote the Declaration of Independence
Letitia Penn's slate house, now in Fairmount Park
Betsy Ross House, where the first American flag probably was made
Old Christ Church

PIKE

Site of early settlement, at Milford
Site of Indian battle, at Minisink, New York, just over the state line, near Lackawaxen
Site of an early community settlement, Lackawaxen township, between Shohola Creek and Lackawaxen River
Stone fort at Matamoras, built in 1742 by Simon Westfall
Site of early settlement, at Dingman's Ferry
Site of early mills at Vandemark's Creek, Milford
Monument to Tom Quick, the Indian slayer of the Delaware Valley, Milford

POTTER

Monument to Civil War soldiers, Coudersport
Tablet to David Zeisberger, first white man to travel down the headwaters of the Allegheny River, Coudersport

Site of Ole Bull's castle and colony at Oleona
Coudersport-Jersey shore turnpike, line of early pack-horse trail
Peaslee Hill, highest point in eastern Pennsylvania; intersection of the St. Lawrence, Mississippi, and Atlantic drainage basins

SCHUYLKILL

Site of Fort Henry, south of Pine Grove
Site of Fort Dietrich Snyder, top of Blue Mountain
Site of Fort Clinton
Site of Fort Lebanon, near Auburn
Site of Fort Franklin, near Snyder's in West Penn township
Location of first chartered railway in the United States, 1826, in Black Valley, from the Swatara mines to the Union Canal
Mahanoy plane, built by Stephen Girard at Frackville
Henry Clay monument, at Pottsville
Red (Zion) Church, near Orwigsburg, 1755
Point of Rocks, six miles west of Pine Grove

SNYDER

Home and grave of Governor Snyder, at Selinsgrove
Site of Indian massacre, on Penn's Creek, near New Berlin
Scene of fight of settlers with Indians, at Selinsgrove
Old blockhouse, near Kreamer

SOMERSET

Sites of ancient forts, near Casselman River
Site of pioneer settlement at Jersey Church, near Wisina, Lower Turkey Foot township
Washington's Road, southwest corner of the county
Site of old fort, near Stoyestown, 1758
Site of Fort Squaw, near Somerfield
Old toll house on National Road, at Addison
Line of Bouquet Road, through the county, now the Lincoln Highway

SULLIVAN

Estate of Dr. Priestley, at Fordsville
Daniel Ogden, first white settler of the county, at Hillsgrove, probably in 1786
Friends Meeting House, in use prior to 1805, near Eldredsville
Home of George Edkins, about 1806, in Shrewsbury township
Aristide Dupetit Thouars, a Frenchman, settled at Dushore, 1794
Celestia, a Seventh-day Baptist settlement, was laid out by Peter Armstrong. He believed that property should not be owned by individuals, and, therefore, he deeded his to Almighty God on June 14, 1864. Later the land was sold for taxes

SUSQUEHANNA

Great Bend, earliest white settlement in the county
Encampment of General Clinton, 1779, on his way to join General Sullivan's expedition against the Indians
Home of Joseph Smith, founder of Mormonism, McKune
Home of Galusha A. Grow, speaker of the National House of Representatives during Lincoln's administration and sponsor of the Homestead Act.

TIOGA

Place of council — Cornplanter, Red Jacket, and five hundred Indians with Colonel Pickering, 1790, at Tioga
Old Indian camping grounds, at Ansonia
Station on underground railroad, at Covington
Camp of General Sullivan's expedition, Red Bank
Discovery of bituminous coal beds, Blossburg
Old Pine Creek Church, at Ansonia
Site of old log tavern, at Liberty

UNION

Shikellimy's old town, Oak Heights, near Lewisburg
Scene of Indian massacre, at French

APPENDIX

Jacob's mill, near end of Brush Valley Narrows
Scene of Indian attack, Smith's mill
Scene of Indian raid, near Winfield
Site of Fort Menninger, near mouth of White Deer Creek; guns made here during the Revolution
Leroy massacre, Limestone township

VENANGO

Site of Fort Franklin, Franklin Avenue west of Thirteenth Street
Site of Fort Machault, Franklin, Elk Street, near Sixth Street
Site of Indian village, on Sugar Creek
Sites of French forts, near Franklin, below French Creek
Site of Fort Venango, Elk and Eighth Streets
Site of log cabin where first court was held in the county, Liberty Street near Twelfth Street
Site of "Old Garrison," at foot of Eleventh Street, Franklin
Indian picture writings, on Indian God Rock, Allegheny River, six miles south of Franklin

WARREN

Site of Cornplanter Indian Reservation, and home of Cornplanter, five miles above Kinzua Creek, Elk township
Site of Indian village, at Conewango
Site of blockhouse, 1795, at Warren

WASHINGTON

House of David Bradford, Washington
Old Le Moyne House, Washington
Site of Globe Inn, Washington
Auld House, Washington
First Women's Seminary, Washington
Log College, Canonsburg, oldest school building west of the Alleghenies
Scene of skirmishes in the Whisky rebellion, Parkinson's Ferry, Monongahela City
Site of Fort Beeler, near Candor

WAYNE

Old house at Milanville, loopholes near roof
Old octagonal schoolhouse, Mt. Pleasant township
Site of early settlement, at "Cushetunk," near mouth of Corkins' Creek
Site of boundary stone, northeast corner of the State Railroad, Honesdale to Carbondale, where first locomotive in America was used
Home and burial place of Samuel Meredith, first treasurer of the United States, Mt. Pleasant township
Birthplace of David Wilmot, Bethany borough

WESTMORELAND

Grave of General Arthur St. Clair, at Greensburg
The Old Spring, Hannastown, north of Greensburg
Battle of Bushey Run, near Harrison City
Old Hannastown, where first court of English-speaking race was held west of the mountains; destroyed by Indians in 1782
Miller's station near Greensburg — place of Indian massacre
Site of Fort Ligonier, at Ligonier
Course of Forbes' Road, from Bedford to Fort Duquesne
Frontier blockhouses, in various parts of the county
Course of Braddock's Road, through the county
Course of Glades Road, through the county

WYOMING

Line of old Indian trail, through Factoryville, Clinton township
Line of old Indian trail, from Old Forge to Wyalusing
Site of home of Tedyuscung, noted Indian chief
Camping place of General Sullivan's army, 1779, Tunkhannock
Tunkhannock viaduct, near Nicholson, largest concrete bridge in the world

Sites of Indian villages, along creeks in Lemon township

YORK

General Wayne's headquarters, York
Residence of James Smith, signer of the Declaration of Independence
Meeting place of Continental Congress, county court house, York, 1777-1778
Site of Thomas Cresap's fort, in Lower Windsor township
Rendezvous of Wayne's troops before Battle of Yorktown, on Penn Common, York
Building in which was developed the Conway cabal against Washington
Oldest house in York, 1743, Queen Street, near Market
Mary Ann furnace, owned by George Ross, the signer of the Declaration of Independence, West Manheim

Valley Inn, four miles east of York, built thirty years before the Revolution
Cavalry battle, Civil War, at Hanover
Confederates under General Gordon, at Wrightsville
Raid by Stuart's Confederate cavalry, at Dover
First stone house in York County, 1734, Springetsbury township, a mile from Stony Brook School
Site of first German settlement, East Manchester township
Site of Hessian prison camp, Revolutionary War, Springetsbury township
Site of the Paine House — used as a depository for records when the Continental Congress met at York

Course of Mason and Dixon's line, in all the southern counties of the state as far west as the Monongahela River

INDEX AND PRONOUNCING VOCABULARY

KEY TO PRONUNCIATION

ā, as in āle; ȧ, as in sen'ȧte; â, as in câre; ă, as in ăm; ȧ, as in fi'nȧl; ä, as in ärm; à, as in àsk; a̍, as in so'fa̍; ch (= tsh), as in chair; ē, as in ēve; ė, as in ė-vent'; ĕ, as in ĕnd; ẽ, as in re'cẽnt; ē, as in fērn; g (hard), as in go; ī, as in īce; ĭ, as in ĭll; j (= dzh), for g, as in gem; k, for ch, as in chorus; n (ordinary sound), as in no; ŋ (like ng), for n before the sound of k or hard g, as in bank; N, representing simply the nasal tone of the preceding vowel, as in ensemble (äN'säN'bl'); ō, as in ōld; ȯ, as in ȯ-bey'; ô, as in ôrb; ŏ, as in ŏdd; o̍, as in co̍n-nect'; ō̇, as in sō̇ft; oi, as in oil; o͞o, as in fo͞od; o͝o, as in fo͝ot; ou, as in out; s (sharp), as in so; t͡h, as in t͡hin; ū, as in ūse; ů, as in ů-nite'; û, as in ûrn; ŭ, as in ŭp; ṳ, as in cir'cṳs; ü, as in mē-nü'; z (like s sonant), as in zone.

Academies, 218
Acadia (ȧ-kā'dĭ-ȧ), 228, 232, 234-235, 238, 253
Adams, John, 355, 366-367; first Vice President, 381
Adams, Samuel, 364
Agriculture, 85-86, 96, 111-112, 115, 197-198, 222; in the English colonies, 243; in New England, 205; in New France, 242-243; in Pennsylvania, 150-152, 166, 207; in the South, 101, 180, 183, 205
Airplanes, 223, 349, 351
Albany (ôl'bȧ-nĭ), N. Y., 62
Albany congress, 361
Algonquin (ăl-gŏŋ'kĭn) Indians, 51-52, 143-145, 244-246
Allan, Ethan, 288
Allegheny (ăl'ė-gā'nĭ) Mountains, 195, 329
Allegheny River, 165, 246-249
Allentown, Pa., 345, 348
Altamaha (ôl'tȧ-mȧ-hô') River, 104
America, named, 22-24
American Revolution, *see* Revolutionary War
Amherst (ăm'ẽrst), General Jeffrey, 253-255
André (än'drä), Major John, 318
Andros (ăn'drŏs), Governor Sir Edmund, 361
Annapolis convention, 372
Antilia (ăn-tĭl'ĭ-ȧ), 37-38

Appalachian (ăp'ȧ-lăch'ĭ-ăn) Highland, 194-195, 371
Apprentices, 180
Arizona, 40, 389
Arkansas (är'kăn-sô), 43
Arkansas River, 55, 56, 57
Arnold, General Benedict, 309, 316-318
Articles of Confederation, 331, 342-343, 369-372, 375
Ashley River, 99
Atlantic Coastal Plain, 194
Audubon (ô'do͞o-bŏn), John James, 392
Automobiles, 220-221
Azores (ȧ-zōrz'), 13, 22, 45
Aztecs (ăz'tĕks), 31-34

Bacon, Nathaniel, 91-92
Bacon's rebellion, 91-92
Balboa (dä bäl-bō'ä), Vasco Núñez de, 24-25
Baltimore (city), 194, 342
Baltimore, Lord, *see* Calverts
Barbados (bär-bā'dōz), 99
Barcelona (bär'sė-lō'nȧ), 18
Barren Hill, Pa., 333
Barry, John, 326-327
Bedford, Pa., 195
Bergen (bûr'gĕn), N. J., 134
Bemis Heights, N. Y., 308-309
Berkeley (bûrk'lĭ), Governor Sir William, 91-92, 97, 134-136
Bethlehem, Pa., 156, 158, 207, 345
Bimini (bē-mē'nė), 41

xiii

xiv   INDEX

Blockhouse, 227, 242
Block Island, 48
Blue Ridge, 195
Bon Homme Richard (bô-nôm' rē'shär'), 324-326
Boone, Daniel, 195-196
Boonesborough, Ky., 196
Boston, Mass., 118, 122, 193, 234, 266, 278-281, 287-294, 296; British troops quartered in, 276, 284
Boston Massacre (măs'á-kēr), 276-277
Boston Tea Party, 278-279
Braddock, General Edward, 250-252, 288
Bradford, Governor William, 112-115
Brandywine, Battle of, 301-303, 332, 340, 348
Brazil (brá-zĭl'), 43
Breed's Hill, 289-290
Bristol, England, 64-65
Brittany (brĭt'á-nĭ), 47, 49
Buffalo, N. Y., 225
Bunker Hill, Battle of, 288-290
Burgoyne (bûr-goin'), General John, 284, 306-309, 313, 316; surrender of, 309
Burlington, N. J., 136
Bryn Mawr (brĭn mär'), Pa., 166
Byllynge (bĭl'ĭng), Edward, 136
Byrd, Governor William, 184

Cable, 225
Cabot (kăb'ŭt), John, 64-66
Cabot, Sebastian, 66
California, 40
Calvert, Cecil (kăl'vērt, sĕs'ĭl), 94-97, 99, 171-172
Calvert, George, 94
Calvert, Leonard, 94-97
Cambria, Pa., 166
Cambridge, Mass., 124, 215; elm, 291, 293
Camden, S. C., 320, 335
Canada, 51, 54, 56, 66, 232-235, 241-244, 306, 342
Canary (ká-nā'rĭ) Islands, 13, 16
Canonicus (ká-nŏn'ĭ-kŭs), 113

Cape Ann, 115
Cape Breton (brĭt'ŭn) Island, 235-236
Cape Cod, 48, 108
Cape of Good Hope, 8, 26, 28, 29, 44
Cape Verde (vûrd) Islands, 22, 28, 45
Caravan, 1, 8
Caribbean (kăr'ĭ-bē'ăn) Sea, 20
Carlisle (kär-līl'), Pa., 195
Carolinas, *see* North and South Carolina
Carpenters' Hall, 281, 341
Carteret (kär'tēr-ĕt), Sir Philip, 97, 134-135
Cartier, Jacques (kär'tyā', zhäk), 49-50, 59
Carver, Governor John, 109
Cathay (ká-thā'), 47
Catholic Church, 39-40, 94-97
Cavelier, René Robert, *see* La Salle
Chambersburg, Pa., 195
Champlain (shăm'plān'), Samuel de, 50-52, 59, 244-246
Charcoal, 152, 208
Charles River, 115, 118, 289
Charleston, S. C., 99-100, 278, 319, 321
Charter of 1606, 82
Château-Thierry (shä'tō'-tyĕ'rē'), 350
Chesapeake (chĕs'á-pēk) Bay, 60, 82, 94, 173, 302-303
Chester, Pa., 140, 143, 303
Chew house, 303-304
Chief, Indian, 145
China, 6, 47
Church of England, 94, 106, 210
Cibola (sē'bô-lä), 39
Cipango (sĭ-păŋ'gō), 14, 17
Clark, George Rogers, 310-313, 329
Clinton, General Sir Henry, 284, 307, 314-318
Clothing, colonial, 177-179, 199-204
Colonial life and customs, 177-225
Colonial literature, 219
Colonial recreations and amusements, 179, 189-192
Colorado (kŏl'ô-rä'dō) River, 38-39
Columbus, Bartholomew (kô-lŭm'bŭs, bär-thŏl'ô-mū), 14, 64

INDEX

Columbus, Christopher (krĭs'tô-fēr), 3, 7, 9, 10, 12–25, 43, 64
Commerce, 2–8, 12, 52, 56, 60–61, 66, 81–82, 96, 132, 152, 180, 206–207, 233, 239, 273, 314, 325, 329, 370; affected by Navigation Acts, 89–91, 206, 265–266, 275–276; of Philadelphia, 153
Committee of Correspondence, 276–277, 279, 362
Committee of safety, 284–285
Communication, 223–224, 273, 349
Concession, the, 134–135
Concord (kŏŋ'kŏrd), Mass., 285–288, 293
Conestoga (kŏn'ĕs-tō'gà), Pa., 162–164
Conestoga Indians, 162–164
Congress, the, 333, 341, 375, 379
Connecticut (kŏ-nĕt'ĭ-kŭt), 118, 133, 173–174, 212, 360; settlement of, 124–126
Connecticut River, 124
Conservation Laws, 389–390, 394–396
Constitution, the, 338, 374–380; ratified, 377–379
Constitutional Convention, 337, 356, 372–377
Continental Congress, *see* First and Second Continental Congress
Continental money, 155, 331, 343, 370–371
Conway cabal (kà-băl'), 343
Cooper, Sir Ashley, 97
Corn, 83, 96, 111–112, 115, 152, 197–198
Cornplanter Indians, 164–165
Cornwallis (kôrn-wŏl'ĭs), General Lord, 299–301, 319–323, 328, 333, 338, 369
Coronado (kō'rŏ-nä'thō), Francisco de, 37–39
Cortés (kôr-tās'), Hernando, 30–36
Council for New England, 115
Countess of Scarborough (skär'bŭr-ŏ), 326
Creek Indians, 104
Croatoan (krō'tŏ-ăn'), 74–75
Cuba (kū'bà), 17, 30, 41
Cumberland, Md., 195, 247
Cumberland Gap, 195–196
Cusco (koos'kō), 36
Customs duties, 153, 275–279, 370

Darien (dä'rĕ-ĕn'), 24
Davenport, the Reverend John, 126
Dawes, William, 285
Declaration of Independence, 171, 295–297, 337, 342, 344, 347, 355, 366–369
Declaration of Rights, 342, 362
De Kalb (dĕ kălb'), Baron Johann, 334–335
Delaware, 173, 292, 377
Delaware Bay, 173, 326
Delaware River, 61, 129, 134–136, 140–142, 146, 147, 158, 171, 173–174, 233, 299, 301, 325–326, 347
Delaware Water Gap, 135
Department of Forests and Waters, 397
De Soto (dĕ sō'tō), Hernando, 41–43, 57
Detroit, Mich., 310, 312–313
Dias, Bartholomew (dē'äsh, bär-thŏl'ō-mū), 44
Dinwiddie (dĭn-wĭd'ĭ), Governor Robert, 247, 249
Discovery and exploration, 10–77, 230–231; Dutch, 60–63, 128; English, 64–76; French, 46–59, 246–248; Portuguese, 43–45; Spanish, 10–46
Disputes between states, 371; Connecticut and Pennsylvania, 173–174, 371; Maryland and Pennsylvania, 171–172; New York and Pennsylvania, 126
Dorchester (dôr'chĕs-tēr), Eng., 115
Dorchester Heights, 291, 294
Drake, 325
Drake, Sir Francis, 67–70, 73
Duke of York, 132, 134, 140, 174; Duke of York's Laws, 132–133
Dunkers, 155
Dunmore, Governor John Murray, 279–281
Dutch claims, 62–63
Dutch explorers and settlers, 60–63
Dutch settlements, 60–63, 128–134, 140, 143, 174, 360
Dutch West India Company, 61

xvi   INDEX

East India Company, 81, 240
East Indies (ĭn′dĭz), 17, 18, 20, 22, 24, 29, 63, 131
East Jersey, 99, 135-136, 138, 360
Easton, Pa., 299
Education in the Middle colonies, 217-219; in New England, 214-217; in Northwest Territory, 372; in the South, 217
Effingham, 326
Electric lights, 221
Elizabeth, N. J., 134
England, 64-76, 80-83, 117, 119, 124, 138, 152-153, 168, 206, 230-239, 261-369
English claims, 65-66, 80-127, 129, 241-245, 248
English discoverers and explorers, 64-76
Ephrata (ĕf′rä-tä), Pa., 155, 157
Erie, Pa., 246
Erie Canal, 225

Fairmount, Pa., 155
Fallen Timbers, Battle of, 341
Federal Hall, 379, 381
Federalist, The, 374
Ferguson, Colonel Patrick, 320-321
First Continental Congress, 280-282, 283-284, 337, 341-342, 362-363
First law-making assembly, 88
First union of the colonies, 126-127
Fisheries, 47, 59, 205, 241, 243, 314, 328
Flag, national, 290, 325, 342, 345-347
Florence, Italy, 22
Florida, 40-41
Flour and grist mills, 152, 198, 208
Foods of the colonists, 196-199
Forbes, Colonel John, 252-254
Forests and lumber, 389-390; in New England, 206, 394; in Pennsylvania, 207, 394-397
Fort Christina, 142
Fort Duquesne (dōō-kān′), 249-254
Fort le Boeuf (lē bĕf′), 246
Fort Mercer, 347

Fort Mifflin, 347
Fort Nassau, 62
Fort Necessity, 249-250
Fort Orange, 62, 128
Fort Pitt, 250, 253
Fort Stanwix (stăn′wĭks), N. Y., 347
Fort Ticonderoga (tī-kŏn′dēr-ō′gȧ), 288, 306
Fort Venango (Vĕ-naŋ′gō), 246
Fountain of youth, 41
France, 46-59, 230-239, 313-315
Franklin, Benjamin, 219, 295, 313-315, 325, 334, 363, 368, 373-374, 377-378; as envoy to France, 337-338, 343
French aid to America, 309, 311, 313-314, 325, 328, 332-333, 338, 343
French and Indian War, 66, 240-260, 268, 310
French claims, 48, 59, 66, 241-245; end of, 258
French discoverers and explorers, 46-59, 246-248
French Protestants, 50, 99-100
French settlements, 50-59, 181-182, 231-239, 241-258
French treaty of alliance, 311, 313-315
Friends, 138-147, 211, 367; in New England, 119
Frontenac, Count de (dē frôn′tē-nȧk′), 54
Frontier rangers, 162, 164
Fundamental Orders, 125
Furniture, colonial, 186-189
Furs and the fur trade, 57-59, 112, 131, 152, 164, 168-170, 182, 222, 241, 243, 398

Gage, General Thomas, 284-290
Gama, Vasco da (gä′mä, väs′kō dä), 8, 26, 44-45
Game laws, 397-398
Gates, General Horatio, 319-320, 335, 343
Genoa (jĕn′ō-ȧ), Italy, 7-8, 12
Georgia, 43, 210, 281, 319, 363; settlement of, 101-104

INDEX

German colonists, 104, 153-162; from the Palatinate, 160-161; from the Rhine Valley, 147-150, 157; from Salzburg, 104
Germantown, Pa., 157-158, 173, 208; Battle of, 303-304, 340, 348
Germany, 4, 350-351; *see* German colonists
Gilbert, Sir Humphrey, 70-71
Gist, Christopher, 247-249
Gladstone, William E., 378
Glassworks, 157
Gloucester (glŏs'tēr), N. J., 61
Gold, search for, 24, 34, 36-39, 41, 52, 57, 83, 182
Golden Hind, 68
Granada (grȧ-nä'dȧ), Spain, 15
Grand Canyon (kăn'yŭn), 39
Grasse, Admiral de (dē gräs'), 323
Great Khan (kän; kăn), 6-7, 17, 65
Great Lakes, 53, 54, 56, 59, 194, 241, 243-244, 258
Great Law, 143, 212
Great Meadows, Pa., 249
Great Valley, 149, 195
Greece, 4
Greene, General Nathanael, 321-323
Grenville, Sir Richard, 71-72, 74
Griffin, 53, 54
Guiana (gē-ä'nȧ), 76
Gwynedd (gwĭn'ĕd'), Pa., 166

Habana (hä-bä'nä), Cuba, 41
Haiti (hā'tĭ), 17, 18, 20, 24, 30
Half Moon, 61
Halifax, Nova Scotia, 291, 294, 297
Hamilton, Alexander, 374-375
Hancock, John, 284
Harris, John, 167-170
Harris, John, Jr., 169-171, 192
Harrisburg, Pa., 168-170
Harris's Ferry, 167-168, 170
Hartford, Conn., 124-125, 360
Harvard College, 215
Hat making, 152, 222, 265

Hennepin (hĕn'ē-pĭn), Father Louis, 56-57
Henry, Patrick, 270, 280, 283-284
Hermitage Estate, 155
Holland, 60-63, 66, 81, 106-108, 231
Holme (hōm), Thomas, 145
Holy Experiment, the, 138, 140
Honduras (hŏn-dōō'rȧs), 20
Hooker, the Reverend Thomas, 124-125
Hornbook, 216-217
Houses, colonial, 182-189
Howe, Admiral Lord, 291, 295, 297
Howe, General William, 284, 294, 297-304, 307-309, 314, 316
Hudson, Henry, 60-63, 128
Hudson River, 60, 62, 108, 129, 134, 194, 225, 306-309
Huguenots (hū'gē-nŏts), 99-100
Hutchinson, Anne, 122-123
Hutchinson, Governor Thomas, 284

Iceland, 13
Illinois (ĭl-ĭ-noi'; -noiz'), 311-313
Illinois River, 56, 196
Inca (ĭŋ'kȧ), 36-37
Indentured servants, 180-181
Independence: growth of idea of, 363-367; won by colonies, 328-330, 332; *see* Declaration of Independence
India (ĭn'dĭ-ȧ), 22, 24, 26, 29, 44, 45, 240-241; *see* East Indies
Indians, 17-19, 24-25, 32-42, 49, 162-165, 173-174, 231-233; relations with the English, 51-52, 83-85, 89, 91, 95, 103-104, 108, 111-113, 118-119, 121, 126, 231-232, 241, 245-246, 310, 341; relations with the French, 51-59, 165, 182, 231-232, 241, 245-246; relations with the Spanish, 32-43, 182; relations with John Harris, 167-170; relations with William Penn, 143-147, 159; relations with the Moravians, 159, 162
Indigo, 101, 205, 265
Intercolonial Wars, 230-239
Invincible Armada (är-mä'dȧ), 73, 74

INDEX

Irish Quakers, 147
Ironworks, 152, 157, 208, 222, 265
Iroquois (ĭr'ô-kwoi) Indians, 51, 52, 143–145, 244–246
Italy, 4–8

Jamaica (jȧ-mā'kȧ), 22
James River, 82, 86
Jamestown, Va., 78, 80, 82–93, 115
Jay, John, 374
Jefferson, Thomas, 296–297, 355, 367–368
Joliet (zhô'lyā'; jō'lĭ-ĕt), Louis, 56–57
Jones, John Paul, 324–326

Kansas, 39
Kaskaskia, Illinois, 311–312
Kelpius, John, 153–155
Kensington, 143, 145
Kentucky, 195–196, 310, 321
King Charles I of England, 96, 116–117, 134, 231
King Charles II of England, 91, 97, 134, 138, 140, 231
King Ferdinand of Spain, 14–20
King Francis I of France, 49
King Frederick the Great of Prussia, 240
King George II of England, 102
King George III of England, 293, 328, 331, 366
King George's War, 235–239, 240
King Henry VII of England, 64
King James I of England, 76, 82, 91, 231–233, 251
King John of Portugal, 14, 18, 43, 45
King Louis XIV of France, 55, 56, 231
King Philip's War, 118–119
King's College, 218
Kings Mountain, Battle of, 321
King William's War, 231–233, 360
Knox, General Henry, 318
Kosciuszko (kŏs'ĭ-ŭs'kō), Thaddeus, 317, 334

Labor, 34–37, 39–40, 88–89, 104, 155, 166–168; in the colonies, 180–185; *see* Slavery

Labrador (lăb'rȧ-dôr'), 48, 65
La Chine (lä shĭn) Rapids, 50
Ladrone (lȧ-drōn') Islands, 28
Lafayette (dē lä'fȧ-yĕt'), Marquis de, 306, 332–335, 343
Lake Champlain (shăm-plān'), 51, 52, 306
Lake Huron (hū'rŏn), 51
Lancaster (lăŋ'kȧs-tēr), Pa., 164, 195, 343, 344, 348
La Salle (dē lȧ sȧl'), Sieur de, 53–59
Las Vegas (läs vā'gȧs), 40
Laws and law enforcement, 383–401
Leather and tanning, 152, 208, 222
Lee, General Charles, 316
Lee, Richard Henry, 295–296, 367
Lehigh River, 158
Lenni Lenape (lĕn'ĭ lĕn'ȧ-pē), 145
Lexington, 326
Lexington, Mass., 285, 288, 293
Leyden (lī'dĕn), Holland, 106–107
Liberty Bell, 343–345, 347
Lincoln, Abraham, 196
Lincoln, General Benjamin, 319
Line of demarcation (dē'mär-kā'shŭn), 22, 45
Lisbon (lĭz'bŭn), Spain, 18
Little Egg Harbor, N. J., 135
Livingston, Robert R., 355, 367
Locomotives, 223
Loe (lō), Thomas, 138
London, England, 108, 118, 150
London Company, 84–89, 108
Long Island, 48, 129, 133, 134, 297–299, 300; Battle of, 297–300
Long Island Sound, 125
Lorraine (lō-rān'), 22
Lost colony, 73–75
Louisburg, Nova Scotia, 235–239, 254–255, 266
Louisiana (loo-ē'zē̇-ăn'ȧ), 55, 56; state, 101
Lumber mills, 152, 205, 208, 222
Lutherans (lū'thēr-ȧnz), 160–163

Madeira (mȧ-dē'rȧ) Islands, 48
Madison, James, 373–375

INDEX

Magellan (må-jĕl′ăn), Ferdinand, 25–29
Magellan, Strait of, 26–27, 69
Maine, 48, 82
Manhattan Island, 60; purchase of, 62
Manufacturing, 222; in the Middle colonies, 206–208, 243; in New England, 205–206, 243; in Pennsylvania, 152, 155–157, 208; laws against, 265–268
Maps:
  Toscanelli's world, 13
  Voyages of discovery, 21
  Routes of the early Spanish explorers and of the Frenchman La Salle, 35
  Routes of the French explorers and the French line of forts, 58
  The Charter of 1606, 82
  Early settlements in Pennsylvania, Maryland, and Delaware, 97
  Captain John Smith's map of New England, 110
  Early New England settlements, 116
  Early settlements in Pennsylvania, 150
  Pennsylvania in 1791, 172
  Scene of the last French war, 242
  Claims of the British, French, and Spanish in North America in 1750, 245
  French forts in the West and Braddock's route, 247
  Bunker Hill and Boston, 288
  The campaign in New York, 298
  Valley Forge, Philadelphia, and Brandywine, 302
  Burgoyne's expedition, 307
  The expedition of George Rogers Clark, 311
  The Revolutionary War in the South, 320
  North America according to the Treaty of 1783, 329
  State forest lands in Pennsylvania, 395
Maria Theresa (må-rī′å tĕ-rē′så), 240
Marquette, Father Jacques (mär′kĕt′, zhäk) 56–57
Marshall, Edward, 146

Marshall, Chief Justice John, 344
Maryland, 99, 171–172, 209–210, 372; settled, 94–97
Mason and Dixon's line, 173
Massachusetts Bay colony, 106–120, 125, 126–127, 132, 147, 209, 212–213, 283, 290, 294, 297, 360, 362–363; settlement of, 106–120; governs Connecticut settlements, 124
Massasoit (măs′å-soit′), 111
Mayflower, 108–110
Mayflower Compact, 109
May, Captain Cornelius, 61, 62
Mediterranean (mĕd′ĭ-tēr-ā′nē-ăn) Sea, 4–8
Memphis (mĕm′fĭs), Tenn., 43
Merion, Pa., 166
Merrimack (mĕr′ĭ-măk) River, 115
Mexico (mĕk′sĭ-kō), 30–36, 43
Mexico, Gulf of, 41
Mexico City, capture by Cortes, 33–34
Middle Ages, 3–8, 108
Middle West, 54
Minuit (mĭn′ū-ĭt), Peter, 62, 142
Minute men, 284–290
Missions and missionaries, 36, 39–40, 56–57, 159, 162, 165, 182
Mississippi River, 41–43, 54, 56–59, 194, 241, 243–244, 250, 258, 310, 329
Missouri (mĭ-sōō′rĭ; -zōō′rĭ), 196
Mobile (mō-bēl′) Bay, 43
Mohawk River, 194
Molasses Act, 266
Monmouth, N. J., 316
Monongahela (mō-nŏn′gå-hē′lå) River, 173, 246, 249
Montcalm (mŏnt′käm′) General Louis Joseph, 255–258
Montezuma (mŏn′tĕ-zōō′må), 31–34
Montreal (mŏnt′rĕ-ôl′), 50, 54, 238, 360
Moors, 14–15
Moravians, 155–159
Morgan, General Daniel, 319
Morris, Gouverneur, 377
Morris, Robert, 338–340, 345–346, 368
Morristown, N. J., 301, 334

INDEX

Muhlenberg (mū'lĕn-bûrg), Doctor Henry M., 160–161
Muhlenberg, the Reverend Peter, 161–162

Nain, Pa., 164
Narragansett (năr'à-găn'sĕt) Bay, 48, 125
Narragansett Indians, 118–119
National parks, 388–389
Naval stores, 267
Navigation Laws, 89–91, 99, 152–153, 265, 266, 275–276, 278, 283–284
Negroes, 86–87, 180–181, 205
Netherlands, the, *see* Holland
New Amsterdam (ăm'stēr-dăm), 62, 91, 122, 124, 126, 128–133; becomes New York, 132
New Bern, N. C., 100
Newcastle, Del., 140, 171, 174
New England, 99, 106–117, 134, 205–206, 209, 231–234, 283–284, 294, 297, 306–307, 360; growth of, 117; settlement of, 106–127
New England Confederation, 124, 359
New England farmhouse, 182–183, 185
New England Primer, 216
Newfoundland (nū'fŭnd-lănd; nū'-found'lănd'), 47, 48, 60, 70, 235, 328
New France, 50–59, 61, 242–244
New Haven colony, 125–126, 133, 215, 360
New Jersey, 99, 134–136, 299–301, 316, 340; *see* East and West Jersey
New London, Conn., 198
New Mexico (mĕk'sĭ-kō), 38, 39, 40
New Netherland (nĕth'ēr-lănd), 60–63, 134–136
New Orleans (ôr'lē-ănz), 243
Newport, R. I., 122
New York, 132–134, 193, 223–225, 297, 299, 301, 314, 316, 318, 360; first U. S. capital, 381
New York Bay, 48, 134, 297
New York State, 51, 52, 149, 194–195, 297–299, 306–309; campaign in, 297–299

Niagara (nī-ăg'à-rà) Falls, 54, 56–57
Nicolls (nĭk'ŭlz), Governor Richard, 132, 134
Niña (nē'nyä), 16
Nonimportation agreements, 275, 279, 281–282, 342
Norristown, Pa., 304
North Carolina, 48, 196, 205, 319–321, 379; settlement of, 97–101
Northwest passage, 49, 51, 69–70
Norway (nôr'wā), 48
Nova Scotia (nō'và skō'shyà; -shà), 232–238, 291
Novaya Zemlya (nō'và-yà zĕm-lyà'), 60

Occupations, 220–223; in the Middle colonies, 206–208; in New England, 205–206; in the South, 204–205
Oglethorpe (ō'g'l-thôrp), General James Edward, 101–104
Ohio (state), 310
Ohio River, 54, 59, 241, 243–244, 247, 249, 311
Ordinance of 1787, 371–372
Oregon (ŏr'ē-gŏn), 69
Orinoco (ō'rĭ-nō'kō) River, 76
Ottawa (ŏt'à-wà) River, 51

Pacific Ocean, discovery of, 24–25, 27–28
Pack horses, 169, 192–193
Palatinate (pà-lăt'ĭ-nåt), the, 160–161
Palos (pä'lōs), Spain, 9, 16, 18
Panama, Isthmus of, 22, 24, 28, 41, 67
Paoli (pà-ō'lĭ) Massacre, 348
Paper mills, 152, 155, 208, 222
Parker, Captain Jonas, 285
Parliament of England, 89, 91, 96–97, 117, 231, 243, 264–282, 361–369; struggle between the king and, 264–265, 329–330
Pastorius (păs-tō'rĭ-ŭs), Francis Daniel, 157–158
Patroon (pà-trōōn') system, 128–129
Paxton men, 162, 164
Penn, Admiral Sir William, 138–140

INDEX

Penn, William, 136, 138-155, 165, 171-173, 360, 393-396, 398
Pennsylvania, 138-175, 196, 210-211, 247-248, 299; disputed boundaries, 171-174; growth of, 149-150, 208; manufacturing in, 208; settlement of, 138-174; in Revolutionary War, 337-348; ratifies the Constitution, 377; University of, 218-219; wild life in, 390-398
Pepperell (pĕp'ēr-ĕl), Sir William, 236, 237
Pequot (pē'kwŏt) Indians, 118, 360
Perkiomen (pûr'kĭ-ō'mĕn) Creek, 160
Peru (pĕ-rōō'), 36-37
Philadelphia, 143, 147-159, 164, 169, 171, 192, 193, 195, 278, 281, 290-291, 299, 304, 306, 314-316, 333-334; commerce of, 207; growth of, 149, 208, 347; British capture of, 301-304, 325, 326, 342, 344, 347-348; Continental Congresses in, 341-342; Constitutional Convention in, 356, 372; University of, 218-219
Philippine (fĭl'ĭ-pĭn; -pēn) Islands, 28
Phips (fĭps), Sir William, 232
Pietists (pī'ĕ-tĭsts), 153-155
Pilgrims, 106-115, 209
Pillory, 213
Pinta (pēn'tä), 16
Pinzón (pēn-thōn') brothers, 15
Pitcairn (pĭt'kârn), Major John, 286
Pitt, William, 253-254
Pittsburgh, 195, 249
Pizarro (pĭ-zär'rō), Francisco, 36-37, 41
Plains of Abraham, 255-256
Plymouth, England, 108
Plymouth, Mass., 109-118, 124, 126, 360
Plymouth Company, 82
Pocahontas (pō'kȧ-hŏn'tȧs), 84-85
Polo (pō'lō), Marco, 5-8
Ponce de León, Juan (pōn'thä dā lä-ōn', hwän), 40-41
Pope Alexander VI, 45
Portages, 192
Port Royal, Acadia, 50, 232

Port Royal, S. C., 100
Portugal (pōr'tû-gȧl), 13, 14, 25-28, 45, 64, 66
Portuguese discoveries and explorations, 43-45
Potatoes, 73
Potomac (pō-tō'mȧk) River, 94, 195, 372
Pottstown, Pa., 160
Powhatan (pou'hȧ-tăn'), 84-85
Prince Henry the Navigator, 43-44
Princeton, Battle of, 299-301
Princeton College, 218
Printing press: at Ephrata, 155; Franklin's, 219
Protection of wild life, 390-398
Providence, R. I., 121-122
Prussia (prŭsh'ȧ), 240
Pueblo (pwĕb'lō) Indians, 37-39
Puerto Rico (pwĕr'tō rē'kō), 41
Pulaski (pṳ-lăs'kĭ), Count Casimir, 334-335
Punishments for offenders, 83, 101-102, 119-120, 212-214
Pure Food Laws, 390, 392-393, 399
Puritans, 106-120, 208-210

Quakers, *see* Friends
Quebec (kwĕ-bĕk'), 49, 50, 54, 230, 232, 234, 238, 316; British capture of, 255-258
Queen Anne's War, 233, 235
Queen Elizabeth of England, 60, 67, 69-71, 81, 82
Queen Isabella (ĭz'ȧ-bĕl'ȧ) of Spain, 14-15, 16, 18, 19, 20
Queen Mary of England, 231, 233
Quivira (kē-vē'rȧ), 39

Radio, 225, 349, 351
Radnor, Pa., 341
Railroads, 223
Raleigh (rô'lĭ), Sir Walter, 70-76, 80
Ranger, 324
Redemptioners, 87, 168, 181, 207
Red Jacket, 165
Redstone, Pa., 311

INDEX

Religion, 32, 126; freedom of, 97, 103, 108, 133–134, 136, 143, 153–161, 243; in New England, 208–209; in the South, 209–210; in the other colonies, 210–211; persecution for, 81, 94, 118, 120–123, 138; taught to the Indians, 36, 39–40, 56–57, 110, 159, 162, 164–165, 182; differences in religious beliefs, 359

Revenge, 73

Revere (rē-vēr'), Paul, 188, 285, 287

Revolutionary War, 155, 161, 165, 231, 261–335, 362–363; Pennsylvania's part in, 337–348

Rhode Island, 119, 126, 210, 373, 379; founding of, 120–124

Rice, 101, 205

Roads, 192–196, 221–223, 349

Roanoke (rō'a-nōk) Island, 71–75

Rochambeau (dē rō'shän'bō') Count de, 323, 333

Rodney, Caesar, 292

Rome, 4

Ross, Colonel, 345–346

Ross, Mrs. Betsy, 345–347

Rural life, colonial, 221

Russia (rŭsh'a), 48, 81

Sachem (sā'chĕm), Indian, 145

Saguenay (săg'ē-nā') River, 51

St. George River, 95

St. Lawrence, Gulf of, 49

St. Lawrence River, 50, 52, 59, 234, 258

St. Marys, 95

Salem, Mass., 115, 118–121

Samoset (săm'ô-sĕt), 111–112

San Francisco (săn frăn-sĭs'kō), 40, 69

San Salvador (sän säl'vá-dōr'), 16

Santa Barbara (săn'ta bär'bá-ra), 40

Santa Fe (săn'ta fā'), 40

Santa Maria (sän'tä ma-rē'á), 12, 16, 17

San Xavier del Bol (sän hä-vyär' dĕl bōl), 40

Saratoga, Battle of, 306–309, 316

Savannah (sa-văn'a), Ga., 103–104, 335

Savannah River, 43, 104

Saybrook, Conn., 124

Schenectady (skĕ-nĕk'ta-dĭ), N. Y., 232

Schoolbooks, colonial, 216–217

Schools, 39, 190, 214–219, 387

Schuyler (skī'lēr), General Philip John, 319

Schuylerville (skī'lēr-vĭl), N. Y., 319

Schuylkill (skōōl'kĭl) River, 147, 164

Scotch-Irish settlers, 148–149, 218, 244

Scottish colonists, 100, 104

Scrooby (skrōō'bĭ), England, 106

Search for a northwest passage, 49, 51, 69–70

Second Continental Congress, 171, 174, 290–291, 294–297, 304, 313–314, 325, 331, 337–338, 342–347, 362–372, 375; at Baltimore, 342; at Lancaster, 343–344; at York, 343; at Princeton, N. J., 343

Seneca (sĕn'ē-ka) Indians, 164–165

Separatists, 106

Serapis (sē-rā'pĭs), 324, 326

Shackamaxon (shăk'a-măk'sŏn), *see* Kensington

Sherman, Roger, 355, 367

Shipbuilding, 205–207, 353

Shippen, Peggy, 316

Shirley, Governor William, 236

Shrewsbury (shrōōz'bēr-ĭ), N. J., 134

Six Nations, 165

Slavery, 34, 86–87, 104, 173, 180–181, 182, 184–185, 376, 377; in Pennsylvania, 166; prohibited, 372

Smith, Captain John, 77, 83–85, 110–111

Social classes, colonial, 179–182

"Sons of Liberty," 363–364, 366

Soul-drivers, 168

Southampton (south-ămp'tŭn), Eng., 108

South Carolina, 65, 82, 205, 319, 321; settlement of, 97–101

South Sea, *see* Pacific Ocean

Spain, 14–19, 22, 26, 30, 41, 45, 60, 64, 66–70, 235, 328

Spanish claims, 22, 45, 245, 248

Spanish settlements, 181–182

Speedwell, 108

INDEX xxiii

Spice Islands, 26, 28
Spinning and weaving, 152, 158, 199–200, 225
Sports and pastimes, *see* Colonial recreations
Squanto (skwän'tō), 111
Stagecoaches, 193–194
Stamp Act, 264, 268–270, 362; repeal of, 274–275; resistance to, 261, 269; Stamp Act Congress, 269–270, 361–362
Standish, Captain Myles, 109, 112–113
Starving Time, 85
State parks and forests, 389, 396, 400
Steuben (stū'bĕn), Frederick William, Baron von, 305–306, 333–334
Stiegel (stē'gĕl), Henry William, Baron, 155–157
Stocks, 213
Stony Point, Battle of, 340–341
Strait of Gibraltar (jĭ-brâl'tēr), 67
Strait of Mackinac (măk'ĭ-nô), 54
Stuyvesant (stī'vĕ-sănt), Governor Peter, 129–132
Submarines, 351–352
Susquehanna (sŭs'kwĕ-hăn'à) River, 167–169, 195
Swamp, the, 160
Swedish settlements, 129, 141–143, 151, 174
Swiss colonists, 99–100

Tampa Bay, 41
Taos (tä'ôs), N. Mex., 38
Taxation without representation, 267, 270–271, 331
Taxes, 133, 210, 217, 265–282, 331, 361–362, 370–371; colonial evasion of, 266–268; on tea, 277–278, 362
Tedyuscung (tĕd-ūs'kŭng), 159
Telegraph, 225, 349, 351
Telephone, 225
Tennessee (tĕn'ĕ-sē'), 43, 195
Texas, 101
Thanksgiving Day, 112, 118
Tobacco, 73, 85–86, 96, 180, 183, 267; tax on, 90–91, 265; used as money, 86

Tories, 316, 329, 341
Toscanelli (tŏs'kà-nĕl'ĭ), 13
Town life, colonial, 220
Town meeting, 364–365
Trappe (trăp), Pa., 161
Travel and transportation, colonial, 192–196, 222–224
Treaty elm, 143–145
Treaty of 1783, 165, 328–330, 338
Treaty of Tordesillas (tôr'dē-sē'yăs), 45
Trenton, N. J., 146; Battle of, 299, 301
Trinidad (trĭn'ĭ-dăd'), 20
Troubles between Spain and England, 60, 66–70
Tucson (tōō-sŏn'), Ariz., 40
Turks, 8

Union, the idea of, 358–363; early attempts at, 124, 126–127, 279, 359–360
United Colonies of New England, 126–127
United States, 326
University of Pennsylvania, 218–219
Upland, Pa., 143

Valladolid (väl'yä-ŧħô-lēŧħ'), Spain, 22
Valley Forge, 302, 304–306, 332–334, 340, 348
Venice (vĕn'ĭs), 5–7
Vera Cruz (vĕr'à krōōz'; vā'rä krōōs'), 33, 67
Vermont, 51
Verrazano, Giovanni da (vĕr'rät-sä'nō, jō-vän'nē dä), 46–48
Vespucci, Amerigo (vĕs-pōōt'chē, ä-mĕr'ĭ-gō), 22–24
Victoria, 28
Vincennes (vĭn-sĕnz'), Ind., 312
Virginia, 61, 73, 94–96, 99, 147, 149, 196, 212, 247–251, 267, 270, 294, 297, 306, 319, 362; settlement of, 80–93
Voltaire (vŏl'târ'), François Marie Arouet de, 143
Voyages of discovery, 21; Columbus's, 16–21, 64; Dutch, 60–63; English,

64–76; French, 46–59; Portuguese, 8, 43–45

Waldseemüller (vält′zā-mül′ẽr), Martin, 22–23
Walking Purchase, 145–147
Warfare, contrast in, 348–352
Warren, Joseph, 284
Warwick (wŏr′ĭk), R. I., 122
Washington (city), 194
Washington, George, 247–252, 262, 290–293, 297–309, 316–318, 323, 332–334, 338, 340, 343, 345–346, 348, 356, 374; made commander in chief, 290, 342; made president of Constitutional Convention, 373; elected President, 379–381
Water power, 152, 205, 207, 222
Wayne, General Anthony, 333, 340–341, 348
Wayside Inn, 188
Weehawken (wē-hô′kĕn), N. J., 134
Weiser (vī′sēr; wī′zēr), Conrad, 159–160
Welcome, 140–141
Welsh Quakers, 147, 165–166
West Indies, 41, 66, 67, 314, 342; trade with, 153, 197, 206, 266
West Jersey, 99, 135–136, 138, 143, 360
Westover, 184
West Point, N. Y., 317–318, 334

Westward movement, 149, 194–196, 244, 246
Wethersfield, Conn., 125
White, Governor John, 74–76
White, the Reverend John, 115–117
White Plains, N. Y., 316
William of Orange, 231, 233
Williams, Roger, 120–122
Wilmington, Del., 302
Wilson, James, 375
Windsor (wĭn′zẽr), Conn., 124–125
Winthrop (wĭn′thrŭp), Governor John, 117–118, 198
Wireless, 225
Wissahickon (wĭs′a-hĭk′ŏn) Creek, 155
Witchcraft, 119–120
Wolfe, General James, 255–258
Women arrive in America, 87–88
World War, 350–351
Wrightstown (rīts′toun), Pa., 146
Wyalusing (wī′a-lōō′sĭng), Pa., 164
Wyoming (wī-ō′mĭng; wī′ō-mĭng), Valley, 173–174

Yale College, 215
Yankee-Pennamite War, 173–174
Yardley, Governor Sir George, 88–89
York, Pa., 343, 348
Yorktown, Va., 322–323, 333, 338

Zinzendorf (fŏn tsĭn′tsĕn-dôrf), Count von, 158–159